Final Passages

POSITIVE CHOICES
FOR THE DYING
AND THEIR LOVED ONES

Judith Ahronheim, M.D., and Doron Weber

Produced by The Philip Lief Group, Inc.

SIMON & SCHUSTER

New York · London · Toronto · Sydney · Tokyo · Singapore

SIMON & SCHUSTER
Simon & Schuster Building
Rockefeller Center
1230 Avenue of the Americas
New York, New York 10020

Designed by Irving Perkins Associates
Manufactured in the United States of America

1   2   3   4   5   6   7   8   9   10

Library of Congress Cataloging-in-Publication Data is available.

ISBN 0-671-78025-5

Produced by The Philip Lief Group, Inc.

The authors acknowledge with thanks permission from the American
Psychiatric Association to reprint a portion of the "Diagnostic Criteria for
Major Depressive Episode" from *Diagnostic and Statistical Manual
of Mental Disorders, Third Edition, Revised*, Washington, DC;
American Psychiatric Association, 1987.

Lines from "Do Not Go Gentle into that Good Night" by Dylan Thomas,
from *Poems of Dylan Thomas*, copyright 1952 by Dylan Thomas, are
reprinted by permission of New Directions Publishing Corporation.

Acknowledgments

Many professionals contributed their time and attention to the preparation and review of this manuscript. We are indebted to all of them and would like to acknowledge especially the following people:

GERALD BLANDFORD, M.D.
  Clinical Professor of Medicine,
  Albert Einstein College of Medicine; Medical Director,
  Nathan Miller Center for Nursing Care, Inc.

FRANK BRESCIA, M.D. Medical Director
MICHAEL J. BRESCIA, M.D. (cofounder)
JAMES CIMINO, M.D. (cofounder)
DAVID WOLLNER, M.D. and Staff
  Calvary Hospital, Bronx, New York

GEORGE FULOP, M.D.
  Assistant Professor of Psychiatry,
  Geriatrics & Community Medicine,
  Mt. Sinai Medical Center

M. ROSE GASNER, J.D.
  Bioethics Consultant
  Formerly, Director of Legal Services, Society for the Right to Die

JAMES R. KNICKMAN, PH.D.
  Professor, Robert F. Wagner Graduate School of Public Service
  New York University

MARGUERITE S. LEDERBERG, M.D.
  Associate Attending Psychiatrist,
  Memorial Sloan-Kettering Cancer Center;
  Clinical Associate Professor of Psychiatry,
  Cornell University Medical College

BRENDA MAMBER, CSW
  Social Work Supervisor
  Jacob Perlow Hospice

DIANE MEIER, M.D.
  Associate Professor of Geriatrics and Medicine
  Mt. Sinai Medical Center

RUSSELL PORTENOY, M.D.
Director of Analgesic Studies,
Memorial Sloan-Kettering Cancer Center;
Associate Professor of Neurology,
Cornell University Medical Center

JAMES STRAIN, M.D.
Professor and Director,
Division of Behavioral Medicine and Consult Psychiatry,
Mt. Sinai School of Medicine

PETER STRAUSS, J.D.
Partner, Trusts and Estates Department
Fink Weinberger, PC

JANE WEBER, ACSW
Executive Director
Jacob Perlow Hospice
Beth Israel Medical Center

At Simon & Schuster, Fred Hills, a consummate professional, gave us the benefit of his strong commitment, sharp eye and seasoned editorial judgment. Our gratitude to Daphne Bien for her assistance in reading and commenting on the manuscript, and to Steve Boldt for copyediting. We would also like to acknowledge Lee Ann Chearneyi for her fine editing and involvement throughout the book; to Philip Lief, for his early and continuing support; and to Julia Banks and Gary Sunshine.

Judy Ahronheim would like to thank her husband Gerry, once again, for his insights and his patience. He understands this field so well and has the willingness to share his insights time and again. She would also like to convey special gratitude to Calvary Hospital, Beth Israel Hospice, and all others who concentrate on providing comfort care to patients and their families. A very personal thank you is reserved for Hospice Care Inc., of Madison, Wisconsin, who were there for Marilyn Malone and her family.

Doron Weber would like to especially thank Lee Ann for helping and encouraging him to develop the original idea for this book. Among those who helped sustain him during the writing, a special thanks to Billy and Beth and Kelsey and Siobhan, and to Turpin and Caroline. Also to Rose and Willie and to Nancy. A salute once again to his parents, Helga and Robert, and sister Anat. And the biggest, most heartfelt thanks to Shealagh, his wife, and Damon, his son, who put up with the long, intense hours. Finally, in memory of Danny and Jerry, still deeply missed.

Contents

Preface

This book originated from our sense that dying patients and their families—as well as the rest of us who must someday face the challenge of illness and death—have special needs and concerns that are not being adequately addressed. Both individually and collectively, we appear to be in a period of uncertainty and confusion about how to face the ends of our lives. As with other aspects of modern life, modern death is infinitely more complex, technological, and impersonal than it used to be. Hard choices must be made—medical, ethical, legal, financial, and emotional choices—and many of us are not adequately prepared to confront them.

Unfounded fears and worrisome misconceptions abound. Lack of knowledge about specific diseases and the natural aging process is one problem. Lack of understanding about such subjects as pain control and the treatment of clinical depression is another. Lack of information about the alternatives and resources available—such as hospice care and comfort care, living wills, and durable powers of attorney for health care—is yet another. We have also neglected to deal frankly and directly with the emotional pain of death and with the challenge of integrating it into our lives. These gaps and shortcomings have contributed to a crisis atmosphere, a sense that few options are available to help us cope with the inevitable, terrifying prospect of illness and death.

As with any crisis, when people are frightened and ill-informed they may seek quick or simplistic solutions. Suicide rates among the elderly have recently increased for the first time in thirty years. There has also been a disproportionate amount of publicity surrounding a few unusual and extreme cases of suicide and assisted suicide. These cases are compel-

9

ling and demand our attention but they point to the problem rather than the solution. Whether suicide, with or without the help of a physician, is *ever* a rational choice and an acceptable medical option is a matter of intense and continuing debate. There are genuine and deeply held beliefs on both sides of the issue and we do not presume to resolve these differences. But one thing we believe, and almost every medical and lay expert in this field can agree on, is that most people who turn to suicide are not fully informed and have not adequately explored other medical options that could give them new hope for going on with their lives.

This book was written as an antidote to the hopelessness, helplessness, and sheer confusion experienced by millions of us today as we face the end of life. We have tried to provide dying patients and their loved ones with responsible information to guide them through life's most frightening passage and to help them take control of the dying process. Throughout the book, we demonstrate that it is possible to live out all phases of life and to face the end with courage, dignity, and a minimum of pain. We believe that greater knowledge about illness and death, and about the wide range of options and resources available to us, can restore a measure of balance and hopefulness to what is, after all, a part of all our lives.

CHAPTER ONE

Facing Death

Tess, a retired schoolteacher, was born at the turn of the century in Pennsylvania. Thanks to the discovery of vaccines, she was spared from smallpox in her youth. Tess married Alan Fields in 1924 and had two children. Her life was saved again, this time by antibiotics, when she cut her hand and developed a serious bone infection in 1950. In 1971, Alan died, leaving Tess some money and wonderful memories. Her children had both moved to California and urged their mother to join them, but Tess liked her life the way it was. She received immunizations in her middle years and was able to travel not only to Europe but to Africa and in 1985, at the age of eighty-five, to China, where she visited the Great Wall. In 1988, she developed fainting spells and a pacemaker was implanted in her heart; later that year she was able to travel to India and visit the Taj Mahal.

In 1990, while planting geraniums on her porch garden at home, Tess tripped over one of her flower pots on the front walk and broke her hip. She underwent surgery under general anesthesia and now walks with a cane. Despite the fragile balance of her health, Tess is determined that she will not be a burden to her children, themselves now in their sixties, living far away at the other end of the country, with financial and health problems of their own.

Tess is not bitter and knows that without the miracle of modern medicine she would not have led the full, exciting life that she has. But as she enters her tenth decade of life, she finds she has outlived not only her husband but all her close friends. Worried about living alone, Tess is afraid she may fall again, remains concerned about her heart, and often wonders if she should go into a nursing home. Understandably, the thought of leaving her much-loved house and flower garden is deeply upsetting, and she is determined to preserve her savings so she will be able to leave some money to her daughter and son. Tess has also begun worrying about what might happen if she becomes seriously ill. Would she suffer much? At times, she has even contemplated taking an overdose of sleeping pills and slipping quietly away. This goes against her nature, but Tess wonders whether it might not be more natural than the things she has read about: machines and tubes you can't get free of. She has considered asking her doctor for help, "just in case," but has not broached the subject with him yet. Perhaps she never will. Tess does not like to be dependent on anyone, not even her doctor. And she still thinks life is worth living.

George, once a successful businessman, was an active, distinguished-looking seventy-eight-year-old widower. He lived in a retirement community where the women outnumbered the men six to one. He had many female admirers (all widowed) but refused to marry again "out of respect" for his late wife, Vera. George had cared for Vera during a long illness and watched as she slowly deteriorated from a degenerative illness of the spine until she became paralyzed from the waist down.

George developed a bad cough and about a year ago went to the doctor. Lung cancer was diagnosed. George wanted to make it and agreed to undergo radiation therapy. During the treatment, George developed a serious, unexpected complication that produced the same type of paralysis his wife had suffered. He quickly became bedridden and severely depressed. When a large bedsore forced him to lie on his stomach, George's withdrawal from those around him set in. His doctor reassured him that although his paralysis might not go away, his tumor was gone and rehabilitation would enable him to function reasonably well. There was no reason to believe that he would not be able to return to the life he'd created for himself at the retirement community, and his many friends there were supportive. But George had been through all this with Vera and did not want to face life in a wheelchair. He simply gave up, refused any further treatment, and died shortly thereafter.

In recent years, millions of us in the United States (and elsewhere) have become increasingly anxious and concerned about situations like these. Most of us know someone like Tess or George, and we worry about the same questions they do:

- How should I die? And when?
- Can I refuse any medical treatment I don't want? Can I request to have every form of medical treatment available?
- Will it hurt? How much pain will I have to suffer?
- Will I die alone?
- How much will my dying cost? Will I have any money left to leave my family?
- If I decide it's time to go, will my doctor help me?

We worry about these questions for a very good reason; they are new questions that did not even exist fifty years ago. Unsettling, even terrifying, they bring us each right up against our deepest fears and limitations.

Let us admit it from the outset. Talking about death—our own or that of our loved ones—is a frightening and humbling experience. Who wants to think about the end of life? It compels us to conceive of a world where we no longer exist. We are forced to imagine our extinction and the end of everything we hold dear. And not only must we face this grim reality, but now we are being told that we must plan and prepare for death with painstaking deliberation.

Why? Why can't we let life come to a natural conclusion? Why must we—Tess and George and the rest of us—be so concerned about how we will die and who will take care of us?

What we are experiencing amounts to a serious crisis of confidence in our current medical system and in the medical profession. We no longer completely trust the system or the professionals who handle our end-of-life dilemmas. We fear the unchecked growth of technology and the loss of a personal connection between ourselves and our caregivers. And in a larger sense, we appear to have lost faith in our society's ability to care for the most basic needs of all its citizens. We no longer believe in the idea of a social safety net that will catch us or a morally responsible community watching over and protecting our interests. We feel somewhat abandoned.

Yet it is not just society but we as individuals who are failing. We are failing in our capacity to confront our inevitable death and the death of our loved ones in a way that is personally meaningful to us. We have allowed death to become impersonal, like the technology and the institutions of which it is increasingly a product, because we are not emotionally prepared to face it and to talk about our feelings with others. We have not been able to integrate the specter of our dying into the larger picture of our living.

We are running scared. We are confused. We are ill-informed. And in our fear, confusion, and ignorance, some of us are resorting to extreme measures that are often inappropriate. These highly publicized cases have only heightened our disquiet.

In June 1990, fifty-four-year-old Janet Adkins flew two thousand miles to Michigan so that retired pathologist Jack Kevorkian could help her kill herself before her Alzheimer's disease got any worse. Mrs. Adkins simply refused to accept the inevitable mental deterioration that was part of her disease process. She was the first person to use one of Kevorkian's "suicide machines"—others have done so since—and the resulting publicity ignited a national controversy. Dr. Kevorkian was charged with first-degree murder for Mrs. Adkins's death. However, a Michigan judge threw his case out because Michigan had no law regulating assisted suicide. The judge ruled that Mrs. Adkins intended to commit suicide, and it was her decision to push the button that started the lethal injection. Kevorkian's device was carefully designed, enabling Mrs. Adkins to control the final infusion of potassium chloride that killed her so that she literally died by her own hand. As this book goes to press, Kevorkian has once again been charged with first-degree murder for helping two more women end their lives.

Shortly after the Kevorkian-Adkins case, Bertram Harper traveled from California to Michigan with his hopelessly ill wife so he could help her to die. He had heard assisted suicide was not illegal there. Mrs. Virginia Harper had terminal cancer and had tried once before, alone and unsuccessfully, to take her life. When Mrs. Harper's pills failed to do the job alone, Mr. Harper fastened a plasic bag over his wife's head and held her in his arms until she died. The Michigan district attorney subsequently arrested Mr. Harper and charged him with first-degree murder, although he was later acquitted after the jury deliberated for only two hours.

A few months later, people across the country read about "Diane," a forty-five-year-old woman suffering from severe leukemia. Diane took her life with an overdose of barbiturates prescribed by her physician rather than undergo further chemotherapy and a series of exhaustive treatments that would have given her, at best, a one in four chance of survival. Dr. Timothy Quill went public with her story, describing in the *New England Journal of Medicine* his moral conflict as Diane's physician and his final decision to supply her with enough pills to end her life.

These cases are unusually dramatic examples of a nationwide anxiety surrounding death and dying—extreme cries of protest, pain, and anger directed at a system that has turned its back on us. Another form of protest captured America's attention when a cofounder of the Hemlock Society, a group advocating suicide for the hopelessly ill, published a suicide manual that shot to the top of national best-seller lists. The ultimate do-it-yourself book, Derek Humphry's *Final Exit* instructs terminally ill patients about how they can take their lives. Humphry coolly discusses the full range of suicide techniques (including hanging, drowning, electrocution, self-starvation) and provides precise and detailed drug dosage charts for what he terms successful "self-deliverance." The book's unexpected and wide popularity has stimulated a national debate about the growing dimensions of our apparent preoccupation with suicide.

Meanwhile a major study by the Centers for Disease Control (CDC) appearing in the *American Journal of Public Health* in September 1991 found a significant new increase in suicide rates among elderly people. Between 1980 and 1986, the suicide rate for Americans over sixty-five years rose 21 percent, with those over eighty experiencing a 38 percent rise. The sudden and dramatic increase reverses thirty consecutive years of declining suicide rates among older people. Along with other, recent developments such as Humphry's popular suicide manual and the sympathetic media treatment of child psychiatrist Bruno Bettelheim's suicide, these figures were interpreted by an accompanying editorial in the *American Journal of Public Health* to suggest that as a society we appear to regard suicide as a rational choice and an increasingly acceptable option for those who are elderly or terminally ill. However, University of Rochester psychiatrists Yeates Conwell and Eric Caine, in an October 1991 editorial in the *New England Journal of Medicine,* cautioned that it is difficult to determine whether suicide is *ever* rational. Conwell and Caine argue that the psychological effects of chronic disease, as well as personal biases about aging and old age, affect the determination of a suicidal person's "rationality."

The suicide debate is only one part of our growing need to control end-of-life situations. It is a drastic symptom of a larger health-care crisis within our midst. What exactly is happening and when did things start to go wrong?

Dying Alone in an Institution and the Fear of Technology

The last half-century has witnessed a dramatic change in our attitude toward and experience of death and dying. This transformation has occurred because of social, technological, and demographic changes in our lives, changes that have affected how and where and when we all die.

Death, like birth, has moved out of the home and into the health-care institution. Until World War II, most of us still died at home in our own beds. Tess's mother, who died in 1938, spent her last hours in the house where Tess still lives today. But Tess's husband, who succumbed to a stroke in 1971, was taken by ambulance to the hospital emergency room. Alan remained in the intensive care unit for ten whole days before he died.

Today, 80 percent of us, or about 2 million Americans each year, will spend our final days in a health-care institution, usually a hospital, sometimes a nursing home. In this sense, our dying has been removed from the context of our everyday lives.

As a result of this isolation, most of us have little or no direct contact with dying people. And because we live longer —at the beginning of this century, the average life expectancy at birth in the U.S. was forty-seven years—death is a less common event. At the same time, the extended three-generation family is a thing of the past. Our grandparents no longer live with us or are in nursing homes, and so we don't experience their aging and their final years. Our parents often spend their mature years in retirement communities far from us. In addition, fewer of us live on farms or in rural environments where we share in the natural life cycle of other species. Death has become a stranger to our lives, an unnatural, much-feared, and little-seen intruder.

With the rise of the modern health-care institution, we have effectively quarantined the dying, as if death were a contagious disease that might infect us as well. Strict boundaries are drawn around the terminally ill. In a sterilized atmosphere, they are shut in and we are shut out. Medical professionals, people who specialize in *death management*, are assigned to take care of the dying while we linger, uncomfortable and helpless, in the background.

Our modern doctor is the sworn enemy of death, a specialist waging battle in the medical arena. To lose a patient is to fail. All effort is organized and centered around the science of saving lives. In this all-out war, the human needs of the individual patient or family may often be forgotten or ignored.

Today's medical battlefield is equipped with a powerful arsenal—a vast array of drugs that can, when used appropriately, save lives that would previously have been lost. Tess is only one beneficiary of this progress. Vaccines and antibiotics have helped us control many infectious diseases such as polio, smallpox, and tuberculosis. In previous years, these devastating diseases reached epidemic levels and affected millions of lives. President Franklin Delano Roosevelt, one of Tess's heroes, contracted polio in 1921 and spent much of his presidency confined to a wheelchair. The availability of the Salk vaccine in 1954 resulted in the ultimate eradication of polio.

In addition, our rapid advances in medical technology have completely changed the practice of medicine. Respirators take over breathing if the lungs fail. Cardiopulmonary resuscitation can restart a heart that has stopped beating. Dialysis does the work of the kidneys, cleansing the blood and preserving life until the organs recover or a transplant donor is found. These technological breakthroughs have enabled us to keep people alive while their underlying conditions are treated and even cured. Truly miracles of science and modern ingenuity, they represent historic progress in the treatment of acute illness and injury and the prolongation of life.

But the use of sophisticated medical technology, while giving us greater options, has also generated new fears and dilemmas. On the eve of the twenty-first century, it has spawned our modern nightmare of a being in a limbo hooked up to machines—alive and not alive. This fate befell Karen

Ann Quinlan and Nancy Beth Cruzan, two tragically injured young women who became national symbols of a person's right to die. Twenty-one-year-old Quinlan suffered a respiratory arrest and permanent brain damage at a party in 1975, where she is believed to have consumed a lethal combination of alcohol and barbiturates. Twenty-five-year-old Cruzan was injured in a car accident in 1983 and suffered severe brain damage from oxygen deprivation. Both women were maintained on life-sustaining equipment for many years despite permanent unconsciousness with no chance of ever recovering. In 1976, the parents of Karen Ann Quinlan won the right to disconnect their daughter from a respirator although she lived for nine more years in an unconscious state, sustained at a seventy-pound weight by artificial feeding. In 1990, the parents of thirty-two-year-old Nancy Beth Cruzan went all the way to the U.S. Supreme Court—and then back home to Carthage, Missouri, to find more witnesses—before they were allowed to remove the feeding tube that had maintained their daughter in a permanently unconscious state for almost eight years. Nancy Cruzan died peacefully twelve days later, on December 26, 1990.

Because we now have the technological option to keep dying patients "alive" almost indefinitely, we also have to decide when and if to use this technology. Death is rarely, if ever, allowed to come naturally. Francine, a woman with emphysema whom Tess knew, suffered a massive brain hemorrhage at the age of seventy-two. Her breathing was supported by a respirator for several months although she remained unconscious. Finally, her kidneys failed and doctors began dialysis, a common medical response, even though this treatment could not restore her damaged brain and lungs. Her husband, John, did not order the doctors to stop treating her —and thus let Francine die—because he loved his wife and wanted to do everything possible for her. But in the years following her death, he often blamed himself for allowing Francine to be subjected to such prolonged and fruitless overtreatment.

Just as in Francine's case, in the overwhelming majority of institutional deaths today—70 percent or about 1.4 million a year according to the American Hospital Association—the doctor, the patient, or the patient's family will have to make some kind of decision about when death should come. More and more, we are being called on to plan or "negotiate" our dying. The negotiation usually involves a decision whether to use life support or to take it away—and this decision determines the timing of our death. Thus technology has given us a tremendous new power—the ability to influence when and how we, or a loved one, will die.

Along with this power, we have created a heavy responsibility. We now have an obligation to understand not only how medical technology is used for its own ends, but how to harness it to reflect our personal values and needs—essentially how to put medical technology's use *to our own ends*, or those of our loved ones. We need to find a way to make our dying both continuous and consistent with our living and to restore to death the dignity and integrity of life.

For over seven years Nancy Cruzan lay in a state of permanent unconsciousness from which she would never recover, her life sustained by a feeding tube surgically implanted in her abdomen. She was, in the words of Supreme Court justice William Brennan, a "prisoner of technology." It took many appeals and extensive legal battles—even beyond the Supreme Court—before the legal system and the health-care system would limit the use of technology in her case.

When the *Cruzan* case reached the U.S. Supreme Court and gained nationwide publicity, millions of Americans rushed to fill out living wills and durable powers of attorney for health care in the hopes that they might avoid a similar fate. While each has its limitations, both of these written documents—known as advance directives—ensure a greater degree of individual control over medical decision-making at the end of life. (See Chapter Eight for a full discussion of advance directives.)

The Aging of America: New Milestones and New Fears

At the age of ninety-two, Tess is a living example of advances in modern medicine. More than once, a disease that would have claimed her in previous generations was held off. Tess is part of the growing number of Americans whose life expectancy has increased dramatically. The elderly (those sixty-five and over) are now the fastest-growing segment of our society. Eleven percent of all citizens or about 25 million Americans are in this age group today. By the year 2020—in less than thirty years—this number is expected to double to 52 million Americans. Among the elderly, those such as Tess who are eighty-five and older—known as the oldest old—are the fastest-growing age group of all. The U.S. Census Bureau estimates that the number of Americans age eighty-five and over, about 4 million today, will more than quadruple in the next fifty years, reaching 17.8 million by the year 2040.

The aging of America is one ironic outcome of our medical progress. We have succeeded in extending the average life span of our citizens, regarded by social scientists and other medical experts as a key indicator of national health. As a result, while many older people, including the oldest old, are in excellent health, an increasing segment of our population consists of people like Tess, individuals who live longer lives but accumulate more illnesses and losses along the way. The health problems of those like Tess, George, and Francine, and the difficulties associated with their aging, increasingly dominate our medical system and challenge our national consciousness.

The most common killers in the United States today—heart disease, cancer, Alzheimer's disease—usually develop over time, giving us advance notice about our condition. We know we face declining health and possibly disability from these diseases. And like Tess, we may become fearful and apprehensive about our future well-being.

In fact, concern about health is the single most common,

identifiable reason for suicide among those over sixty-five. Many people like Tess and George may have to face chronic pain from their medical problems, physical infirmity that reduces their previous level of activity, or mental deterioration that may impair judgment. They must deal with these problems at a time when their personal, social, and financial resources may be dwindling, and when they may perceive they have less and less to look forward to. These losses may lead to feelings of helplessness and despair. In George's case, the prospect of life confined to a wheelchair was not worth fighting for, especially since he had watched his wife, Vera, slowly deteriorate in a similar situation. We don't know if George would have actually committed suicide had he been in a position to do so, but he failed to put up even the slightest resistance to his predicament.

For most of us, pain, and the fear of pain, is one of the most frightening consequences of growing old or sick. "Will it hurt? How much will I suffer?" may be the most common questions asked by seriously ill patients. In one survey in the medical journal *Cancer*, 69 percent of cancer patients admitted they would consider suicide if their pain was not adequately treated. While many of us might be determined to cope with a serious or terminal illness, much of our resolve may fade in the face of uncontrolled pain and suffering. Yet most of us are not aware that pain, whether from age-related disability or terminal illness, can usually be controlled using modern methods of pain relief.

Other psychological and social factors play an important role in our reactions and behavior when sick. For example, a diagnosis of serious or terminal illness—particularly cancer or AIDS—may lead some people to contemplate and commit suicide *before* any symptoms appear. In the case of AIDS, the social stigma of having the disease may also increase the likelihood of self-destruction. How many people who commit suicide stop to consider alternative solutions or are even aware that other forms of help are available before resorting to such a drastic act?

Physical infirmities and social isolation, which often increase with age, can also lead to depression, and many people have ended their lives because they were depressed. Although George's decision to give up may have felt right to him, thousands of other people have been treated for depression and have gone on to live satisfying lives. Sylvia, a depressed ninety-year-old heart patient, was "adopted" by a student Geriatric Interest Group. Simply by allowing medical students to interview her, Sylvia recognized she could be an important part of someone else's life, which added meaning to her own. Depression has often been viewed as an inevitable consequence of the infirmities and losses that may accompany old age, a time when we lose our traditional roles and familiar social identity gained through work, family, or the community. We even *expect* to be depressed and assume it is a normal state for us. Today, however, we are giving more attention to identifying and treating depression as an illness. Depression can also be treated when it worsens the suffering of those who are terminally ill or when it interferes with a peaceful end to a long life.

Doctors and Patients: Why Can't We Talk About Death?

A young doctor developed serious complications after he underwent a liver biopsy for what turned out to be nothing more than a harmless lesion. He spent a total of four months in the hospital and underwent several dozen procedures. For thirty-one days he lived in an intensive care unit (ICU), with tubes placed down his mouth and nose, connected to a mechanical respirator that took over his breathing.

Dr. Edward Viner survived to write about his experiences in "Life at the Other End of the Endotracheal Tube: A Physician's Personal View of Critical Illness" published in *Progress in Critical Care Medicine*. Even though Viner did not have a terminal illness, his experience made him keenly aware of how the dying would feel in this kind of predicament. He describes how he became preoccupied with death and dying but hesitated to let his doctors and nurses know about his feelings. He began to contemplate suicide and asked the nurses repeatedly whether the windows were kept locked. When he finally got up the courage to raise his fear of dying with the doctors and nurses at his bedside, Dr. Viner reports how each person in the assembled group "physically drew back in response." Ironically, Edward Viner felt sorry for his caregivers because he had "laid such a difficult situation on them."

It is clear that the medical profession is not doing all it can and should to help us cope with death and dying. Doctors no longer provide all the treatment, guidance, knowledge, and moral support dying patients and their families crave. Not even when their patient is another physician, as in Dr. Viner's case. Sometimes it appears that when dealing with death, physicians, nurses, and other health professionals suffer from the same confusion, ignorance, and fear we all feel.

Death makes many physicians feel helpless and inadequate. It is often the last subject they want to bring up, because it implies failure. That may be one reason why the physicians and nurses treating Dr. Viner in the ICU drew back when he talked about his fears about dying. They may have felt personally rebuked, as if he had told them they were not doing their job.

As fellow human beings, many doctors avoid talking about death because it forces them to confront their personal, often unexamined, emotions about mortality. Dr. Viner himself had never really considered his feelings about dying until he ended up in the intensive care unit as a patient. It was much easier for him to console his patients with anecdotes and statistics than it was to face death himself. At the end of his illness, his attitude had markedly changed: "I am able to talk more easily with sick people now that I have been there and I understand that these patients are preoccupied with the fear of dying and want to talk about it."

Many physicians also feel that dwelling on death is unhelpful to their patients because they want to encourage them in every way to affirm life. This emphasis on "accentuating the positive" can do more harm than good when it ignores the patient's distress and evades direct questions and concerns. If you are worried about a possible brain tumor, you will be more interested in the results of your CAT scan and your prognosis than in listening to your doctor spout generalities about "mind over matter." Many physicians, however, take their cues from patients, revealing only what they feel the ill person can handle about his or her condition. Patients may often resent this form of selective disclosure. Most of us want, and should have the right, to know *everything* about our illness.

Another problem is that many patients no longer have the luxury of a personal or primary care physician who has treated them and their family over a period of years. Medicine has become more specialized and fewer general practitioners (GPs) are available, so each one must now see more patients in less time. Private offices are run like businesses, where the patient often feels like an item on an assembly line. At ever-increasing numbers of health clinics, patients may be treated by a series of different physicians, leading to a lack of continuity of care. For all of these reasons it is increasingly difficult to establish and maintain a personal, ongoing rapport with a single doctor.

Those patients who do have a doctor often find it hard to get an appointment. When they finally see the doctor, they may feel rushed and intimidated, as if an invisible meter is running. They forget to ask the most important or appropriate questions. Many try to please their doctor by playing the "good patient." Even Edward Viner felt bad for his doctors because he had "laid such a difficult situation on them." Another patient we know, an elderly woman with asthma, Catherine, did not understand her doctor's instructions about her prescription because he "always seemed so rushed and I hated to pester him." When her asthma inhaler did not work, Catherine stopped using it and her asthma got worse. She did not realize that the medicine in the inhaler would prevent her attacks only if she used it regularly over time; that particular medicine was not designed to produce instant results. Catherine's doctor seemed annoyed with her for failing to understand this, which then made her even more reluctant to ask him questions.

Not all patients are as deferential as Catherine. People have grown angry at the limited time and attention they get from their doctor and its disproportionately high cost. While many of us are still in awe of physicians due to their knowledge, doctors have slipped down a few notches in our estimation because we sense that something is missing. The physician is no longer viewed as the all-knowing and all-powerful figure who can do no wrong. Some of the traditional trust implicit in the patient-doctor relationship has eroded. We have all become a little more skeptical and even suspicious about the medical profession's compassion and capabilities.

Final Passages: Toward a New Dialogue and a New Understanding

Confused and frightened by the prospect of long-term illness and suffering, inadequately informed about existing alternatives and options, frustrated and angered by the legal and medical obstacles strewn in their path, an increasing number of patients across America feel they must take end-of-life matters into their own hands. To them, it seems there is nowhere else to turn. Some of these patients have chosen to die, either alone or with the help of a physican or loved one. They have opted for a premature death rather than face the prospect of long illness, infirmity, and suffering—while loving relatives and concerned doctors skirt the law and even risk jail to help them.

Unfortunately the now highly publicized cases of suicide and assisted suicide—domesticated by Derek Humphry's do-it-yourself suicide manual and Jack Kevorkian's homemade suicide machine—have the potential of spawning a spiral of imitation, or at least of creating serious confusion and uncertainty. They represent progressively more isolated and extreme acts, yet they appear in the media as increasingly commonplace. They have focused our attention on an urgent problem, but they have also distorted the issue by highlighting the most radical and extreme solutions. When fear and unbearable suffering *seem* to have no outlet, some patients may seek drastic remedies.

The effect may be to create an aura of inevitability and desirability around suicide for people facing end-of-life situations. We may seem to be giving people a choice of how to die without first giving them a choice about how to live better: through improved medical treatment and care, better social and family support, and a greater personal understanding of their condition with all its limitations and possibilities.

Patients and their families must know that there are ways other than suicide to live and die with courage and self-dignity—and with a minimum of pain. We start at the beginning, with the realization that we will all die. But there are ways to make death a part of life and to prepare ourselves and our loved ones for it. With proper care and medical attention, patients who learn they have a terminal illness or become incapacitated in later life need not react with feelings of hopelessness that lead to depression and suicidal urges. A wide range of options and resources are available for the dying and their loved ones. In today's climate, we have lost sight of how life could, and should, end. It is time to give back to our dying a human, or a humanly understandable, face.

CHAPTER TWO

Learning the Facts: What You Should Ask Your Doctor (and How)

"A doctor who cannot take a good history and a patient who cannot give one are in danger of giving and receiving bad treatment."

—Anonymous, quoted in Paul Dudley White,
Clues in the Diagnosis and Treatment of Heart Disease

Margot, a sixty-two-year-old retiree who loved the Florida sun, noticed a sore on her forearm. When the sore didn't heal after several months, her husband became concerned. He urged Margot to go to the doctor, but she refused. "What if it's cancer?" he asked bluntly. "Don't be ridiculous," Margot replied, ignoring the American Cancer Society's warnings about "a sore that does not heal." It's always "them," her husband would say later. "Never *me*. I think that was her attitude." Margot died of malignant melanoma eighteen months later.

Melanoma is a virulent form of skin cancer that can be cured if detected early enough. Had Margot not ignored the early signs of the disease, or been better informed, or less fearful, she might be alive today. But she was afraid to ask a question or seek help that could have saved her life. In some cases, such as Margot's, medical knowledge can literally be lifesaving; in others, such as Ruth and Mark's, it cannot alter the underlying nature of the disease, but it can help us cope with the fears and anxieties engendered by serious illness.

Ruth was eighty years old and lived alone. Her son, Mark, a successful architect, visited her frequently in the rambling house where he had grown up, and Ruth was always happy to see him. But she seemed to be getting very forgetful, and Mark was worried about it. He noticed more and more frequent lapses of memory. Ruth loved to tell Mark stories of his childhood antics and repeated them endlessly, unaware that she had just told him the same story. Mark grew concerned his mother might leave the stove on and start a fire; or that she would be victimized by muggers, burglars, or other opportunists.

Not the least of Mark's concerns was that his mother was losing her mind. His fears mounted when Ruth began to complain about people stealing from her. She confided in a whisper that the cleaning woman was dishonest and should be "let go." There were other incidents involving stealing. Mark eventually reported a $3,000 jewelry theft to the insurance company, and Ruth was reimbursed in full. Six months later the jewelry was found—his mother had misplaced it, along with numerous other "stolen" items.

Ruth continued to enjoy her son's visits. She was oblivious of and unconcerned about the "theft" and the insurance claim, for the simple reason that she had forgotten all about it as soon as it happened. Mark, on the other hand, had a very different reaction. A good and honest sort, he returned the money to the insurance company, with a red face and profuse apologies. If only that were the end of it, he thought.

Mark took his mother to a psychiatrist, who evaluated her carefully. There was no evidence that Ruth was "crazy," Mark was told, but she should be seen by an internist, to make sure everything was all right medically. After a physical examination and a series of tests, Ruth was given a clean bill of health. So what is wrong with my mother? Mark wanted to know. When he was told she probably had Alzheimer's disease, Mark was badly shaken. He was filled with dread and anxiety. Had he lost his mother forever? And did this mean he, too, would develop Alzheimer's?

Thousands of people every day are seeking answers about health, disease, and aging. But they may not have a specific question, or they have so many they do not know where to begin. Many things can go wrong with the body or even the mind, and fears persist until answers are found. Illness and old age pose new hurdles and challenges that need to be understood before they can be overcome. Many people who are not adequately informed and prepared may feel confused and desperate when confronted with a medical crisis or an end-of-life situation. Without enough knowledge to explain and clarify our condition, many of us may begin to feel helpless and depressed because we believe that nothing can be done for us. These feelings may even lead some of us to contemplate suicide or some other drastic remedy that appears to solve our problems. Numerous reports in medical journals tell of people jumping out of windows, shooting themselves, or otherwise panicking and resorting to desperate measures at the mere suggestion that they might have cancer or another serious illness. One such report recounted the tragic story of a seventy-year-old man who was feeling fatigue and had a cough. Fearing the worst, the man decided to end it all with suicide. The pathologist who performed the autopsy could find no evidence of any serious disease at all. It turned out that the dead man had never bothered to visit a doctor.

Why did this man, for whom many options might have been available, choose to take his life? Did he have a previous bad experience with a doctor? Was his fear of cancer so intense that he could not confront the possibility of having it? Had he seen someone else linger in pain from the disease and vowed never to undergo a similar ordeal? Was he clinically depressed? Or was he misinformed about his medical condition and the options available to him?

It would be a terrible waste for us to give up or jump to hasty conclusions because we lack a full understanding of our medical situation and the alternatives available to us. We need to ask better questions and to demand better answers that make sense to us. What does my diagnosis really mean? What can I do about it? There would be fewer things that we *had* suddenly to accept about illness if we had more knowledge about it.

Although many ailments cannot be completely cured, *it is never correct to say that nothing can be done.* Some constructive step, some skill of the doctor, nurse, or other health professional, can always be tapped to help the situation, not in a minor way, but in a major way.

The first step toward help is to get the facts; and the quickest and safest way to get the facts is to ask your personal doctor, who is familiar with your case. Later in this chapter we will discuss how to make the most efficient use of your physician and to get the answers you need. Our intention is to help you find ways to get the facts about *your* disease. But first we have included some general facts about the most common illnesses that lead to death or disability and raise fears in all of us. (A full list of organizations that provide help for a wide variety of illnesses is in the Appendix.) While many diseases discussed here as examples, such as cancer, heart disease, and Alzheimer's disease, are indeed serious, they are not death sentences. Many of us may live for years with one of these diseases and enjoy a quality of life that is acceptable to us. Even people infected with the AIDS virus may survive for a long time without becoming sick. Other people may care for a loved one who is seriously ill and enable him or her to make the most of their remaining life. But we need to understand what we are up against and what we have to look forward to. "Real fears," William Shakespeare wrote in *King Lear,* "are less than horrible imaginings." Often our greatest obstacle is our "horrible imaginings" about the unknown—which turn out to be far worse than reality. How much pain will cancer cause me? Will they abandon and laugh at me if I have Alzheimer's? In place of concrete knowledge about our actual medical condition and prognosis, we substitute half-truths and popular myths that terrify and isolate us. And these fears and terrors, if they are allowed to stalk us, may contribute to depression and hopelessness and ultimately even to suicide. All too often, it is a simple breakdown in communication. We fail to understand what the normal course of an illness is, the nature of its symptoms, and what we can do about them. And often, too, doctors or other caregivers may not be able or available to correct our misperceptions. They may not provide a complete picture of our medical condition and its implications, leaving us stranded with only partial information so that we are more likely to panic and jump to the wrong conclusion. It is both helpful and reassuring to learn as much as we can about our specific medical condition. And reassurance can be as healing as medicine, but it has no side effects.

Alzheimer's disease

As our life expectancy has increased and more people survive into old age, there are more cases of Alzheimer's disease and more need for us to learn to live with this disease. In fact, as many as 4 million Americans experience Alzheimer's disease or similar problems at the end of life—a worsening forgetfulness and gradual loss of thinking and reasoning capacity, or what used to be called senility. Mark will have to learn to adjust to his mother's illness, but because he is a concerned and involved son, his mother will suffer less than it might at first appear. While there is as yet no cure for this disease, much can be done to make Ruth feel comfortable and to improve her quality of life. Perhaps just as important, Mark can gain a greater sense of control over her situation and so alleviate his own sense of anguish and helplessness and improve *his* quality of life.

Alzheimer's disease has been around for centuries, but an aging population as well as new knowledge about the disease have brought with them more awareness. In 1907, Dr. Alois Alzheimer described the case of a middle-aged woman with senility. When she died at the age of fifty-five, he examined her brain and wrote about his findings. Through the years, this rare condition became known as presenile dementia, to distinguish it from the far more common senile dementia (senility). Then, only about twenty years ago, research scientists found that the majority of old people with senile dementia had exactly the same changes in the brain as Dr. Alzheimer's patient had, and not "hardening of the arteries," as previously believed. In other words, Alzheimer's disease was the most common cause of their senility. Today the term *dementia* is preferred over *senility* because the condition is not confined to the old nor is it accepted as part of normal aging.

These and more recent findings have received a great deal of publicity, but apart from the aging of our population, Alzheimer's disease itself is not on the rise. It is true that "hard," calcified arteries in or near the brain may increase the risk of strokes, and these may produce a condition called multi-infarct dementia, which sometimes causes the same symptoms as Alzheimer's disease. Strokes, however, seem to be on the decline rather than on the increase.

Severe forgetfulness is not a part of normal aging. Although many people late in life develop some problems with memory, most remain mentally clear. This is true even for 50 percent or more of people in their nineties. Ruth's problem is not rare in someone her age, but it is not normal. It will probably progress slowly, but since she is no longer young, there is a possibility that she will die from an unrelated cause rather than Alzheimer's disease itself. If not, her memory and confusion will probably worsen, as well as her coordination and walking, and Mark and others will be doing more and more to assist her in her daily activities. It is worth pointing out that most people with Alzheimer's eventually die from pneumonia or some other form of infection; or because their confusion may make them prone to accidents, such as falling, they may die from complications of traumatic injury, such as a serious fracture. There is no hard evidence that the disease itself ends a person's life directly.

Because Alzheimer's disease affects the brain, it may manifest itself in unpredictable ways, causing changes in emotions or personality. People we thought we knew so well—as Mark thought he knew his mother, Ruth—may now appear to act in odd or "uncharacteristic" ways. In *The 36-Hour Day*, an excellent guide for families of Alzheimer's patients, the authors, Nancy L. Mace and Peter V. Rabins, suggest that "adaptation is the key to success." They recommend that we accept changes in behavior as long as they are not harmful; we must let go of our previous conception of the loved one and try to make the best of a new situation. Generally, it is best to create a structured environment with regular routines so the patient knows what to expect, from knowing exactly where the furniture is to when it is time for meals or medication. We should only make changes when the routine is not working, and if it seems overwhelming, try to concentrate on just one change that will make life a little easier. Other useful suggestions are to get enough rest ourselves, maintain a sense of humor, share our experiences with other families, and get an ID necklace or bracelet with our telephone number for the confused person in the event he or she wanders off and gets lost. Mace and Rabins also remind us to "talk *to* the confused person. Speak calmly and gently. Make a point of telling him what you are doing and why. Let him have a part in deciding things as much as possible. Avoid talking *about* him in front of him, and remind others to do the same." We can never be sure how little, or how much, the Alzheimer's patient understands, and it is important to treat him or her as a dignified, autonomous human being.

As long as Ruth receives regular medical care to prevent serious medical illness and is kept in a safe and comfortable environment, it is very possible that her remaining years will be as free of suffering as is possible for someone her age. Ironically, as Alzheimer's disease progresses, it tends to protect in certain ways. Ruth, for example, was unaware of the embarrassing situation surrounding the insurance claim. Because this incident was so upsetting to Mark, and because he loves his mother a great deal, it is difficult for him to understand his mother's lack of concern. Another patient, Maria, appeared to be unaware that her youngest son had died of cancer, although it had been explained to her on several occasions.

One potential cause of suffering for people with Alzheimer's disease is the imposition of painful medical treatments that, because patients are confused, they do not understand. For this reason, many family members and their doctors feel strongly that those with Alzheimer's disease or other forms of dementia should avoid any uncomfortable treatment that would fail to make them feel better or improve their quality of life. The federal government and state agencies have become aggressive watchdogs over the nursing-home industry. Restraints, once commonly used, are now forbidden except in highly unusual circumstances, and nursing-home staff are learning creative new ways to help people with Alzheimer's disease cope with and adjust to their confusing environment. Invasive treatments, even those that are life sustaining, may not be forced on patients against their wishes, even if patients may no longer have the ability to make health-care decisions for themselves. (See Chapter Eight for details on legal protections such as living wills and durable powers of attorney for health care.)

People with severe Alzheimer's disease sometimes get agitated because, in their confusion, they may not understand what is going on around them and many ordinary events may seem frightening. The agitation may also be a sign of medical illness, a painful condition, or even constipation, and attending to that problem may ease the agitation. Removal of physical restraints, or when possible, of uncomfortable treatments —such as bladder catheters or feeding tubes—may help. Modification of the environment, a pleasant visitor, a meal, or even a massage may be very soothing. Low doses of sedatives may also help. Strong sedatives ("major tranquilizers" or "neuroleptics") have gotten a lot of bad publicity because inappropriate use has created serious complications in many patients, leading to charges that these tranquilizers turn people into "zombies." However, when used judiciously and at doses carefully tailored to meet someone's individual needs, these sedatives can actually be soothing to the patient. Examples of sedatives that may be helpful in small doses are the major tranquilizers thioridazine (Mellaril) and haloperidol (Haldol) and the minor tranquilizer lorazepam (Ativan).

There is presently no cure for Alzheimer's disease, although experimental therapies are under active investigation in research centers across the country. The idea of a progressive deterioration of this sort is intolerable to some people, as it was to Janet Adkins, who sought assistance in ending her life before further mental and physical deterioration occurred. Her story is discussed in detail in Chapter Three. But many positive things can still be done for people with this disease. Ruth should receive regular medical care from someone experienced in dealing with the disease, such as a geriatrician. If there are sudden changes in behavior or rapid deterioration in memory, the doctor will look for reversible medical problems that could do this and will provide guidance on avoiding situations or medications that could cause problems in the future. A social worker, city or county office on aging, senior resource center, or state chapter of the Alzheimer's Association (see Appendix) can help Mark find out about community services and home care so that Ruth will be able to stay at home in her familiar environment as long as possible. It is not too late to do important financial planning and to make arrangements for future health care (see Chapter Nine). Ruth should receive visitors who engage her in one-on-one conversations in which she is called upon to discuss pleasant memories or significant events from her younger days, which she remembers best, and which may be very interesting for others to hear about.

If her condition deteriorates, she should continue to be

stimulated by things that are pleasant but not intellectually taxing, such as her favorite music, good food, and physical comfort. Mark should discuss his mother's end-of-life treatment preferences with a doctor in the event she develops a life-threatening medical problem. All effort should be expended to keep her as comfortable as possible and to treat her with the compassion and dignity she would have wanted.

Mark needs reassurance for himself, too. His concern that he may get the disease like his mother is understandable. However, it is presently not possible to predict who will develop this condition. There is good evidence that a few cases of Alzheimer's disease run in families, but even in these families not everyone inherits the disease. In the vast majority of cases, no consistent hereditary pattern has yet been identified. Regardless of someone's family history, the greatest risk factor for developing Alzheimer's disease is a very long life. Although many cases develop in people who are in their seventies and a few sooner, only about 10 percent of people under eighty are affected. Some experts argue that if we all lived until age one hundred and twenty, we would all have Alzheimer's disease or some form of dementia, but of course this cannot be proved. While mild memory loss is not uncommon, today the vast majority of those over eighty never experience significant memory loss or other symptoms of dementia.

Acquired Immune Deficiency Syndrome (AIDS)

People with AIDS face problems that go far beyond the devastating disease itself. They have to face the social stigma of having AIDS, job discrimination, the difficulty of obtaining insurance coverage, and abandonment by friends and even close relatives. Belatedly, the federal government is waking up to the fact that this is a disease that affects us all, and medical care is being made more easily available. Most major urban hospitals today are able to provide state-of-the-art treatment. Clinics on site may be staffed with professionals who can provide financial counseling to individuals with inadequate insurance coverage. People with very limited resources may qualify for Medicaid (called MediCal in California), which pays for all outpatient as well as in-hospital care. Those with no insurance at all are not denied medical care at public hospitals, where the complex medical problems faced by patients with AIDS have been treated most frequently. Unfortunately, the resources of these and other hospitals that serve AIDS patients are being stretched to the limit and other avenues of care must be found for victims of this epidemic.

Many communities have established special housing units for people who need a supportive environment. These facilities and programs are geared to providing health care as well as to meeting the emotional needs of people with AIDS. Those seeking health-care facilities and opportunities should contact local community organizations, churches, hospitals, hospices, and outpatient clinics to find out what is available in their communities (see Appendix).

Many people with AIDS have become estranged from families who would otherwise be providing emotional support as well as housing. Counseling and social-work interventions, available at many health-care clinics, can sometimes help to overcome the obstacles that have gotten in the way of supportive relationships. These problems include lack of information about the disease and the way it is transmitted so that sometimes false assumptions are made; or personal anger, shame, and rejection because the person infected with AIDS was indulging in "unacceptable" behavior that was hidden from their loved ones. When these obstacles are appropriately addressed, the relationships may often be restored, giving the ill person crucial emotional support and perhaps a home.

Spouses or other individuals who have been intimate with someone infected with AIDS are often reluctant to be tested themselves. They are terrified of discovering they are "positive" for the AIDS virus (called HIV), and question what use this knowledge would have. But not everyone who has sex with an HIV-infected person becomes infected, so there is always a possibility that having the test will be a great relief.

Testing positive is certainly not good news, but knowing the truth will lead to proper treatment, as well as to practicing safe behaviors to prevent the further spread of the disease. Many infected people remain well for long periods of time, with seven to ten years being the average. Medicine is available today that may delay the onset of illness even longer. In addition, although there is no medical proof, it is logical and compatible with what is known about other diseases that a healthy lifestyle is important for anyone who is HIV positive. Adequate rest, avoidance of stressful activities, proper nutrition, and cessation of smoking protect the immune system in other ways and could help to delay the disease's progression and reduce severity. It is also worth pointing out that no epidemic in world history has ever been uniformly fatal. There are always some people who, for whatever reason, are able to live with the disease and carry on with their lives. In fact, people with no symptoms who have carried the AIDS virus for over ten years have been identified. Although they are still capable of transmitting the disease to others—they must not donate blood, for example—it is possible they will never develop symptoms of AIDS.

Since 1985, when mandatory AIDS testing began, it is extremely rare to get AIDS from a blood transfusion. If you are concerned, however, you can predonate your own blood a few weeks before an operation or store and freeze it several months or even years in advance; you can also ask a close friend or relative to provide a designated donation on your behalf.

The person with AIDS suffers not only from a devastating illness but also from ostracism by a society in fear for itself. Short of a vaccine or cure—currently being pursued by researchers across the globe—hope lies in our ability to care for and comfort those who are stricken.

Cancer

Cancer is perhaps one of the most dreaded of all diseases, but it is not one disease. Cancer takes many forms and in many cases is curable. This is partly due to our ability to detect cancers earlier and earlier, before they become so advanced that they cannot be cured. Examples are cancer of the breast, colon, cervix of the uterus (womb), skin, and prostate. For instance, although blood in the stool can be due to a number of noncancerous and often minor problems, it may be the first sign of a malignant (cancerous) tumor, most often of the colon. Early cancerous and precancerous tumors can be removed—often without an operation—and the condition completely cured.

Breast cancer detected on a routine mammogram is often completely curable, and cure rates are increasing. As with all cancers, regular checkups and early detection are the key. Some women do not need to have a mastectomy (removal of the breast) for a cure; and many who do have a mastectomy are able to undergo surgical reconstruction of the breast, if they desire it. For those women who develop painful tumor spread, there are effective medicines and other techniques that can prevent and treat pain. Today, most if not all cancer patients can be made comfortable. (See Chapter Four for a fuller discussion of pain control.)

Prostate cancer is usually detected with a simple rectal examination, which takes less than a minute. Regular examinations each year are critical because early prostate cancer is completely curable. While there is evidence that the majority of elderly men harbor small islands of cancer cells in the prostate gland that cannot be detected with a rectal examination, in most of these cases clinical disease never develops. Although sensitive blood tests for the detection of prostate cancer are available, these tests are not presently recommended for routine screening purposes because of their inexact nature and because they may detect these islands of cells, whose significance is unknown.

Symptoms related to the prostate gland are usually due to benign and not malignant disease. For example, men who have trouble passing urine or urinate frequently most often have benign enlargement of the prostate gland, a common and noncancerous condition called benign prostatic hyperplasia (BPH).

Routine cancer checkups are important for everyone, regardless of their age. If your doctor tells you that you might have cancer, it is important to get treatment promptly. In addition to cancers mentioned above, other potentially curable forms of cancer include cancer of the testes, lymphocytic leukemia, and Hodgkin's lymphoma. Deep cancers, such as cancer of the pancreas, ovary, and lung, are more difficult to diagnose early because tumors in these parts of the body cannot be accurately visualized and located while they are too small to produce signs or symptoms. Sometimes they are cured when tumors are found during an operation for another problem. In some cases, lung cancer can be detected on a chest X ray while it is still curable. Other forms of cancer, though not usually curable, can be controlled or remain mild for so many years that the person survives long enough to die of an unrelated cause. Examples of these cancers include chronic lymphocytic leukemia and some forms of lymphoma. It is unlikely that all cancers will be curable or even preventable in our lifetime, but new research brings new hope for all cancers every day.

What if your doctor suggests treatment other than surgery, or in addition to it, such as radiation or chemotherapy? Will it produce a cure? Will the treatment be worse than the disease? Is the treatment even worth it? One woman frankly said she would not "consider it" at her age because she was seventy-five. But advanced age alone is not a contraindication to good anticancer treatment because many elderly patients benefit greatly from these treatments and tolerate them as well as younger patients. Although radiation and chemotherapy are double-edged swords, if prescribed appropriately they can reduce pain, prolong useful life, and sometimes even result in cure. The outcome is entirely dependent on the type of cancer the patient has and how advanced the problem is. If a positive outcome is a good possibility in your case, you should seriously consider radiation or chemotherapy. You must ask your doctor what the purpose of the treatment is, what it is expected to do, what might happen if you do not undergo the treatment, and whether there are alternative treatments you can consider, such as surgery or hormonal therapy. You should be aware that truly "alternative" treatments such as exotic diets, meditation, and megavitamins do not cure cancer, although they make the person who believes in them feel better psychologically and this may lead to some improvement. However, psychological support should be given as an adjunct and *not as an alternative* to treatment that has proved effective.

Radiation is less likely to cause serious side effects than chemotherapy. However, it can cause fatigue, or inflammation of normal tissue that is close to the cancerous tissue under treatment. When adverse symptoms occur, in most cases they are temporary. You should ask your doctor what kinds of problems to expect and what to do about them if they occur. Cancer chemotherapy consists of the administration of one or more toxic medicines that obliterate tumor. Although certain forms of chemotherapy can be very well tolerated, most medications can harm normal tissues in parts of the body remote from the tumor—the blood being the most vulnerable in general. Other tissues can be harmed as well, depending on the specific medicine used and the dose. Once again, it is important for you to consult a physician, probably a cancer specialist (oncologist), as to what types of symptoms the chemotherapy is most likely to cause. Nausea and vomiting are common side effects that occur right after chemotherapy is administered, but they can also occur just *before*, something called anticipatory vomiting. Highly effective medications are available that can reduce vomiting and nausea considerably (see Chapter Four). Because chemotherapy can cause a reduction in the numbers of important blood cells, the doctor may recommend frequent blood tests for a few weeks following the chemotherapy sessions so that any serious problems can be anticipated and appropriate action taken. For example, a drop in the white blood cell count can lead to serious infections so that prophylactic (preventive) antibiotic treatment might be recommended.

For someone who has already undergone chemotherapy or radiation treatments for cancer and doesn't want to continue, it is important to discuss these feelings directly with a responsible and attentive professional, such as a primary care physician, oncologist, radiation specialist, or chemotherapy nurse. Has the first run-through produced serious side effects? Can these side effects be avoided in the future? What is the possible outcome of further treatments? A cure? An additional ten years or one year or one month? It is important to get all the medical facts before one makes a decision. These are important questions to ask whether a person is twenty or ninety years old.

Chapters Four and Seven discuss a wide range of options in detail for people who are seriously ill, confused about where to turn, or feel that they have lost hope. Remember that there is always something that can be done.

Heart Disease

Many people, particularly those with a family history of heart disease, often become concerned about pain or tightness in their chest area. It's important to keep in mind that chest pain can be caused by a number of problems that have nothing to do with the heart: these include problems with the stomach, esophagus (food tube), chest muscles, or lining of the lung. However, chest pain may be an indication of underlying heart disease, and it is advisable to visit a doctor, such as an internist, for an evaluation if it persists. Fortunately, today there are highly effective treatments for this problem, and many heart attacks can be prevented. If pain is related to coronary heart disease, which is due to blockages in the coronary arteries nourishing the heart, the treatment approach might include changes in diet, weight loss, medications to lower the blood level of cholesterol, or a graded aerobic exercise program, prescribed by and under the supervision of a cardiologist. Exercise programs can be designed for coronary heart disease patients of *all* ages.

Coronary heart disease can also be treated with angioplasty

or open-heart surgery. In angioplasty, a balloon-tipped catheter is inserted directly into the coronary arteries: the balloon is inflated and the blockage is cleared. Coronary artery bypass grafting (bypass) is a surgical technique that uses an open vein taken from a patient's leg and substitutes it for a blocked coronary artery. These methods have been used successfully in people of all ages. Other forms of open-heart surgery have met with similar success. Contrary to some views, age need not be a barrier. One distinguished ninety-year-old man was dissuaded from undergoing a bypass procedure because some doctors and nurses believed he was "too old." The man died of a heart attack a few months later. Another man, an eighty-nine-year-old professor, had his diseased aortic valve replaced in a major operation and continued to do important work until he died at the age of one hundred and three.

An increasingly common and successful treatment for heart disease involves the use of a pacemaker. A pacemaker is a small device, not much larger than a thick, round silver dollar, implanted underneath the skin and connected to thin wires that lead into the heart through large blood vessels. The outline of the pacemaker is barely visible on the surface of the skin. Inserting a pacemaker is a simple procedure nowadays, performed by a cardiologist or cardiac surgeon, and most often the patient doesn't even have to spend the night in the hospital. Battery replacements are even simpler and can be done as a short outpatient procedure. Later on, the battery can be checked by telephone and the pacemaker can remain in place for years, usually without problems of any kind.

People with pacemakers can lead a completely normal life. Those who require pacemakers generally do so because the heart's own electrical system is "frayed," and heartbeat may fail to occur often enough. However, the heart muscle and other vital structures of the heart may be completely normal. Placement of a pacemaker in an otherwise healthy heart is analogous to replacing the battery in a beautiful classic car.

Other forms of heart disease exist, but new treatments come into being every day. Heart disease has for years been, and will continue to be, a fruitful field for research. This research, coupled with changes in our lifestyle, has led to decreased mortality from virtually all types of heart disease in this country.

Infirmities of "Aging"

There are many infirmities that people associate with getting old. While not immediately life-threatening, many of these impairments may appear overwhelming and undermine our joy and faith in life. Sometimes, they may make us question the value of carrying on at all. An eighty-seven-year-old woman named Elizabeth, who was basically healthy but suffered from many physical ailments connected to her advanced years, confessed one day: "I'm old. Nothing works anymore. I can't hear. I can't see. My hands and shoulders are riddled with arthritis. I can't move around or drive. All my friends are dead or in the same situation. The only thing I have to look forward to is getting sick and dying."

Although many people may have bad moments when they feel like this, a persistent and overwhelming sense of despair may be a sign of a treatable clinical depression. The first thing Elizabeth needs is to see a health professional, preferably her personal physician. If depression is diagnosed, then appropriate treatment should be initiated, as we will discuss in detail in Chapter Five. But apart from any possible depression, Elizabeth obviously has some other problems that need attention. A senior resource center or local office on aging can be excellent sources of help, and she or an interested family member should contact them for assistance. They often have solutions to the problem of getting around the community for routine chores and activities, for health care (including treatment for depression), and for maintaining social contacts or establishing new ones. In addition to recognizing and assisting when problems exist, they can identify the person's positive capabilities and capitalize on these. For example, someone with poor vision or hearing may be physically fit enough to participate in full or modified exercise classes designed for seniors.

An older person is commonly the sole survivor of long

friendships and powerful family ties. New social contacts are extremely important in these situations, and often middle-aged or younger individuals become fast friends and a source of support and good times. Community and church organizations also provide help by getting services to the home, including meals, activities, and health care.

Hearing and visual impairments should be addressed head-on. Hearing loss can be very frustrating, and the hearing impaired sometimes find themselves left out of conversations, or out of frustration, they simply stop listening and withdraw. It is not uncommon for someone to avoid using a hearing aid, claiming that "it doesn't work." Because a hearing aid may amplify extraneous, unwanted noise as well as the sounds people want to hear, many individuals become annoyed and refuse to use one. Another important factor, not frequently recognized, is that older hearing-impaired individuals often have problems with "discrimination," which means they may hear individual sounds but may not be able to tell the difference (discriminate) between closely related sounds or words. For example, they may confuse certain rhyming words such as *sin* and *thin*. It is important to get the speaker to look directly at the person who is trying to hear, to enunciate clearly, and to avoid mumbling. Simply talking louder may distort the quality of the sound and actually *reduce* the ability of the listener to understand the spoken words.

If someone is not using his or her hearing aid, it is important to find out why. Perhaps she thinks it doesn't work because she is using it incorrectly; perhaps the battery needs changing or the apparatus needs cleaning or repair. Or she may not like the way it looks and would be willing to wear a different style. One woman in her nineties with severe hearing impairment obtained significant help from a new style of hearing aid worn on the chest and connected by wire to the in-ear portion. However, she did not like to use it because she was forced to learn a new method of using the aid when she was talking on the telephone. In these circumstances amplification of the telephone receiver with an additional device can be very helpful. So can a little patience, because the technique can be mastered and the results are well worth the effort.

Elizabeth, who seemed so depressed, also complained of visual problems, which need to be examined. If cataracts (clouded lenses of the eye) are present, surgery can bring significant and sometimes dramatic improvement in vision. Because most cataracts occur in older individuals, cataract operations were practically designed for the elderly. Many extremely old patients have regained adequate or even excellent vision after cataract surgery. Nowadays, most patients can even avoid having to wear cataract spectacles because a replacement lens is implanted directly and permanently in the eye during the operation. This is particularly useful for those who are very aged or debilitated and might have difficulty managing contact lenses.

Is the visual problem due to degeneration of the macula— an area of the retina governing direct, central vision? One woman with macular degeneration became extremely depressed because her doctor told her nothing could be done about her condition. One form of this impairment, "dry" macular degeneration, progresses slowly and interferes with central vision but not peripheral vision. There is presently no cure for this condition, but patients often have many years during which to adjust and learn techniques to overcome this deficit. Patients with poor vision should ask an eye doctor to refer them for a low-vision evaluation. An ever-increasing number of special lenses, visual aids, and rehabilitation techniques have helped a lot of people enjoy their lives again. In addition, there is some evidence that wearing sunglasses to avoid bright sunlight can slow the progression.

Another and potentially more severe form, "wet" macular degeneration, comes from the growth of tiny, frail blood vessels in the retina of the eye. Serious loss of central vision can occur rapidly if one of these vessels bleeds. In this form of macular degeneration, visual loss can often be prevented with laser treatments that obliterate the dangerous vessels. Low-vision aids and visual rehabilitation should also be given to people who have lost vision due to this form of the disease or to any other eye problem that is not reversible.

Elizabeth's concern about her arthritis is understandable. Arthritis is very common in older people, and although it is more often mild than severe, it can produce significant disability. Many people fear the prospect of painful, crippling arthritis that may confine them to a wheelchair in late life and turn them into invalids. But pain relief from arthritis is achievable—the management of chronic pain, using not only medications but a wide variety of methods, is discussed in Chapter Four—while modern surgical and rehabilitation techniques and devices can make a significant difference in our ability to function even in very old age. The vast majority of those with arthritis will never become disabled. Osteoarthritis, by far the most common form of arthritis, is usually mild and noncrippling. For people with severe arthritis of the knees or hips, surgery may offer an excellent and dramatic solution to restore mobility. Like many operations for degenerative conditions, total hip and total knee replacements are surgical procedures most often used in people who are over sixty-five. Although these operations should only be performed if other methods have consistently failed to help, many older people have successful hip or knee replacements that dramatically improve their quality of life.

Elizabeth is fortunate in at least one aspect: she can still think and reason. This is a precious gift that should be valued. She will be able to form and enjoy new social contacts that someone without this capability could not appreciate. In addition, because of her age, she has accumulated a lifetime of knowledge and experience that younger people lack. She has something to teach and pass on. If she is able to "see" this about herself, she will be able to help others, which will bring a new dimension into her life.

Parkinson's Disease

For people in the advanced stage of Parkinson's disease, the loss of mobility and flexibility can be debilitating. In addition to being physically restricted, patients undergo an enormous emotional toll, wondering if they will ever be able to move around the house again. One important step is to visit a doctor, probably a neurologist, to ensure they are on the best regimen of medications. Many are available today, and many patients have achieved a great deal of relief from antiparkinsonian medications alone. Each regimen must be tailored to the person's individual needs. Are they taking a medication such as Sinemet? If so, do they need to take it more frequently or at different times of the day than at present? Would they benefit from the addition of a second drug, such as selegiline (also called deprenyl or Eldepryl), bromocriptine (Parlodel), or one of several other available drugs? Are they taking medication that might reduce the effectiveness of these medications or directly worsen their symptoms, such as a strong tranquilizer like haloperidol (Haldol) or a gastrointestinal drug called metoclopramide (Reglan)? Have they consulted an occupational therapist who could advise them how to improve their activities of daily living and recommend assistive devices such as grab bars to use in the bathrooms or other areas inside and outside the house? Smooth sheets, even satin ones, might make it easier for them to slip in and out of bed. They might want to take up an active exercise program to forestall the development of rigidity and maintain muscle strength.

They might also see about using community services provided for others with various medical problems. Perhaps their local senior resource center or office on aging can give them some tips. Because they have had to give up driving, they may feel increasingly isolated and cut off. Shopping, going to the doctor, attending a church or synagogue, participating in social events, or simply maintaining contact with the outside world is often dependent on one's ability to drive from one location to another. A driving service through a church or youth group, a "dial-a-ride" low-cost car service, or even a reliable taxi company in the community may help them negotiate this barrier and overcome their isolation. Or they might employ a trusted friend—or the friend's son or daughter—to drive them places for a modest fee. Perhaps they can receive one meal a day from a "meals on wheels" service, which might reduce their shopping needs. It will also make them realize they are not alone and others are concerned for their well-being.

Parkinson's disease is under active research, and new techniques such as the transplantation of chemically active tissue into the brain may offer hope for the future. While there is as yet no cure for Parkinson's disease, much can be done to improve patients' quality of life and show them that they still have value for others and new satisfactions, however small, to look forward to for themselves.

Beyond those questions relating to specific medical illnesses and conditions—and the ones we have just discussed are a mere sample—patients need to know how to communicate better with their physicians. A woman named Linda reacted this way to her illness: "I fell on the floor when I got out of bed yesterday. My doctor just told me I had a stroke. I can't move my arm and can barely lift my leg. I'm eighty; my life is over."

What Linda's doctor has not yet told her—and what she did not know to ask—is that there is a possibility she will get significantly better. It is impossible to predict the extent or rate of recovery when someone has a stroke, but it is likewise impossible to predict that there will be no recovery. Many patients do, in fact, recover from stroke. After six weeks of rehabilitation, Linda walked out of the hospital with the help of a cane. Her nephew bought her an antique walking stick as a get-well present. She now jokes that she uses it "only because it looks chic." Linda is also receiving medication that will reduce her risk of having a stroke in the future. Her life is far from over, and she has much to look forward to, but incomplete information and lack of full communication with her physician almost led her to lose hope.

The patient-doctor relationship is the cornerstone of good medicine, but it requires open discussion and understanding between all parties. Patients are entitled to a full and clear explanation of any problem that concerns them, but they should also learn how best to approach their physician on a personal and professional level. It is useful for patients to keep the doctor's perspective in mind when going for a visit. An awareness of the doctor's particular circumstances and professional attitudes may help bridge the gap that sometimes leads to misunderstandings. If you view your doctor as someone essentially well-meaning and dedicated but limited by certain constraints, this approach may assist you in securing the kind of treatment and cooperation you want. Some doctors may appear to lack compassion when their only shortcoming is an abrupt or stiff manner; once the patient breaks through this barrier, the therapeutic interaction and communication improve. Other physicians may truly lack empathy and sensitivity toward their patients. *Those patients who are unhappy or dissatisfied with their physicians should not hesitate to seek more sympathetic and cooperative doctors.*

Many patients are upset because physicians always seem rushed and unwilling to take enough time with them. "Why don't any of my new doctors seem to care?" is a common complaint today. There may be many reasons why doctors seem rushed. First and foremost is the large number of patients that need care. It is difficult, if not impossible, for a doctor to say no to someone who is sick. Urgent situations and dire emergencies crop up regularly and often necessitate changes in scheduling. Sometimes these emergencies demand squeezing new patients in and delaying other patients who are scheduled for routine visits. Due to the large and ever-changing nature of their caseloads, physicians are constantly scrambling to balance seeing new and unexpected patients who need immediate attention with more routine office visits. As a result, regular patients may often be inconvenienced and experience long and frustrating delays. When the doctor does appear, pressures from a previous patient or anticipation of an upcoming problem may all impinge on the doctor's concentration and allotment of time to the present patient. Ideally of course, physicians are adept at clearing their minds and focusing their full attention and medical know-how on each patient, but they are also human and subject to emotional pressures that carry over from one patient to another.

The physician's training under the present health-care system also tends to emphasize the importance of doing hard science over personal interaction with the patient. A doctor's primary energies are usually devoted to practicing scientific medicine (performing the biopsy, getting the results) rather than to addressing the emotional consequences of the news, or getting the patient to ask unspoken questions ("Will I suffer?" "Will I live?" "How long?"). To sit down and talk, to hold a patient's hand and go over things carefully, takes far more time and is not financially rewarding under the current system. Unfortunately, there are doctors who simply don't want to spend a lot of time with their patients; others would like to give more time but have too many patients competing for too few appointments. Fewer doctors today work out of private offices where they can exert some control over time spent in the office; more and more doctors work within large organizations such as clinics or health maintenance organizations (HMOs) where they are required to see a set number of patients in a specific amount of time (often up to six in one hour) and where the office closes up at five P.M. and may not be open at all on weekends. Patients who have simple problems and few questions may not feel as rushed as those who have a lot of medical problems, a lot of questions, and complicated treatments or complex medication regimens. Unfortunately, patients with the greatest need for time, especially older people, will be the very ones whose needs may not be met.

Those doctors who do work out of private offices, and particularly those who see a large number of Medicare or Medicaid patients, have government limits set on their fees. While this can be good for the federal budget, it puts pressure on the private practitioner to see larger numbers of patients in the same amount of time. For example, Medicare, the federal health-insurance program for the elderly, reimburses doctors on the basis of how many patients they see and what technical procedures they perform, not for how much time they spend with each patient. So, broadly speaking, a doctor who sees a single older Medicare patient for one hour—questioning, examining, counseling, or comforting—may earn as little as one-sixth of the amount his colleague earns because he sees six younger patients for ten minutes each. The system simply does not reward the more caring physician who takes time out to talk and explain things to his patient. Although many consumers feel that doctors should concentrate on giving better care, even if they make less money, many physicians feel that, in a purely monetary sense, they are *penalized* for providing this kind of personal care. On the other hand, if physicians perform certain procedures for their patients, such as a colonoscopy or bronchoscopy, they will be much more amply rewarded for the time spent.

Despite some modest recent changes in federally mandated fee structures that benefit general and family practitioners, those doctors in general care still earn significantly less than their counterparts in the various specialties. When it comes to making home visits, Medicare reimburses doctors as much as one-third less than physical therapists, occupational therapists, and nurses. The current health-care system continues to encourage physicians to perform more technical tests and procedures, which are handsomely reimbursed, and to spend less personal time with patients, which is not financially beneficial to doctors. Of course there are many dedicated physicians who provide their patients with excellent care and adequate time, at home and elsewhere, but they do so by swimming against the current. Your doctor's individual personality and motivation—the reasons he or she became a physician in the first place—may often determine the quality of care you receive.

In addition, today doctors feel they must see a lot of patients to offset rising malpractice insurance costs, which range from $10,000 to $100,000 a year. The fear of being sued also forces doctors to perform even more tests and procedures. This practice, known as defensive medicine, is used to rule out any remote possibility the doctor may have overlooked and to establish evidence that the doctor behaved in a professional and conscientious manner. These tests and procedures, which often involve the latest equipment and technology, can be expensive, time-consuming, and even dangerous. Unfortunately, defensive medicine is usually more effective in easing the doctor's anxiety than in helping the patient.

It is true that there may be explanations for a doctor's resistance to your needs, for his or her lack of availability, and even for an apparent lack of interest in you as a person. But this is small consolation if you are sick or frightened and have questions that demand answers. What can *you* do to make sure your needs as a patient are answered?

Even before going to see the doctor, you need to prepare yourself and plan how to best use the limited time with your physician. Try to be as precise as possible in describing your specific condition or complaint. Do not be embarrassed about the details. For example, if you suffer from urinary incontinence, you should tell your doctor you have trouble controlling your bladder and wet yourself on occasion. In many cases, help is available for this problem but many people are too embarrassed to broach the subject. Remember that the doctor's main function is to serve you, but to do that effectively he or she needs as much information as possible. For urinary incontinence, a doctor may recommend that you keep a "bladder diary" so you can record and time your symptoms and so better understand your problem and get appropriate treatment. In all medical conditions, you need to be a good detective about your body and a ready witness with your personal medical testimony. Once you give an accurate account of your condition, make sure to ask appropriate questions about your diagnosis and treatment. Do not be satisfied with generalities. On what basis is the doctor making a diagnosis: tests, symptoms, or an educated guess? If tests are ordered, what are they, why are they being given, and what are the alternatives, if any? Why is the doctor suggesting a particular therapy, and what is his or her experience with this treatment?

You should be assertive about your questions and insist on answers from the doctor, answers that you can understand and that make sense to you. Do not be intimidated if a doctor seems brusque or overly businesslike. This is not always easy, as we saw with Catherine, the elderly woman in the last chapter who did not understand how to use her asthma medication. But Catherine eventually recognized that her doctor was not inaccessible, only overworked. She discussed her feelings with the office nurse, who suggested Catherine write down her questions in advance and bring them with her on her next visit. She could also bring another person with her, a close friend or relative, who would take notes during the exam and ensure that any questions or concerns Catherine had were brought up during the visit. In the event Catherine still forgot an important question, or a new issue came up that needed clarification, she was able to make arrangements to call the doctor back after five o'clock. There was more time then, the nurse explained, because office hours were over and other patients would not be waiting to be seen. To her surprise, Catherine found that her doctor was eager to answer her questions; she was even more surprised that much of what he had to say was reassuring.

Seek a time that is best for both you and your doctor to discuss specific questions that might take more time than usual. Basic questions can be answered during an ordinary office visit—or in the hospital, during a bedside visit. It is very helpful if patients or family members write down their questions in advance so they will not forget to ask them. One of the questions should be: "When is a good time to speak to you if I have more things to ask you about?" Once you establish an answer to this all-important question, you will know when and how to reach your doctor if an important issue comes up that you did not remember when the doctor was right there.

When visiting your doctor, try to make eye contact and get the physician to look at you. If your doctor seems distant, you can physically draw nearer by pulling your chair closer. Make the doctor take note of you as an individual in your own right. You are not only an equal but you are the paying customer whose needs must be met. Without being unpleasant about it, keep in mind that you have the power to take your business elsewhere. As you are paying for the physician's services, demand that you get your money's worth. If the doctor says something you did not hear or fully understand, insist that it be repeated and explained. You should not leave the doctor's office until you are satisfied and your basic questions and concerns have been answered.

Of course many questions can and should be addressed to people other than the doctor. Questions about medications can often be answered by a nurse in the office or the hospital; questions about appointments or about your bill will be answered most swiftly and accurately by a designated person in the doctor's office, or in the hospital, by personnel in the billing office.

In a big clinic or HMO there may be different people at the front desk and a number of people answering the telephone. This may often lead to confusion and frustration. It is a good idea to establish a relationship with one or two people *by name*. That way a question can be directed to that same person, who will remember you or your question and will be able to help you more efficiently, either by answering your question directly or by steering you to the appropriate person who can help. Always be assertive but polite even if you are frustrated or upset. Receptionists and clerks are only human and will respond best to someone who is not only forceful but takes their busy situation into account.

If you think you have good reasons for switching doctors, you should do so. Patients often change doctors for a variety of reasons—personality conflicts, lack of confidence in the doctor, financial reasons—and doctors realize this and accept it. Even if you run into resistance, the choice of doctors is yours to make. Your new doctor's office can request copies of your previous doctor's records with your permission. This transfer of information is important to ensure good continuity of care, and you do not have to make the request by yourself —the office secretary will do it. If you belong to a large clinic or HMO, you still have the option of switching doctors within that group. You should not feel guilty or embarrassed about leaving a doctor who fails to meet your needs. It is likely that your previous doctor receives new patients from other doctors, and it is even possible that your new doctor "loses" patients to other doctors. It is vital that you, the patient, feel comfortable with your doctor.

Finding a new doctor you can have confidence in is not as tall an order as you might think. One of the best methods is the word-of-mouth approach. Ask a number of your friends, particularly your contemporaries, whether they have a doctor they can recommend. If you have a specialist that you trust (say a urologist, an eye doctor, or a cardiologist), he or she might be able to refer you directly to a good general internist or family practitioner. There is no charge for this referral; all your doctor needs to do is give you the name and number of the new doctor. You can usually call his or her office directly for an appointment. It will be up to you to determine how you feel about this new doctor.

If the word-of-mouth approach is unsuccessful, check the *Directory of Medical Specialists*, available in many community libraries and all medical libraries, to find the names of doctors in a particular field. This directory provides a small "biography" of each doctor listed, giving his or her year of graduation, medical school, and history of professional affiliations.

The directory only lists doctors who are certified in their particular specialty so you will know if they have satisfied all the requirements for certification. Don't be put off by the word specialist if you are looking for a generalist or primary care physician. General internists and family practitioners are listed under the specialties of "Internal Medicine" and "Family Practice." Certain diseases tend to be treated by particular specialties (see Appendix), but it is usually best to get a referral from your primary care physician.

You can also get names of doctors from your state or local medical society. Unfortunately, not all doctors are members of these organizations, and often some of the best doctors fail to join local groups, so they may not be listed. National organizations maintain lists of doctors in specific specialties. However, membership in national organizations does not always require a screening procedure, so unless the organization can give you reliable information about the doctor's background and credentials, this may not be too helpful.

You can also find the name of a doctor by calling your local hospital. Today hospitals require doctors to fulfill strict criteria before they will grant or renew admitting privileges, although bad apples sometimes crop up. To get an "inside" scoop on a doctor, it is sometimes helpful to ask nurses or even other doctors who work in a hospital about the person you have in mind. You can also ask for other recommendations, should they know of someone better suited to your needs. Make sure the person you ask is someone you yourself trust.

Obtaining a doctor's name from a professional organization, hospital, or individual will not, of course, tell you in advance whether you will feel confident or comfortable with that particular doctor. Every patient—and every doctor—is different, and not every doctor will be the "right match" for you.

One factor you might take into account is how long the doctor kept you waiting. While unexpected delays can occur, note whether the doctor apologizes for your wait once he does see you. You can also speak to other patients in the waiting room and ask their opinion of the doctor. Personal anecdotes and individual tones of voice ("He's just wonderful, I send all my family and friends here" or "Believe me, if I had any other choice, I'd go elsewhere") can speak volumes. Once your appointment begins, observe how well the doctor listens or whether he or she tries to control the medical interview. Do you feel you've had a chance to explain what is bothering you? Is the doctor answering you directly and personally or are you getting standard and impersonal responses? Another factor to consider is the doctor's availability. Is the doctor readily reachable outside office hours or does he or she discourage outside contact? In an emergency, would the doctor or a partner be there for you, or would you have to contend with an answering service and a new physician who is not familiar with your case? You might also consider how convenient the doctor's office is to where you live or work. If you plan on regular visits and each visit requires a large outlay of time and money or missing work, you might want to look closer to home. On the other hand, you may feel that this physician's outstanding abilities and sympathies merit the extra effort and expenditure.

You should not rely on the yellow pages of your telephone book or other forms of advertising to find someone with good credentials. Although most reputable private doctors are listed in the yellow pages, it is an advertising guide where doctors provide their own names, and disreputable doctors show up now and again, as in any advertisement.

In the end, trust your intuition. Patients are usually right about their doctors. If your instinct tells you that a physician is not "right" for you, then look elsewhere. It should not matter that the doctor has a big reputation or an impressive patient list. If you are uneasy or uncomfortable with a physician in any way—even if you can't quite put your finger on the reason why—then speak up and address your problem directly. If the doctor is not answering your questions or providing the feedback you need, change doctors. Keep looking until you find someone who meets your needs and responds to your concerns.

Above all, don't let hopeless feelings become a trap that

convinces you there is nothing left to be done, that no one will ever understand you, and that some drastic remedy like suicide is the only alternative you have. It isn't. There are doctors out there who can respond and answer your particular needs. They can help point you to other available—and viable—options. But you have to go seek out the appropriate physician and engage him or her in a personal dialogue. Don't shortchange yourself. Your life, under any circumstances, has value; and you must find a medical professional who recognizes and respects that fact and is willing to work with you to preserve and enhance it in keeping with your values.

CHAPTER THREE

Extreme Options: Suicide, Physician-Assisted Suicide, and Euthanasia

"It is not a thing to do while one is not in one's best mind. Never kill yourself when you are suicidal."

—Edwin Schneidman, *Suicide*

Jeanette, a bright and outgoing college senior from Minnesota, began to notice clumsiness in her hand while writing an examination. When the weakness did not subside after a few days, she visted her family doctor. He admitted her to the hospital for tests, including a spinal tap, which revealed that Jeanette was suffering from multiple sclerosis. She was only twenty-two years old.

Jeanette's mother had suffered from the same slowly degenerative disease, but she had persevered and enjoyed a reasonably healthy life into her early seventies. Jeanette was determined that she, too, would have a good life. After a course of medical treatment, her hand improved. She got married, had two children, and pursued a successful career in advertising. She continued to participate in a wide variety of activities and was regarded by all her friends as a vivacious and energetic person.

In her forties, Jeanette's health began to deteriorate at an acclerated pace. She grew easily fatigued and developed bladder problems. She became a little shaky and eventually needed a cane for walking. Her speech became slightly slurred, and she once again had difficulty with her handwriting.

Jeanette's progressive illness took its toll on her personal and professional life. Her husband divorced her and shortly after married a younger, healthy woman. Her children, now college age, seemed to keep their distance and remained more aloof than usual. The advertising agency where she had successfully worked for fifteen years began to give her the worst accounts and then finally asked her to leave. Shortly after this devastating news, Jeanette suddenly lost vision in one eye. Jeanette's entire life slowly fell apart.

When Jeanette approached her long-time physician—Dr. Marshall, the same physician who had admitted her to the hospital twenty years before and had known her since her teens—her mind was made up. She had decided that life was no longer worth living and she wanted his help in terminating her existence. She knew that assisting a suicide was against the law in Minnesota, but there were ways around it. She had heard about similar cases through the media, and she was sure Dr. Marshall would help. He had always been progressive and open-minded in previous treatment decisions.

Jeanette was stunned when Dr. Marshall refused her request outright. He had always seemed so accessible, talking to her about living wills and the rights of patients. But here, for some reason, he drew the line.

Dr. Marshall told Jeanette that the recent personal losses brought about by her illness were making her depressed and in no condition to make a reasoned judgment of this magnitude. What if she changed her mind once her depression lifted? Even if she did not, it was his role to help her regain health and a measure of happiness, not to assist in her death. Jeanette grew angry and claimed he had promised never to let her linger on life support if she was dying and had no chance of recovery. Dr. Marshall said he would still honor that request, but physician-assisted suicide was different. Jeanette was seriously ill but she was not dying. In his medical opinion she had many more years of life, however compromised, to enjoy. Dr. Marshall would help relieve her discomfort, but he would not kill her.

Dr. Marshall explained there was a fairly good chance Jeanette's vision would improve. He urged her to take medication that he would prescribe for her depression and then to resume treatment for her illness. There were many therapies, some still experimental, that she had not tried. Multiple sclerosis is thought to be an autoimmune disease in which the body's natural defenses attack myelin, the white coating of nerve fibers in the brain and spinal cord, as though it were foreign tissue, causing it to disintegrate, thus interfering with transmission of nerve signals. One of the promising treatments is a synthetic protein that suppresses the malfunctioning immune system. Research on a number of other drugs and treatments was under way as well.

If Jeanette did not wish to try these new treatments, she could still practice some stretching and muscle-strengthening exercises to help keep her muscles in working order. She could take muscle relaxants to alleviate her muscle spasticity. She also had much to gain from occupational therapy, which would improve her ability to perform the activities of daily living. The local MS society sponsored helpful group therapy sessions for patients, and these were free of charge. Dr. Marshall could also recommend a psychologist, who might provide Jeanette with some useful psychotherapy.

Dr. Marshall did not wish to minimize the severity of Jeanette's illness or the anguish of her losses. These were real and profound. But Jeanette's mind was still fully alert and there were activities she could participate in. Her children loved her, she had loyal, caring friends, and it was not like her to give up so easily. Dr. Marshall, a long-time friend, believed he could still help Jeanette find some meaning and satisfaction in her life. His medicine had much to offer. But it could not be the agent of her death and assist in her suicide.

* * *

Jeanette sought one kind of help from Dr. Marshall—assistance in taking her life—but she received another: help in coping with a serious disabling illness and carrying on with her life. Initially she resisted his advice and resented his refusal to help her kill herself. In her anger and sense of betrayal, she went so far as to get the name of another physician reputed to be more sympathetic to such end-of-life requests. But after seriously considering the idea of changing doctors, she decided to stay with Dr. Marshall and to follow his advice. He had never led her astray before. And if he was so convinced that her life was still worth living—when one door closes, another opens, he was fond of repeating—then perhaps she would try to live up to his expectations.

It was all a question of how you looked at it: the glass was either two-thirds empty or one-third full. After much agonizing, Jeanette decided to concentrate on the one-third she still had left. Her vision did in fact improve significantly. One of the real surprises for her was how much closer she grew to her adult children, James and Margaret, as they finished college. They began confiding in one another, and Margaret revealed she had "shrunk" from Jeanette in her teens because she feared she, too, would be affected by multiple sclerosis, just like her mother and grandmother. Dr. Marshall explained that it is very rare for members of the same family to be afflicted by MS, and the chances that either Margaret or James would develop the disease were slim indeed. Jeanette's renewed closeness with her grown children was alone worth the many setbacks she had suffered. It was as if all the affection and pent-up feelings of earlier times were suddenly expressed openly and shared among them. As if they were redeeming the past and correcting a wrong turn taken during their adolescence.

Not everyone who suffers a debilitating illness and contemplates suicide chooses the difficult but life-affirming road that Jeanette took. Some people "succeed" in taking their lives or enlisting a physician or friend to help them commit suicide. Sherry Miller, a forty-three-year-old woman suffering from multiple sclerosis, turned to pathologist Jack Kevorkian for assistance in killing herself with carbon monoxide when she decided her life was no longer worth living. Her existence was simply intolerable to her. Others carry on with their lives but suffer unnecessary pain and anguish because they fail to receive proper and compassionate care. Not everyone has a stable long-term relationship with a dedicated personal physician like Dr. Marshall who stays in the same town and continues practicing medicine and seeing the same patients—so that doctor and patient effectively go through life's phases and age together. And even with Dr. Marshall's help, Jeanette's physical symptoms and psychological fear and anxiety did not suddenly disappear. They were just treated and maintained at a tolerable level. But there can be little doubt that in Jeanette's case, as in many other instances, alternatives other than suicide are available for those prepared to face life.

Whether the decision to commit suicide, with or without the aid of a physician, can *ever* be a rational medical option for those facing a serious or terminal illness is a subject of intense and ongoing debate that will be discussed later in this chapter. There are passionate differences surrounding this question among people—even between the authors of this book. But whatever our personal views or feelings, we, along with almost every expert in this field, agree on the most fundamental issue: the overwhelming majority of people who resort to suicide are unaware of the full range of medical options that are available to them—practical options that could provide assistance and hope for carrying on with their lives. They make a desperate and irreversible decision without sufficient knowledge and understanding. And suicide in these cases is *always* a tragedy. If *you* are considering suicide, you should discuss your thoughts and feelings with your physician. Now that the issue has moved to the forefront of public debate, doctors may feel more comfortable and ready to discuss the subject with you. It is important that you be open and frank with your doctor about your fears and anxieties.

Historical and Religious Attitudes to Suicide

Suicide, the intentional taking of one's own life, is a complex and tragic human behavior. It is the ultimate act of self-destruction, and it results in the untimely loss of life—yet it is a voluntary act. No one knows all the reasons why some people choose to end their lives prematurely.

Despite a general prohibition, suicide has occurred throughout human history and in all corners of the world. Among the ancient Hebrews, Greeks, and Romans, suicide, while generally discouraged, was accepted as an honorable way to avoid death by one's enemy and social humiliation. Ritual suicides, for instance, where a widow offers her life when the husband dies, are also recorded in some societies. Some early Christians practiced suicide as a means toward martyrdom and a way to reach heaven. Reacting against this tendency, St. Augustine condemned suicide in the fifth century as a crime and a sin, basing his opposition on the biblical commandment "Thou shalt not kill."

The opposition to suicide intensified during medieval times, with St. Thomas Aquinas branding suicide a cardinal sin—punishable by execution—because it usurped God's power over man's life and death. Dante, reflecting the views of orthodox medieval Christianity, put suicides in the seventh circle of Hell, just below murderers and heretics. Suicide was equated with murder in many parts of Europe until well into the eighteenth century. As late as the nineteenth century in England, the body of a suicide was buried at a crossroad by night with a stake driven through the heart, and suicides were refused burial in consecrated ground. The property of suicides could also legally be confiscated because kings owned the life of their subjects. Anyone who took his life had therefore stolen the "rights" of the king and restitution could be demanded.

Despite such official condemnation, a widespread belief that after the Renaissance suicide was becoming more prevalent led to renewed discussion and less hostile views toward the taking of one's life, although most philosophers and religious leaders stopped short of outright approval. One notable exception was John Donne, the clergyman and poet who became dean of St. Paul's and who wrote the first defense of suicide published in the English language in 1608. John Sym, an English country clergyman who was a contemporary of Donne's, argued that many suicides were sick in mind and could not be held responsible for their behavior; consequently, suicides should not be damned. But the minister was alarmed by an apparent rash of suicides, and his main interest was in the prevention of tragedy. In his *Life Preservative Against Self-Killing*, Sym describes specific warning signs, such as unusual solitariness and sudden changes in behavior, and prescribes practical measures to prevent suicide: melancholic people should avoid dark or steep places, not remain alone, and exercise caution in handling weapons such as knives.

In the eighteenth century, scholars began to pay more attention to the influence of environmental factors such as air, diet, and climate on national character and their role in social and medical problems such as suicide. The French writer and political philosopher Montesquieu argued that suicide among the "gloomy" English resulted from a malady arising from the effects of the local climate on the body and mind and should therefore not be punished. In 1794, E. G. Elvert, a German pathologist, performed autopsies on suicides as he searched for changes in the body that might have affected the mind.

The great moral and political philosopher of the Enlightenment, Jean-Jacques Rousseau, asserted that the fault for suicide lay with society and its ills, not with the individual who took his own life. By the early nineteenth century, suicide was being considered less in moral and theological terms and more as a medical and social problem. Suicide was seen as a consequence of mental and emotional disorder, and thus it was brought into the larger discussion of civilization and madness. In fact, it was regarded by many as a form of insanity, and therefore as a social disgrace more than a sin. This view of suicide was originally confined to the upper classes, but by the twentieth century it had been accepted by popular opinion and by the middle class. Although people still disapproved of suicide, they could attribute it to an individual's mental difficulties, an unfortunate departure from normal behavior, rather than a severe and punishable moral transgression.

With the upheavals of the Industrial Revolution, suicide rates rose and there was great interest in examining the social roots of the problem, particularly in large urban centers. Research began to show that suicide rates increased during hard economic times and decreased during war; that Protestants had higher rates for suicide than Catholics or Jews, as did those who lived in cities as opposed to the country; and that suicide was higher among men, the elderly, and those who were unmarried, widowed, or divorced. Emile Durkheim, a pioneering sociologist, published a landmark work, *Suicide*, in 1897, comparing suicide rates in Europe and the U.S. and developing a general model explaining the reasons for suicide. Durkheim placed more emphasis on the stresses of society than on the individual. "The causes of death are outside rather than within us, and effective only if we venture into their sphere of activity." Sociologists after Durkheim have concentrated more on the interaction between social factors and the psychological state and vulnerability of the individual, and they have cautioned against using the characteristics of a society to explain individual behavior. Psychiatrists, psychologists, and other mental health professionals have also entered the field, contributing greater knowledge about the interplay of psychological, biological, social, and even genetic risk factors for suicide.

Today the medical and mental health community—represented by such groups as the National Institute of Mental Health and the American Psychiatric Association—believes mental illness and substance abuse play a very significant role in the likelihood of suicide. Depressive disorders alone, almost all of which can be treated, are implicated in as many as

60 percent of all suicides. Yet it takes a powerful combination of such predisposing factors and sudden crises to drive a person to commit self-murder. For example, studies have shown that stressful events, depression, physical illness, and loss—even when they occur together—rarely result in a completed suicide if one's social support system is intact and responsive. While death is inevitable for all of us, suicide is not.

Suicide and the Suicide Controversy in the United States

Over thirty thousand Americans die from suicide each year, making it the eighth leading cause of death in the United States and a serious public health problem. Most experts believe that even this number is low because death by suicide may be difficult to establish and is generally underreported. Still, most of us probably know someone who has taken his or her life or have heard about such a person from others.

Suicide rates increase with advancing age, with those over sixty-five showing the highest rates and those over eighty having twice the suicide rate of people sixty-five to seventy years old. In fact, for the elderly, suicide is the third leading cause of death from injury, following death from falls and from motor vehicle accidents. Suicide among the young (those fifteen to twenty-four years old) has surged over the last thirty years and generated widespread concern and many national programs and intiatives. However, older people still kill themselves at twice the rate of youth. Whether because we value the young more or consider their loss greater, older Americans seem to have more cultural permission to take their lives. This is true in most other nations as well. It is a dangerous misperception that we need to address and correct.

Most people who kill themselves—whether alone or with outside assistance—have visited a physician or health care provider in the month before their death. In one survey, 75 percent of elder suicides saw their physician within one month of taking their lives, while 33 percent did so in the last week of life. The medical professional is therefore uniquely placed to respond to the potential suicide patient's call for help and to intervene in a positive manner. This is particularly true for older people, who are far less impulsive than the young and spend a longer time contemplating and planning suicide (one to two months on average). Thus there is a greater likelihood that the elderly or infirm will visit a physician during this period of uncertainty. In most suicidal situations, as we saw with Jeanette and Dr. Marshall, the interaction between patient and doctor is often the last, key meeting point where one human being may influence the end-of-life decision of another. The behavior and attitude of the physician or other health care professional in this scenario is crucial and may ultimately be decisive.

Most people who kill themselves are male: about 80 percent of all suicides in the United States are committed by men. Women tend to attempt suicide more often than men but complete it less frequently. The majority of the thirty thousand completed suicides in the U.S. each year are performed by individuals acting alone, without any outside intervention. The use of firearms is the preferred method for most, who are men (women prefer less violent means, such as drug overdoses). Nevertheless, some patients who suffer from serious illness or disability will approach their physicians, friends, or loved ones and seek their help in killing themselves. While assisted suicide may still involve only a relatively small number of people, the actual number is unknown. Several highly publicized cases such as those involving Dr. Jack Kevorkian and his suicide machines, and a series of new legislative initiatives in California and Washington that sought to legalize assisted suicide and euthanasia, have helped catapult this issue into the national spotlight. In addition, the legal and moral questions raised by suicide, assisted suicide, and euthanasia—and particularly the appropriate role of the medical profession in these matters—have stimulated widespread debate and soul-searching about our values as a society.

While suicide is not a crime in the United States—it has been decriminalized—a person may still be deprived of liberty and forced to undergo psychiatric observation and treatment for attempting it. Americans do not have a legal "right" to commit suicide. The "right to die" usually refers to the right to refuse life support if you are already terminally ill or in an irreversible condition, and life-sustaining equipment is all that is keeping you alive—as in the two most famous "right to die" cases, involving Karen Ann Quinlan and Nancy Cruzan. The guiding principle of the right-to-die movement was the need to protect dying or hopelessly ill patients—especially those who could no longer speak for themselves—from unwanted medical treatment. New legislation, first known as natural death acts, was proposed allowing patients to fill out living wills or appoint legal spokespersons through durable powers of attorney for health care to safeguard their treatment wishes in advance. Almost every state has since recognized these rights and passed laws protecting them. Legally, the right to die has meant the right to let death come naturally, without medical intervention, if that is what the patient wants. (See Chapter Eight for further discussion.)

In contrast, suicide, assisted suicide, and euthanasia involve a more active, interventionist role in the act of dying. Suicide is the act of turning against oneself and committing self-murder. "Assisted suicide," or when the person involved is a doctor, "physician-assisted suicide," refers to enlisting someone else's help in taking one's life by some active means. And "euthanasia" or "active euthanasia," also known as mercy killing, involves active intervention to cause death directly, such as giving a patient a lethal injection.

Suicide is not a crime in the United States but to assist a suicide is against the law. About half the states have laws that expressly prohibit assisted suicide. You can be charged with a felony if you help a patient take his or her life in these states. In the other states, such as Michigan, the law on assisted suicide is unclear, but you may be prosecuted under a general charge of murder or manslaughter. This is what happened to

Bertram Harper when he flew to Michigan in order to help his terminally ill wife to kill herself. Mr. Harper was arrested and charged with first-degree murder, although he was eventually acquitted. In no state is there any legal mechanism that allows a person to request assistance in killing himself or herself, for example, by asking a physician or loved one for a bottle of sleeping pills. There is also no legal method to request that another person help kill a patient, for example, by administering a fatal injection. In Washington State, a grassroots initiative gathered enough signatures from state residents to put the legalization of assisted suicide on the ballot in the fall of 1991. The measure was defeated. A similar initiative in California failed but may be attempted again.

While the law on assisted suicide and euthanasia is being tested in the courts and legislatures, the moral and ethical debate rages on. For some people, the line between allowing seriously ill patients to die and actively bringing on their death is a huge moral gulf, and to cross this line is to begin on the slow "slippery slope" toward involuntary euthanasia as the Nazis practiced it during World War II. In Nazi Germany, mass murder and genocide first started with officially sanctioned killing by doctors of the handicapped and others viewed as medically defective.

Some ethicists and doctors worry that once we gain the right to actively help patients die, we will have the power to decide that some lives are worth saving while others are not. If we allow a physician to administer a lethal injection to relieve the suffering of a competent patient who requests to die, why should we deny this treatment to an incompetent patient suffering from the same illness who cannot speak? Abuses may occur, and weak or "undesirable" groups in our society, such as the physically or mentally handicapped, may gradually be purged under the guise of humane treatment.

Other health experts and ethicists dispute these fears and argue that assisted suicide and euthanasia involve the same basic question of individual rights and beneficence as the right to refuse life-sustaining treatment. The real issue for them, in the words of Margaret P. Battin, a University of Utah philosophy professor and leading expert on dying, is "whether one has the right to determine or control the circumstances of one's death." Individual self-determination and autonomy—the right to make one's own decisions about one's body, free of any constraint—are the overriding considerations here. The principle of beneficence—of being kind and doing good—also requires that physicians should make a patient's death as painless as possible. These libertarians believe that afflicted patients have the right to get medical help in committing suicide or to a peaceful death by lethal injection if that is what they request when they are of sound mind. Giving doctors the right to release people from life altogether, they say, is a necessary form of compassionate care, an essential check on high-tech medicine.

This broad umbrella of autonomy and beneficence may be used to cover a wide spectrum of approaches that are, in fact, fundamentally different: from Dr. Kevorkian's radical use of suicide machines advertised through the media as a public service to Dr. Quill's private prescription of lethal drugs for a patient he had known and cared for across many years. Kevorkian advocates doctor-assisted suicide for people suffering from terminal or severely painful diseases and calls euthanasia the "last civil right." Turning the "slippery slope" argument on its head, he criticizes the medical profession for behaving like immoral Nazi doctors and *not* helping such people die. Just as doctors in Nazi Germany should have refused orders to torture and conduct experiments on their victims, Kevorkian argues "our civilization is equally culpable because we have equally immoral laws which, on the contrary, force doctors not to do what they should be doing."

Kevorkian, in the view of most doctors, lawyers, and ethicists, has crossed the line into very dangerous territory. He is currently facing first-degree murder charges. The three cases, to date, where he has helped women take their lives have all involved patients who had serious illnesses but were not dying. Whether these patients had really explored and exhausted other options, or whether they could have been helped in other ways, is not clear because Kevorkian appears to have such an overriding personal agenda. To some, he is a hero because he provided these patients with exactly the help they wanted. However, legitimate doubts and questions have been raised about his methods and motives.

Kevorkian, a retired pathologist, accepted the medical diagnoses made by others and determined each patient's capacity to arrive at a decision to take her life. But Kevorkian made these determinations not as a qualified, practicing doctor committed to saving his patients' lives—nor even as a neutral observer or friend. He was not treating any other patients but was actively searching for people who wanted to kill themselves with the aid of his experimental technology. For example, Kevorkian talked about his suicide machine in the media for over a year before Mrs. Janet Adkins came forward as his first test case. According to one producer, a national television show was waiting in the wings to record Mrs. Adkins's final act on videotape and broadcast it. Only the last-minute qualms of their legal department prevented the filming. Kevorkian thus appeared to be offering death on demand, not medical treatment and care.

Mrs. Adkins's suicide took place outside of the normal patient-doctor relationship and without any of the usual procedures for safeguarding against a physician's potential error in judgment or abuse. As many critics pointed out, Kevorkian had only met Mrs. Adkins once, at dinner the previous night, before agreeing to assist in her death. Questions were asked about whether Kevorkian was a qualified doctor who had enough information to evaluate her mental capacity to make such a momentous decision. Certainly Mrs. Adkins, who had played tennis with her son a week earlier, was in good physical health and functioning well. And even by the standards of the Hemlock Society, of which she was a member, she was not "terminal"—defined by the organization as having six months or less to live—but might easily have lived for many more years. Not a single physician or group in the entire country, including the Hemlock Society, came out in support of Kevorkian's action.

Despite near-unanimous condemnation by doctors, lawyers, and ethicists, Dr. Kevorkian's actions initially met with a positive response from the public. Polls showed that many approved of his behavior or at least felt Mrs. Adkins should have the right to control the end of her life. A January 1991 Gallup poll found that a majority (58 percent) of Americans say that a terminally ill patient has the right to end his or her life "under any circumstances." Mrs. Adkins was said to be in the early stages of Alzheimer's disease, when she could still grasp the fact that she was losing her memory and her ability to think and reason, and she still had some remnant of independence that allowed her to act. She apparently found the reduced quality of her life—and the further inevitable losses to come—intolerable and unacceptable. According to her family, her decision to take her life was consistent with her life-long philosophy and beliefs. Mrs. Adkins's fear and anxiety about debilitating illness, the illness itself, as well as her attitude to life, led her to see suicide as the only way out. But some medical experts have questioned whether Mrs. Adkins, a woman with Alzheimer's—a disease that clouds memory and reasoning—had the ability to make a reasoned decision at all. Others have asked if it was Mrs. Adkins or society that failed to find other options. Marcia Angell, editor of the *New England Journal of Medicine*, wrote in a *New York Times* editorial that the medical establishment's "antipathy" to Kevorkian should not obscure other important questions: "Why would someone like Mrs. Adkins have asked for the services of Dr. Kevorkian? What were her alternatives?" Is it the flaws and inadequacies in our health care system—and the inability of doctors to respond to the genuine needs of aging, demented, or dying patients—that invite the abuses that occurred with Kevorkian?

Nevertheless, it is important to make a distinction between Mrs. Adkins's personal motives and rights and Dr. Kevorkian's professional role in helping her. Kevorkian did not act as a physician who had cared for his patient across the years and developed familiarity and insight into her condition. Dr. Samuel Klagsbrun, a New York psychiatrist who supports physician-assisted suicide in certain circumscribed cases, argues that a doctor who agrees to help a patient "must experience hell before taking action." Klagsbrun believes that "because life is sacred, we must go through pain, doubt, and be filled with questions. We ought to find it impossible to sleep well before as well as after such a decision." Kevorkian's hasty action may make one ask whether he underwent any such period of self-questioning before agreeing to help Mrs. Adkins take her life. Klagsbrun says he must be convinced that a patient's situation is completely devoid of hope before agreeing to help. "There must be no reasonable alternative that the patient, the physician, and the family have not explored." Furthermore, the physician must know the patient "reasonably well" according to Klagsbrun. "This request cannot be evaluated on the basis of a single moment in someone's life, such as a brief consultation. Facing an irreversible decision, I must know that I am not responding to only one moment in the journey of a patient's life." This is precisely what Dr. Kevorkian, after the briefest of consultations, did in fact do: he helped a patient whom he did not know and had only met once before to kill herself.

Klagsbrun's other criterion for assisting a terminally ill patient to die is that the patient "must be free of clinical depression or other perceptual distortions that could potentially improve with treatment." Many clinically depressed patients are certain they want to kill themselves, but once treated with medication or psychotherapy, they change their minds. Klagsbrun, in formulating his set of standards—"the criteria must create a grid which is so fine that haste, nonsense, distortions, and poor judgment cannot get through"—also emphasizes that "one does not give up life without a struggle." The struggle will inevitably involve "suffering," and much depends on how one evaluates the amount of suffering that is tolerable or intolerable to the patient—a process that is highly subjective and problematic. "To the extent that suffering—physical, emotional, and spiritual—can be well-addressed, the wish to die may change dramatically."

According to Klagsbrun, all his criteria for determining when it is permissible to help a patient take his or her life "depend totally on clear communication between patient and doctor over an extended period of time." These criteria were clearly missing in the relationship between Dr. Kevorkian and Mrs. Adkins. Did Kevorkian give Mrs. Adkins a chance to explore other options and consider her decision in the light of medical knowledge and her beliefs about suffering? Or was he too strongly predisposed to find what he wanted—a "guinea pig" for his experimental and as-yet-untested suicide machine—so that he could not act as a responsible gatekeeper? Dr. Arthur C. Caplan, director of the Center for Biomedical Ethics at the University of Minnesota, was one of many experts who questioned whether a "banner carrier for euthanasia" such as Kevorkian could be a dispassionate judge of candidates seeking help in committing suicide.

Even within the context of the debate over physician-assisted suicide, Dr. Kevorkian—tagged by the media as "Dr. Death"—represents an extreme, and somewhat unsettling, position. "He is a man with a cause, and the cause is immoral, unethical, and very dangerous," according to Dr. Caplan. But navy psychiatrist Capt. Kenneth Karols supports Kevorkian: "Veterinarians do this routinely for animals. Should the physician of humans do less?" Certainly Kevorkian is a man with a self-declared mission and a highly controversial program: to offer "death on demand" as a public service for those who no longer want to live. To this end, Kevorkian would like to establish national death clinics or what he calls "obitoria"—staffed by suicide specialists or "obitiatrists"—where patients could check in for a quick and efficient termination of their existence. Kevorkian's radical ideas may be useful for stimulating national debate, but they remain unacceptable as a basis for social policy or as an example of the patient-doctor relationship at its best.

A different aspect of physician-assisted suicide is illustrated by the case of Dr. Timothy Quill, a Rochester physician who helped a long-term patient with leukemia take her life by prescribing a lethal dose of barbiturates. As opposed to Kevorkian, Quill's actions arose out of a long-term relationship with a terminally ill patient, a forty-five-year-old woman called "Diane" who had previously suffered from vaginal cancer, depression, and alcoholism. Diane's chances of surviving her leukemia were about one in four but she did not wish to undergo further chemotherapy and other painful and exhausting treatments, including possible bone marrow transplantation, necessary for continuing life. She told her family of her decision not to seek treatment and then to take her life and asked Dr. Quill to help her. After exploring other options with Diane and wrestling with his conscience, Dr. Quill referred Diane to the Hemlock Society. When Diane asked him for barbiturates, a key ingredient in a Hemlock suicide, Dr. Quill gave her a prescription and explained exactly how to use the pills. Diane died two days later. Dr. Quill wrote about this experience in the prestigious *New England Journal of Medicine* so that the issue of physician-assisted suicide would be brought out into the open.

The district attorney's office convened a grand jury in Rochester to investigate Quill's role in the suicide, but the jury refused to indict him. The New York Medical Society, after examining the case, also decided not to press charges. There was a widespread feeling that Quill's actions were responsible—particularly among medical professionals and particularly in contrast to Dr. Kevorkian. Dr. Quill had a long-term, ongoing relationship with his patient and had explored other options with her and her family before acquiescing in her suicide.

A flood of letters to the editor of the *New England Journal of Medicine* followed Quill's article, although opinion was divided. Jack P. Freer, a doctor from Millard Fillmore Hospital in Buffalo, New York, wrote in support of Quill: "Dr. Quill provided his patient with exactly what was lacking in the more notorious cases involving Jack Kevorkian and the anonymous author of 'It's Over Debbie' [another controversial case involving physician aid in dying]: comprehensive medical care, with the deep concern for the patient's well-being and respect for her choices. The debate concerning euthanasia and assisted suicide will continue, but we now have one additional reference point: a conscientious physician providing excellent medical care."

Other physicians praised Quill's courage and compassion in the treatment of his patient. One man, Dr. Stewart A. King, a retired surgeon with amyotrophic lateral sclerosis (ALS), a fatal degenerative disease, described himself as "essentially quadriplegic and dependent on a respirator;" King fully supported Quill and the position that it is ultimately the individual patient who must decide whether the burden of illness is too great and whether there is "an acceptable reason for carrying on." King was adamant: "Of course, I agree that the decision to seek death must be challenged by the medical profession and the family, but if no valid rationale can be offered for sustained existence, what then? Can the profession justify simply walking away from the problem? I think not." King ended with a personal plea: "When my continued survival is no longer meaningful (to me), I hope that a caring physician will make the transition as easy as possible. I realize that some health professionals will find it impossible to do this, but I hope that they and society will understand the true compassion for their patients' suffering that motivates the physicians who do help those in need."

Dr. Quill claimed that many doctors later told him that they had helped their patients kill themselves but were reluctant to admit this on the record. Quill argued that it is morally right for physicians to assist terminally ill patients whom they know well to die, if the patients request help. He also suggested that more physicians might be willing to assist patients in suicide at the end of life but were afraid to broach the subject with their patients. He called for greater openness and a franker discussion between doctors and patients—and between society and its citizens—on the question of physician-assisted suicide. Kenneth Iserson, a physician from the University of Chicago who responded to Quill in the *NEJM*, echoed the widely claimed notion that doctors do help patients to die: "I have rarely found a primary care physician who has not helped a patient to die who was desirous of ending intolerable pain or disability in the midst of terminal illness." But Iserson stated that most of these physicians assist patients in ways that are subtly, and to many, significantly, different from Quill's, "prescribing narcotics or barbiturates with the explicit caveat, 'Don't take this many, or it will kill you.' " This stratagem may not only alleviate the physician's guilt feelings about the act, but is also used to establish deniability for the physician in the event of a legal investigation into the circumstances of a suicide. Even Diane, wrote Dr. Quill, "was more than willing to protect me by participating in a superficial conversation about her insomnia" when it came to asking for barbiturates. But Quill himself felt it was important "to know how she planned to use the drugs and to be sure she was not in despair or overwhelmed in a way that might color her judgment." He went one step further and insisted on a frank and open conversation, in which his role in assisting Diane to kill herself became explicit:

"In our discussion, it was apparent she was having trouble sleeping, but it was also evident that the security of having enough barbiturates available to commit suicide when and if the time came would leave her secure enough to live fully and concentrate on the present. It was clear that she was not despondent and that in fact she was making deep, personal connections with her family and close friends. I made sure that she knew how to use the barbiturates for sleep and also that she knew the amount needed to commit suicide. We agreed to meet regularly, and she promised to meet with me before taking her life, to ensure that all other avenues had been exhausted." Quill knew he was entering new terrain but felt certain he was acting in the best interest of his patient. "I wrote the prescription with an uneasy feeling about the boundaries I was exploring—spiritual, legal, professional, and personal. And yet I also felt strongly that I was setting her free to get the most out of the time she had left, and to maintain dignity and control on her own terms until her death."

Despite the fact that many doctors find physician-assisted suicide permissible in some individual cases, such as Quill's, there is a general reluctance to legalize it, as the recent failed efforts in Washington State attest. In the words of K. Danner Clouser, a philosopher at the Milton S. Hershey Medical Center, "it is a big leap from the moral acceptability of suicide and assisted suicide to incorporating it into public policy." Many medical professionals who accept physician-assisted suicide on a case-by-case basis feel the danger of abuse would be too great if it became a matter of widespread policy. Rather than being a struggle to make the case for helping a patient die in each individual instance—with physicians "going through hell" to make sure they were doing the right thing—physician-assisted suicide would become too easy, and the temptation to apply it indiscriminately would be great. This attitude has given rise to what some call the "glorious hypocrisy": refusing to legalize or adopt assisted suicide as a matter of policy, but allowing doctors to make individual decisions to help patients die based on the specific merits of a particular case.

While not faulting Quill's role in Diane's suicide, some medical experts cautioned against using such an unusual case as a basis for adopting a public policy of assisted suicide. Dr. Joanne Lynn and Dr. Joan Teno of George Washington University wrote: "Few patients die in such supportive surroundings. Few have a physician who is so thoughtful and skilled or a family that has comparative emotional and financial resources. Instead, pain control and emotional support are given low priority in health care. Under the current health care 'system' most of us will die in old age, with family scattered and resources used up, in the care of anonymous providers with limited skills and commitment. The pressures to allow active euthanasia arise largely from the wholesale inadequacy of the health care and legal systems to care for chronically ill and disabled persons who are slowly dying. These pressures do not arise from the few, like Diane, who have available all that can be done and find it still so inadequate that they prefer an earlier, self-administered death." In this view, the call for assisted suicide is a small part of a much larger and more fundamental problem. And our main efforts should be devoted to the development of more "effective systems of care and support" that could deliver basic services such as housing, food, more doctors, family support, and symptom relief.

Whatever their wider implications for public policy and law, Dr. Quill's actions, in the opinion of many—including one of the authors of this book—suggest that there are certain cases where it may be morally permissible for a physician to assist in the death of a terminally ill patient who is rational, who requests help, and whose suffering is intolerable with no hope of relief. According to an editorial in *The New York Times* "Dr. Timothy Quill . . . took exemplary procedural care and his case poses the issue in its purest form: should doctors be allowed to assist in the suicides of terminally ill patients? If they do it as carefully as Quill did, the answer is probably yes." In this view, it is not *always* wrong for a doctor to help a patient take his or her life—although we have to be extremely careful about defining when and why it is permissible. The decision must come as the final stage in a continuum of care in which patient and doctor have explored every other option over a period of time and have struggled together to arrive at an alternative solution. Family support, treatment for depression, comfort care, pain control, and respect for the patient's end-of-life treatment wishes must all be made available in an effort to avoid such a fate. However, once all these options have been exhausted in the context of a frank, ongoing, and intimate relationship between patient and doctor, and when there is severe suffering with no hope of relief, it may be ethically appropriate for a doctor to help a patient gain release from a life that is intolerable. In this view, if we automatically rule out physician-assisted suicide *in every case*, without examining the particular circumstances of an individual patient, we may be shutting our ears to the very needs of the patients that should be served.

Dr. Christine Cassel of the University of Chicago and Dr. Diane Meier of Mt. Sinai Medical Center made the argument against "inflexible rules" concerning assisted suicide in the September 1990 issue of the *New England Journal of Medicine:* ". . . the medical profession's repeated and firm rejection of any participation by physicians in assisted suicide begins to appear self-serving in its emphasis on a professional scrupulosity that seems blind to the expressed needs of the patients. The public appears to be losing faith in doctors, at least in part because of our paternalistic and sometimes cruel insistence on life at any cost. The very rigidity of this position invites the abuses exemplified by the Kevorkian-Adkins case: when people facing unbearable suffering have no legitimate options, extreme measures result." Cassel and Meier argue that rather than being a first step on a slippery slope, a more open process might make doctors and patients more accountable and help to limit assisted suicide to clearly appropriate cases. They place the patient's needs and values first and criticize American society for refusing to accept death as part of life and thus needlessly prolonging life when dying with dignity may be more important to the patient. "The rigid view that physicians should never assist in suicide denies the complexity of the personal meanings life can have in favor of a single-minded devotion to its maximal duration." They see this refusal as "a reflection of how sterile and technological our profession has become."

Cassel and Meier believe that physicians must become more personally and morally engaged with their patients and with their own feelings about death and dying. "A strict proscription against aiding in death may betray a limited conceptual framework that seeks the safety of ironclad rules and principles to protect the physician from the true complexity of individual cases." Physicians must have the "intellectual and moral vitality" to tackle difficult, ethically complex issues that may challenge their values. "Only then will the profession remain true to its commitment to stand by patients through the whole of life's course, up to and including death."

Cassel and Meier do not endorse wholesale acceptance of physican-assisted suicide. They recognize the dangers of using this as an expedient for cost-cutting and the potential for "neglect or abuse" of our most vulnerable members; and they reiterate the paramount need for better care and support. But they conclude with an appeal for greater tolerance and compassion regarding the role of doctors in helping terminally ill patients to end their lives: "In circumscribed and carefully defined circumstances, however, it may be right to recognize the inevitability of death in a life of unbearable suffering and to help ease this passage."

Not everyone agrees with Cassel or Meier or approves of Quill's actions. Many doctors and ethicists—including one of the authors of this book—argue that physicians should never play a role in honoring patients' requests for aid in dying. The doctor's duty is to heal and save a life and, when this is not possible, to use the many means now available to prevent and alleviate suffering. It is not necessary to resort to euthanasia or assisted suicide to "ease the passage." And to legalize such practices would be to leap over a wide gulf that exists in our society, diverting attention and resources from more fundamental needs that should be addressed: a lack of understanding about adequate pain control, comfort care, and what is already available and protected by law.

Strong opposition by doctors to Dr. Quill's behavior, as well as to the concept of physician-assisted suicide, was also expressed in the letters to the editor of the *NEJM*. One doctor, Lisa Cardo of Albert Einstein College of Medicine in New York, wrote: "It is never the role of a physician to help a patient perform such an act. In fact, it is the role of a physician to prevent suicide attempts whenever there is a possibility that they may occur. In this situation, as in other situations in which physicians are faced with the threatened death of their patients due to illness, it is the role of the physician to apply his or her knowledge, skill and caring to save lives."

A Michigan physician, Michael T. Ross, argued that Quill could and should have done more to try and save Diane's life: "A one-in-four chance of living is a fighting chance for a relatively young woman with as full a life as Dr. Quill describes. Any physician should be reluctant to let a patient like this forgo such an opportunity for life without applying all his or her powers of persuasion and personally invoking the love of family and friends and the expertise and support of a psychiatrist, the patient's nurses, a clergyperson or patient advocate, a social worker, and maybe a patient or two who risked the uncertainty of treatment in similar circumstances. An intense demonstration of caring, listening, and communication might well have helped this woman face her crisis differently or at least with greater solace."

Peter M. Marzuk, a physician from Cornell University Medical College in New York who has studied suicide in AIDS patients, suggested that Quill's "fondness for his patient" may have led to a personal friendship and prevented him from exercising professional "impartiality." Marzuk argued that physicians themselves may feel powerless when faced with their patient's terminal illness and may "project their own hopelessness onto the patient, thus sanctioning or even unwittingly encouraging an assisted suicide." Sometimes when doctors feel they can do nothing about the illness, they "collude with the patient to wrest control of death from the fatal disease." Noting that Quill's patient had a history of alcohol abuse and depression, Marzuk asks whether Quill had done enough to determine that depression and despair were not a feature in Diane's suicidal intentions. "Did he obtain the consultation of a more detached colleague or psychiatrist to determine whether the patient was clinically depressed?" Not only might Quill's identification with his patient have prevented him from a fully accurate diagnosis of her condition, but it may have led him to ignore his own highly emotional state of mind as a contributing factor, according to Marzuk. "Likewise it is important to know that Quill himself was not despairing. Did he speak with other trusted colleagues or friends about his plans, or did he arrive at his decision to assist a suicide in his own mind—alone, helpless, frightened of either choice he would make, as he watched a friend succumb to an illness he could not control?" Marzuk suggests that Quill was trying to join with Diane in cheating death by taking control of her deadly illness. In this view, the idea of rational suicide is based on our effort to convince ourselves that we are in control of our life and our destiny. By planning her death, Diane was trying to be the active agent, rather than the passive victim, of her death; while Dr. Quill, in assisting her, sought to maintain the illusion that they were both in control.

Other experts question whether suicide is ever a rational act. Dr. Kathleen Foley of New York's Memorial Sloan-Kettering Cancer Center, an international expert on pain control, has written and spoken extensively about the relationship of pain management to patient requests for physician-assisted suicide. Foley addressed this issue in the July 1991 *Journal of Pain and Symptom Management*. "Adequate pain relief, control of symptoms, and treatment of psychologic distress," she writes, "clearly alter patients' requests to terminate life." She considers the very concept of rational suicide "an oxymoronic statement," a contradiction in terms, citing the fact that psychiatric illness—namely depression—is what is at the basis of suicidal requests, even among those who are medically ill. Based on her experience with patients, Foley believes that suicidal ideation and requests "dissolve" when pain and other symptoms come under control. Many hospice physicians and experts on palliative (comfort) care—who as a group are less in favor of assisted suicide and euthanasia than doctors in general—echo this stance. Many hospice physicians, who concentrate on alleviating a patient's pain and suffering, often find that because of their emphasis on pain relief and comfort care, persistent requests by patients for aid in dying are rare.

In this view, these requests are based on correctable problems such as depression, pain, and abandonment.

Suicide researchers Drs. Yeates Conwell and Eric Caine say that the issue of rational suicide is still open because "the presence of depression does not imply that a patient's choice [to commit suicide] is irrational, nor does the absence of mental disease imply rationality." They believe rational suicide is a poorly understood issue that requires further study. Was Dr. Quill's patient Diane, a woman with a history of psychiatric illness, truly a "rational" patient? Would someone without her history be considered more rational? How depressed must a patient be, Drs. Conwell and Caine ask, before their depression "precludes rational decision-making?"

A fundamental argument against physician-assisted suicide is perhaps best summed up by Dr. Leon Kass, a University of Chicago physician and ethicist who sees assisted suicide and euthanasia as "a betrayal of the deepest meaning of the art of healing." Kass writes that the physician "serves the sick not because they have rights or wants or claims but because they are sick. Healing is thus the central core of medicine: to heal, to make whole, is the doctor's primary business." In this sense, the doctor serves the cause of healing even more than the individual patient. It is not the patient's autonomy or self-determination that counts as much as the patient's life, of which the physician is the appointed caretaker.

Eric J. Cassell, a physician and professor at Cornell University Medical College, states bluntly that doctors should not be "killers." Cassell, who has written extensively on the nature of suffering, contends that "doctors administering injections is bad for doctors and bad for medicine, not because it is too hard but because it is too easy." Many physicians feel that the unusually powerful and intimate role of doctors with their patients is the foundation of medicine, whose aim is to save lives and relieve suffering. To inject a legal power to cause death into this relationship, where patients are already unusually dependent and vulnerable, would undermine the essential bond of trust and introduce an ominous new element between doctor and patient. It might also have the effect of desensitizing doctors to the value of human life. As Dr. Leon Kass writes: "The patient's trust in the doctor's wholehearted devotion to the patient's best interests will be hard to sustain once doctors are licensed to kill. Indeed, using the taboo against doctors killing patients, the medical profession has its own intrinsic ethic, which a physician true to his calling will not violate, either for love or for money."

According to this argument, if a physician appears sympathetic to the patient's interest in suicide, this may signal to the patient that the physician feels assisted suicide is a desirable alternative. Such an impression may be confusing or upsetting to the patient. Moreover, if the patient decides to reject suicide, will that patient have the same degree of confidence in the physician's commitment to his or her care as before? Imagine that Diane had changed her mind and decided to seek treatment. Would she have retained the same basic trust in Dr. Quill's complete commitment to caring for her health?

Many doctors and ethicists opposed to physician-assisted suicide and active euthanasia are concerned that allowing physician aid in dying would affect the care of those who are most vulnerable. Many people, particularly the very old or very sick, could feel pressured to request death rather than linger and become a potential emotional and financial drain on their families; or a burden on their physicians, who might also seem "tired" of them. Such physically or mentally infirm patients would be susceptible to any suggestion from their physician that suicide might be appropriate, particularly because it is made by the figure whose medical judgment and expertise they most rely on. The *right* to die could thus be interpreted as a *duty* or *obligation* to die. Instead of fostering a community of care and compassion, we would be encouraging individual, isolated acts of self-destruction.

In addition, because of the huge and steadily rising cost of health care and the lack of medical insurance for millions of Americans, physician-assisted suicide could be seen as an economic expedient, a more "cost effective" way of dealing with death. Its implicit message: society prefers to spend its limited resources on other people. Physician-assisted suicide could thus become a shortcut in the dying process and direct our efforts away from providing better pain relief and care for dying patients and giving patients and families more emotional support. It would put a halt to further research for cures and comfort care and act as a disincentive for government or private insurers to fund such measures. And given the crisis in our current health care system, it could lead to our treating life as a cheap commodity, too easily disposed of when it becomes less than perfect or too expensive to sustain.

The Reverend Kevin O'Rourke, director of the Center for Health Care Ethics in St. Louis, Missouri, speaks for many when he asserts: "Hence, 'the call' for assisted suicide by physicians is not only contrary to religious values, it is also denounced by experts in the life sciences, is contrary to beneficent care of patients, and contrary to the best interests of family and society. Fostering assisted suicide would only demonstrate that we have lost the meaning of being human."

The Modern Dutch Experience with Euthanasia

Despite our increased knowledge and research, we have not solved the fundamental problem of suicide nor resolved the debate about its medical, legal, and ethical place in our society. But we do know that for seriously ill patients the request for assistance in dying often masks a need for greater reassurance, better comfort care, and a stronger network of human support. The modern Dutch experience with euthanasia sheds some light on this aspect.

Holland is the only country in the world where physician-assisted suicide and euthanasia are openly practiced today— even though it is still illegal and physicians may be prosecuted unless they abide by strict guidelines. These guidelines specify that the patient must be suffering intolerably with no chance of improvement; that the patient requests aid in dying voluntarily and repeatedly, over a reasonable period of time; that he or she is mentally competent to make such a decision; and that two physicians, one of whom has not been involved in the patient's care, agree that euthanasia is appropriate.

In a nationwide study commissioned by the Dutch government and published in the *Lancet* in September 1991, researchers found that loss of dignity, pain, unworthy death, and dependency on others were the primary reasons given by patients requesting aid in dying. But perhaps most telling was the wide gap between the number of patients who requested assistance from their doctors and the number who actually resorted to physician-assisted suicide and euthanasia.

According to the *Lancet* study, over twenty-five thousand patients a year seek assurance from their doctors that they will assist them if suffering becomes unbearable. About two-thirds of these requests never end up as serious and persistent at a later stage of the disease and are never brought up again: patients find other means of coping with their illness. And even of the serious and persistent requests, about two-thirds of *these* do not result in euthanasia or assisted suicide. In most cases, alternatives are found that make life bearable again (and in some instances the patient dies before any action has been taken).

It is clear that even in Holland, where the legal system tolerates physician aid in dying under certain circumstances, most patients are actually seeking greater reassurance and comfort from their physician rather than a quick and unnatural death. Dying patients need to know they will not be abandoned: that someone will be there for them, ready to relieve their pain and suffering if it becomes unbearable. Those who receive this reassurance are able to face the end of life with far greater equanimity and less need of outside intervention.

Two other points about the Netherlands are worth mentioning. One is that every person in Holland has free access to health care. Thus there is no fear that a patient might request euthanasia to save family members the expense of a long illness. Our concern about America's 34 million unin-

sured citizens—several times greater than the entire population of Holland—does not come into that picture. Nor do the
feelings, pressures, and fears of millions of other Americans
who may not have adequate coverage to pay for relevant services such as at-home physician care, home nursing care,
home respite care, care in a nursing home or other long-term
care facility, dietitian care, rehabilitation care, physical therapy, and psychological counseling. Not only the patient's
treatment choices but the doctor's recommendations are too
often influenced by financial considerations.

Another major difference between the United States and
Holland is that Dutch medical care is still provided primarily
by family physicians who make house calls and usually live in
the neighborhood. Such physicians know their patients and
their families well and are in a better position to act in their
best interests, based on personal knowledge and experience,
rather than a heavy reliance on technological expertise. Physicians are more likely to provide appropriate and individual
care to someone whom they have treated over a lifetime and
whose family they will continue to treat even after the patient's death. And patients will have greater trust in a doctor
whom they have known for twenty-five years and who has
seen them through previous crises. It is believed that most
cases of euthanasia in Holland take place in the patient's
home, in the presence of family members and often with the
patient's pastor or priest in attendance.

The American health care system, while it still has its
Jeanettes and Dr. Marshalls, will require major across-the-
board reforms to attain this level of patient-doctor confidence
and freedom from financial constraints.

Thinking Positively About the End of Life

While the debate about assisted suicide and euthanasia rages
on, much as it has for thousands of years, most of us will still
need to know how to cope with the end of life in a more
natural and less abrupt manner. Most of us will not commit

suicide. We will not enlist others to help us kill ourselves. Thirty thousand suicides a year may be a high figure—even though only a small number of these suicides involve people who are either terminally ill or old and chronically ill—but it is only a tiny fraction compared to the approximately 1.5 million Americans who must make end-of-life decisions each year. It is important to recall that the overwhelming majority of us will make these decisions with our physicians and families in a responsible and time-honored manner. The Kevorkian-like cases may grab the headlines and create a temporary sensation, but these cases are exceptional and should not deflect us from our real challenge: to face the end of life with a maximum of dignity and independence and a minimum of pain and suffering.

As we saw at the beginning of this chapter with Jeanette and Dr. Marshall, physicians may play a vital role in helping us cope with an end-of-life crisis. Doctors may offer general medical knowledge and advice or specific information about new drugs and treatments. But they and the many health professionals who work with them also offer something even more vital and tangible. They can offer an open and compassionate ear and the opportunity to vent painful feelings and seek alternatives by focusing on the future. They can offer hope. Several studies have shown that while people like Jeanette who become depressed due to serious illness are at the highest risk for suicide, depression alone will not lead most patients to take their lives. It takes something else to turn feelings of sadness and loss into an active desire for death. That something is hopelessness. And physicians are well placed to recognize the early signs and symptoms of hopelessness and prevent such seriously depressed patients from turning to suicide.

Hopelessness is the dividing line between depression and suicide. It is at the moment when we lose all hope for the future that life seems most bleak. Our image of ourselves and of the world darkens, relationships cease to have meaning, and we can't imagine any other alternative *except* suicide. In this sense, hopelessness represents a failure of our imagination; we look ahead but see nothing.

Yet as soon as we are given a vision of our future, however altered, our imagination begins to work again. A small crack opens and a new image of ourselves emerges; a fresh outlook on the world is possible. We have a goal, even if it is modest. Life-affirming hope is what Dr. Marshall gave Jeanette—the conviction that things could and would get better.

Dr. Marshall told Jeanette about available drugs and treatments, about exercises and therapies she could undertake. He held out the possibility of improvement. It could be some small improvement in her physical state, such as a steadying in her hand so she could write with a pen. Or it could be the chance to get closer to her children. Or activating the old image of herself as a courageous woman who would fight on against the odds. It might even be the slight physical contact with Dr. Marshall when he squeezed her hand, the knowledge that if he still believed in her and the value of her life, then her very existence must have meaning—both for herself and for those who love her.

CHAPTER FOUR

Controlling Pain and Other Symptoms

Opium: . . . the Creator himself seems to prescribe [it], for we often see the scarlet poppy growing in the cornfields, as if it were foreseen that wherever there is hunger to be fed there must also be pain to be soothed.

—Oliver Wendell Holmes

Barbara, a sixty-nine-year-old woman, had been a heavy smoker all her adult life, and now she suffered from severe emphysema. The slightest amount of exercise would leave her breathless. Barbara rarely left home, but she achieved partial relief from oxygen, obtained from a portable tank she could move around the house and yard.

One day her husband, Tom, noticed that she was becoming groggy. The next morning he found his wife in bed, unresponsive. Emergency personnel arrived within minutes of his call. Recognizing that Barbara was in respiratory failure, they quickly resuscitated her by placing a tube into her windpipe and forcing air into her lungs. In the hospital, pneumonia was diagnosed and Barbara was treated with antibiotics and mechanical ventilation—the tube in her windpipe was connected to a respirator, a machine that would assist her breathing. Soon after being connected to the respirator she was alert, and with the help of the antibiotics, the pneumonia improved. She was cared for by a team of doctors and nurses in the intensive care unit, where great efforts were expended to help her. The doctors adjusted the settings on the respirator in an effort to wean her from it, but every time the settings were lowered and the respirator disconnected, Barbara's condition deteriorated. She remained connected to the respirator and over the next two weeks underwent innumerable blood tests and a variety of other procedures. Eventually, an intravenous line was replaced by a nasogastric tube inserted through her nasal passages so that complete liquid nutrition could enter her stomach.

Hooked up to the respirator with a broad tube in her windpipe, Barbara was unable to speak, but she was fully alert and able to communicate with head movements and by writing notes. She was sore and extremely uncomfortable and could not adequately reposition herself in bed. She felt trapped and required assistance for every aspect of her existence. She asked how long she would have to be "hooked up" and came to realize she could spend the rest of her life on the machine. "I want off," she would write, and finally, "I want to die." In this manner she conferred with the nurses, the doctors, her husband, and her priest, Father John. She was able to make it clear to them that life on "machines" was not worth living. She wanted everything disconnected even if it meant her life would end.

The doctors unanimously agreed it was unlikely that Barbara would survive for more than twenty-four hours off the respirator. And as the days wore on it became increasingly certain that she would not return to even her previous level of function, where most activities were performed with great effort, although she had been free of a respirator and was able to do a few things for herself. Now, this was no life, Barbara felt, and there was no sense in continuing on the machine. Her husband tearfully acquiesced with her desire to be disconnected from the respirator. The doctor assigned to her case, Dr. Wilson, a "pulmonary" or lung specialist, had treated many patients with emphysema. Although he was uncomfortable with Barbara's decision, he said he would not "stand in the way." The patient was fully competent to make her own decisions, he said, and she had the right to discontinue treatment even if it meant she would die.

The respirator was disconnected. Barbara felt breathless and uncomfortable, and shortly thereafter she became agitated. Her husband asked the nurse if they could give her something to make her more comfortable, but the nurse said nothing had been ordered by the doctor. Sedatives and even oxygen, she said, would further suppress Barbara's ability to breathe and might kill her. "But we're going to let her die," Tom said. "Why should she suffer?" The nurse gave Tom a puzzled look, was silent for a moment, and then said it was not her decision.

When Tom went to find the doctor, Barbara begged the nurse to reconnect the respirator. A medical resident was paged and rushed back to the ICU. Within minutes, the respirator had been reconnected. Barbara's breathlessness had ceased, but she was once again a "prisoner," as her husband would later describe his wife's situation.

Several days went by. Barbara had not changed her mind about discontinuing the respirator, even though it would mean her death, but she could not face the fear and misery this appeared to entail, and she dreaded the pain. Her husband continued to visit daily and began to sleep nights on the couch in the ICU's waiting area. Tom attempted to comfort his wife of thirty-five years by telling her how much she meant to him and that he didn't want to lose her. He apologized to her for letting them connect her to the respirator in the first place. She shook her head and became withdrawn.

Tom scheduled a meeting with Dr. Wilson, who suggested Barbara be given antidepressant medication to "pull her through the depression and make her feel better about things." He also agreed to prescribe a mild sedative if she again decided to discontinue the respirator, but he repeated the "dangers" of giving her anything strong. Tom, confused by this logic, repeated what he had said to the nurse: Barbara was not going to survive without the respirator. It didn't make sense to withhold any medication that could make her more comfortable. "You're asking me to kill your wife," the doctor said sternly, and refused to talk further.

Tom sank into despair himself and once again turned to his priest. Tom had been gratified earlier when Father John had reassured Barbara that the church approved of an incurable patient's decision to terminate what it called "extraordinary medical treatment," such as a respirator. Now Tom was relieved to learn that the church did not disapprove of giving medication that would ease suffering, "even if this would hasten a natural death." This was the principle of "double effect," the priest told Tom. Giving Barbara a strong sedative was intended to have one effect, to make her comfortable. But there was a possibility it would have a second, unintended effect, to hasten her death. Only the first effect is intentional, Father John explained. "The sedative is given to ease her suffering while nature is allowed to take its course. Its purpose is not to kill her. That would constitute active euthanasia, an entirely different matter." But in Barbara's case, the priest counseled, it was morally permissible to prescribe morphine for the good effect of easing her suffering, even if it would produce a double effect. The priest offered to speak to Dr. Wilson on the couple's behalf, but the doctor, he suggested, might not be able to overcome his own qualms —moral or otherwise. In fact, repeated discussions with Dr. Wilson left Tom frustrated and angry. The doctor's responses ranged from "We don't allow that in this hospital" to "Euthanasia is illegal" and finally to "Please don't ask me again." Tom would have given up if it hadn't been for his priest, who suggested he seek a second opinion from another specialist in Dr. Wilson's field.

Tom was advised to call the medical staff office, and he was given the names of three other lung specialists who practiced in the hospital. He consulted with Dr. Persico, who visited Barbara and agreed to take over the case. Dr. Wilson happily gave over care to his colleague, stating that he was "glad to be rid of this kind of situation."

Dr. Persico was in his sixties and had recently given up a

practice in Philadelphia to take a job in the suburban hospital where Barbara was a patient. He was familiar with these situations, he told Tom. "We can keep your wife calm and free of discomfort by giving her small doses of morphine. Yes, it might depress her respiration, which could hasten her death by a few minutes, but there is nothing illegal or immoral about that." He was glad to hear that the patient's priest had supported the decision because, although clergy from all other religious groups had supported his patients' end-of-life decisions, not all had been as knowledgeable as Father John had been, and more than one had balked at the idea of giving morphine.

Dr. Persico set aside half an hour of his time and arranged a team conference in the ICU office. Tom and Father John were encouraged to attend. The procedure was explained to all of the staff, including the junior doctors and nurses, who had previously participated in disconnecting respirators, but some were squeamish about the administration of morphine. Dr. Persico explained that the smallest possible dose of morphine would be given prior to disconnecting the respirator. The morphine would enter the brain and make Barbara calm; it would also reduce her feeling of breathlessness. If a small dose was not sufficient, increasing doses would be administered until she felt comfortable. The nasogastric tube would be removed to increase her comfort, and she could have sips of cool liquid if she felt thirsty. Oxygen would be given by a face mask. Although oxygen, like morphine, had the ability to depress her respiration, it would also help to reduce breathlessness. Dr. Persico pointed out to the staff that they seemed comfortable with the idea of giving oxygen, and that they should feel just as comfortable with the idea of morphine: both would give the patient comfort. However, Dr. Persico himself offered to administer the medication if the nurses felt uncertain or had ethical qualms. He agreed to sit with Barbara in her room if she desired, and her husband or others would be allowed to be with her as well.

Later, a bedside discussion took place between Dr. Persico

and Barbara, with Father John and Tom in attendance. That night, morphine was injected until Barbara became calm and drowsy, and the respirator was replaced with an oxygen face mask. Barbara died peacefully a few hours later, her husband and her priest and her doctor by her side.

Many fears surround dying, but perhaps the greatest fear is that death will be accompanied by prolonged suffering and pain. This *could* have been the case in Barbara's situation. In fact, the dying process was more protracted than it should or could have been. There is still, in the 1990s, misinformation and insufficient knowledge on the part of patients, families, and even health professionals concerning the appropriate level of symptom control that is possible or permissible.

It is often misinformed health professionals who convey medical information to hospital attorneys and administrators, a group who play an increasingly strong role in health care decision-making today. Although the primary goal of both doctor and hospital is good patient care, end-of-life decisions are made with an eye to protecting the care providers from legal liability, and they sometimes play it safe at the expense of the patient.

A combination of misinformation, fear of liability, and inexperience led to Barbara's predicament. Once she had reached the agonizing decision to have the respirator disconnected, she was undermedicated. As a consequence, she suffered unnecessarily until she begged to be put back on the very treatment from which she wished to be freed. The doctors and nurses lacked experience and information about the appropriate medical approach in this case and feared that withdrawing the respirator would leave them vulnerable to legal repercussions, or that it would be an immoral act. The majority of clinicians—including cancer specialists—receive very inadequate training in pain assessment and pain management. Lack of knowledge about the appropriate use of analgesics, coupled with a lack of sophistication in diagnosing and treating the psychological complications of terminal illness, may hinder the proper care of patients in pain. Barbara's situation was unusual in that Tom, a family member, thought to ask whether something could be given to help his wife, and even more unusual in that he pursued the matter to its conclusion. Patients and family members tend to have little experience in death and dying, are unaware of medical options, and assume that the doctor knows best and that everything that *can* be done *is* being done. If they are informed enough to prepare a specific question about pain management, the situation may be so frightening or confusing that they are too afraid or intimidated to ask it or don't know whom to ask. Even when they do ask the right question, physicians often don't have the right answer. A doctor who is not expert may increase the patient's fears by not letting him or her know that side effects are usually transitory. A doctor may not know how to adjust the dose, or how to use other medications to counteract side effects—such as using stimulants to counteract the sedating effects of some painkillers.

Another problem in Barbara's case was that Tom himself felt torn. On the one hand, he wanted to keep his wife from suffering, but on the other hand he wanted to keep her alive so he would not lose her. This predicament was reinforced by the doctor's words, which had the effect of placing Tom in the awkward and untenable position of being her "killer." Fortunately, Tom was able to speak to someone who gave him a more realistic perspective. Barbara was dying from emphysema; technology had forestalled her death temporarily; and now, medical skills could be used again to allow natural death to occur comfortably.

Few people involved in this scenario were aware of the legal protections and professional sanctions that would have allowed Barbara an earlier and more peaceful end. Dr. Wilson assumed that giving morphine constituted active euthanasia and that he would thus have been committing an illegal or immoral act. He was so convinced of this that he avoided seeking legal counsel or raising the issue with the hospital's ethics committee. In fact, many recognized professional organizations have addressed the principle of the double effect. As early as 1983 the President's Commission for the Study of Ethical Problems in Medicine and Biomedical and Behavioral Research published the results of lengthy research and deliberations, in which they discussed these issues.

In addressing the use of symptom-relieving medication that might also accelerate death, the report discusses the example of giving morphine to someone in pain: "Were a person experiencing great pain from a condition that will be cured in a few days, use of morphine at doses that would probably lead to death by inducing respiratory depression would usually be unacceptable. On the other hand, for a patient in great pain —especially from a condition that has proved to be untreatable and that is expected to be rapidly fatal—morphine can be both morally and legally acceptable if pain relief cannot be achieved by less risky means."

More recently, national medical organizations, including the Society for Critical Care Medicine and the American Thoracic Society, have published official position statements endorsing the kind of treatment that Dr. Persico made available to Barbara. The use of symptom-relieving medications is important in these end-of-life situations, they state, because medicine's goal is to prevent suffering. Providing adequate pain relief for patients who choose to forgo life-sustaining treatment is considered appropriate care. In the rare instances when these practices have been challenged in the courts, they have been upheld by law. For example, in 1989, a young Georgia quadriplegic, Larry McAfee, won the right to receive morphine if and when he chose to disconnect his respirator. In 1990, the Nevada court ruled similarly in the case of Kenneth Bergstedt. It is unfortunate that some patients must still fight for the right to receive appropriate care, which has medical, legal, and ethical sanctions to reinforce it. Dr. Persico and many of his colleagues had taken this sort of situation seriously for many years, giving morphine, oxygen, and psychological comfort to dying respirator-dependent patients, never doubting its usefulness or the morality of their approach. Patients have now won legal recognition of their rights, and the practice is supported by important organizations in the medical establishment.

The fear of pain and suffering at the end of life is something shared by most of us. Fear of pain can make us feel isolated, angry, helpless, and extremely vulnerable. If it becomes a reality, the fear worsens and the suffering increases. It can become so overwhelming that it undermines our life and paralyzes any other thoughts or considerations that might enable us to cope. Faced with severe and unremitting pain, with no hope of any improvement or relief, some people turn to suicide as the only way out. Many patients can endure almost any intensity of pain as long as they believe that some relief is possible. But when we lose all hope that our pain can be treated, our psychological distress can increase our pain and we are more likely to consider desperate measures. Fortunately, despite the many problems we confront in terminal illness and the end of life, there are many excellent and effective treatments to control pain. These treatments, along with the knowledge that relief is available, can help make the end of life bearable.

Pain Control

Many people worry that they will die in pain. This fear of pain may be particularly strong for those with cancer. But according to experts in the field of pain control, almost all terminally ill patients can experience adequate relief with currently available treatments. In some cases, relief of pain and other symptoms may require total anesthesia, which may not be acceptable to everyone but is a method that works when all else fails.

If pain control is achievable for most cancer patients, and for virtually all who are terminally ill, why do stories abound of patients suffering and dying in pain? Are these stories a myth? Not entirely. In fact, despite the availability of strong painkillers for at least three hundred years, many patients today do not receive adequate treatment for their pain. Pain control is crucial, particularly in those who are hopelessly ill, since unrelieved pain can lead not only to physical suffering but to hopelessness, despair, and even suicide. In fact, unremitting pain is one of the most common reasons given by patients who request euthanasia or physician-assisted suicide.

Persistent pain that cannot be brought under control makes us feel helpless and desperate. Suicide can suddenly appear as our only option, a way of reasserting some control and escaping the horrible agony. In this sense, suicide can seem like a form of treatment—the ultimate "cure"—for our pain. But there are better treatments available that not only relieve our pain but allow us to hold on to an acceptable quality of life. When these treatments are not offered to us, we have to learn to demand them. Patients in pain are inadequately treated for many reasons, but these can all be overcome with care and attention, and importantly, with increasing patient awareness and assertiveness about what can and should be offered. Simone was a cancer patient whose situation illustrates how this awareness might have brought relief earlier than it came.

Simone was seventy-eight years old when she developed cancer of the pancreas. By the time it was diagnosed, it had become incurable. Five years earlier, her husband, Harry, had been diagnosed with prostate cancer, and when the cancer invaded the bone, he had been in a great deal of pain. Becoming more and more withdrawn, Harry drove off into the country one day and shot himself.

Simone had endured back pain off and on for at least ten years, but that was due to an arthritic condition of her spine, and she had seen these episodes of discomfort come and go. When her back ached these days, she would dwell on Harry's solution and try to force it, and the intense pain, out of her mind. She would be strong; she would live with it. But Simone began to feel weak and helpless. Physical therapy exercises now seemed a burden instead of a release. The latest arthritis pill, Ansaid, seemed to upset her stomach, something she had never experienced. Desperate for relief, she went back to her old standby, Motrin, but in higher doses. Despite this, the pain just got worse—the intensity was greater and the quality of it was different from before. Still, when her physician, Dr. Isaacs, would ask about her back pain, Simone would answer, "Oh, it's not so bad." It was the same old thing, she reassured him, the arthritis.

In her overwhelming dread of the physical and emotional pain Simone associated with her husband's suicide, she refused to recognize that the cause of her pain was the cancer. In fact, Simone's pain came from her tumor. The pancreas lies in the back of the abdomen, against the spine, and tumors in the pancreas commonly produce pain in the lower back. By the age of seventy-eight it is not uncommon for a person to have more than one medical condition at the same time, and Simone had two potential causes of pain that occurred in approximately the same part of the body. Because she would not, could not, admit the level of her pain to her doctor, it was poorly controlled. The excessive doses of Motrin, self-medicated, led to an ulcer—a not uncommon complication of Motrin and related arthritis pills. It was only when Simone's doctor discovered the ulcer that he realized something was amiss. He questioned her about her use of arthritis pills and soon realized how severe Simone's pain had been. The treatment of the ulcer would be simple: Simone would avoid Motrin and the ulcer would quickly heal with antiulcer medicine. As for the pain, Simone and Dr. Isaacs had a heart-to-heart talk. Simone received MS-Contin, a long-acting form of morphine, and her back pain vastly improved. "Yes," Dr. Isaacs said, "this pill is safe for your ulcer." In fact, pain relief reduces the risk of getting another ulcer in the future. Simone had assumed there was no solution to her back problem except the extreme one her husband had chosen. Her fears kept her in pain.

The need to be a stoic is not the only barrier people have to appropriate treatment. Fear of addiction is another, major impediment to adequate pain control. This fear is held by doctors, nurses, and patients themselves. After all, the strongest and most reliable pain relievers for most serious pain continue to be narcotics, technically referred to as "opioid analgesics" after the prototype narcotic, opium. This group of medications includes not only the widely used morphine but the illegal drug heroin, which is not available in the United States even for medical use. Although narcotics have been available for several centuries, abuse of opium led to federal restrictions on their sale and manufacture as early as 1908. However, while narcotics are often selected by drug abusers and addicts, their medical use by patients in pain is a totally different phenomenon. The fear people have of addiction from *medicinal* use of opioids is based on false assumptions and lack of research. The question has recently come under scientific scrutiny, and the bulk of evidence put forth by leading pain experts is that true addiction in medically treated patients is very rare. Addiction is rare not only among cancer patients but also among people treated for chronic pain due to conditions other than cancer (nonmalignant pain).

Narcotics have the potential for producing physical dependence in most patients, but physical dependence is vastly different from true addiction. When narcotics are taken regularly after a period of time, sometimes only after a few days, the patient's body grows to depend *physically* on the drug. Abruptly stopping it can result in symptoms such as nausea, vomiting, restlessness, sweating, and shaking. Physical dependence, however, can easily be overcome by reducing the dosages gradually over several days, or longer if the drug has been taken for a prolonged period of time. Almost all patients can be withdrawn safely and effectively from narcotics that are given for medical purposes and will not feel the need to return to the drug unless their medical condition continues to cause serious pain that cannot be relieved by other means.

In stark contrast, addicts seek out their drug of choice, whether it be a narcotic or other addicting substance such as cocaine or alcohol, and the need is for the drug itself, not for pain alleviation. This true addiction is an obsessive mental and physical craving that compels the substance abuser to seek a drug for the "high" or other sensation it produces, and *not* for its medicinal pain-relieving effect. Drug addicts compulsively pursue this high, often jeopardizing the health, welfare, or even the lives of themselves or their families. It is a life-destroying process, not a life-enhancing comfort.

Most experts believe that an adult at high risk of becoming an addict from medical use of opioids would almost always have shown evidence of such tendencies prior to becoming ill, perhaps having exhibited self-destructive or other harmful behaviors previously. He or she might already have had a history of alcoholism or substance abuse. A physician would naturally exercise great caution before instituting an opioid analgesic for a person with a history of drug abuse. However, in the presence of severe pain and medical illness, careful use of the drug even in such an individual would be justified, as long as the patient can use the drug responsibly. Compassion for the patient must be foremost in consideration. However, if you are worried about your ability to safely take narcotics, or are a concerned family member of someone with a record of past abuses or excesses, communicate your doubts to the doctor honestly and openly—so that the best course of action can be mutually decided upon for individual treatment.

In the vast majority of cases, however, opioid analgesics can be given without fear of addiction. Contrary to popular belief, there is conclusive evidence that most war veterans who received narcotics for relief of pain produced by their injuries—and were otherwise not drug users—discontinued use of addicting substances once they returned home. Awareness of this new evidence has only recently begun to filter down to health professionals and patients. Fears and overcautiousness remain. Not only do many doctors and nurses worry that they will cause their patients to become addicted, but patients themselves hesitate to take pain-relieving narcotics when prescribed, either because they themselves fear addiction or simply because they feel that taking narcotics is "wrong."

The doctor's fear that he will turn his patient into a drug addict may lead him to prescribe inadequate doses. This fear may also lead to the faulty practice of administering pain medication on an as-needed basis rather than on a regular schedule. Although it is entirely appropriate to give medication this way for simple conditions, such as an ordinary headache, it is generally inappropriate for patients who are suffering severe and constant pain, particularly those who are terminally ill. If your pain is unrelenting or if you are put in the position of having to beg for pain relief, this can lead to a feeling of utter hopelessness. The as-needed practice (also called PRN, from the Latin *pro re nata*) may be well intended, but it results in undertreatment of pain. It is now recognized that pain medication given on a regular basis, around the clock, significantly enhances pain relief and in the long run leads to lower total dose requirements. This is because when pain is inadequately treated or when medication is withheld until the pain reaches high levels, a higher immediate dose may be required to reduce it. And the longer the delay, the more anxiety you will experience, further accentuating the pain, discomfort, and fear that can lead to thoughts of ending it all.

Around-the-clock dose administration has other benefits. It circumvents practical problems, such as a busy nurse who must prioritize her time and sometimes fails to answer promptly the call of one of her patients who is in pain. It bypasses the personal distaste or fears surrounding narcotic use held by many health professionals or other caregivers, which might prevent prompt administration of a drug ordered by the doctor. It overcomes cultural or communication problems between patient and nurse, when the patient may not express his or her pain in ways the nurse can easily understand; or situations where an inexperienced, overworked, or even an unkind nurse may be annoyed at the calls of a demanding patient and subconsciously (or consciously) wish to "punish" such a "difficult" person. In all of these situations, real pain may remain unrecognized or underrated.

Regular pain medication also prevents you from being put

in the role of supplicant, having to beg for pain medication, or not wanting to be a "nuisance" and suffering in pain rather than ringing the buzzer a second time. Many people feel it is important to be strong or stoic and to bear the pain until they have "earned" the next dose. Simone's experience told her not to complain, and except for an odd set of circumstances, she might have spent her last days in agony. Pain experts recommend that analgesics, including narcotics, be given to the seriously ill on a regular schedule and that the need for higher doses be evaluated on a daily basis. It is important for you to recognize and remember that this is not only a basic patient right, but it is the most appropriate form of medical care.

Along with fears of addiction, there is still a pervasive lack of knowledge about techniques used for pain control. For example, your physician may hesitate to prescribe enough narcotic for fear that tolerance to the dose will develop and escalating doses will be required. Tolerance is a phenomenon, exhibited by narcotics as well as by many sedatives and sleeping pills, in which the body gradually becomes accustomed to the drug's effects, at which point symptoms will reappear unless a higher dose is used. For example, a ten-milligram dose of morphine might adequately relieve cancer pain for a few days, but shortly, higher doses may be needed to relieve the same amount of pain. In fact, while some cancer patients can achieve pain relief with doses of morphine as small as five or ten milligrams, many will eventually require total doses exceeding two hundred milligrams per day, and some higher. These are doses rarely required in other medical conditions, and the thought of prescribing or administering such high doses horrifies the doctor or nurse inexperienced in the treatment of cancer pain. However, for reasons that are not well understood, pain-relieving doses will usually reach a plateau. The plateau differs depending on the severity of the pain, the patient's ability to cope with pain, and on individual physiological characteristics of the particular patient. When doses are increased gradually, and you are informed of possible side effects and observed carefully, safety is assured.

Still, many physicians hesitate to give narcotics because of the potential side effects even though this practice is often inappropriate. Side effects can usually be avoided, controlled, or reversed. Common side effects of opioids include nausea, constipation, drowsiness, confusion, or dizziness. More serious side effects occur at high doses or in people who have never taken narcotics and may be very sensitive to small doses; these effects include respiratory depression and drops in blood pressure. However, what is frequently forgotten or ignored is that tolerance to the most serious side effects occurs faster than tolerance to pain-relieving effects. This is not true of all side effects, such as constipation, and these must be treated or prevented. Patients, too, may be reluctant to receive opioids because of side effects.

Dr. Russell Portenoy, a pain expert at New York's Memorial Sloan-Kettering cancer center, notes that patients often worry that strong painkillers will turn them into "zombies." In fact, he points out, most who achieve adequate pain relief remain clearheaded and able to function. However, if sedation does occur at pain-relieving doses, a "psychostimulant" drug such as methylphenidate (Ritalin) or amphetamine (e.g., Dexedrine) can be given to increase alertness and energy and even elevate mood. Appropriate doses of these psychostimulants can be given to nearly all patients without serious side effects.

Thus, you can be maintained with opioid analgesics in relative comfort for prolonged periods while the side effects are treated or in many cases disappear on their own. Some patients may require or desire sedating doses of medicine—anything from mild sedation to complete anesthesia. However, in the terminal phases of illness it is usually the disease and not the medication that produces sedation or lethargy. This effect of disease itself may actually have the positive effect of easing the dying process.

All in all, opioids are actually among the safest drugs in use today. They are free of most of the side effects caused by well-known painkillers such as aspirin and the pharmaceutical class of drugs known as nonsteroidal anti-inflammatory agents

—the "arthritis pills" that caused Simone's ulcer. Because opioids have been in wide use for many years, their side effects are well known to all physicians and are predictable, often preventable, and rarely serious. If undesired serious side effects occur, they can quickly be reversed with an injection of a narcotic antagonist or antidote called naloxone (Narcan), which is available and on hand in every hospital ward and emergency room.

A different kind of side effect may occur, a desirable one —that of euphoria, or the sensation of feeling very good psychologically. Many people are afraid of this side effect; they believe the euphoria is a "high" and therefore an evil that will lead to addiction. However, in a patient with advanced cancer, it may be difficult to differentiate euphoria as a side effect from simple happiness over the sudden relief of pain. Whatever the cause of euphoria, its appearance should be viewed as a positive event in the life of someone who is seriously ill and particularly so in someone who is hopelessly ill. In these situations, depression, and not its eradication, is the evil to be avoided.

Other side effects of narcotics can be desirable as well. Morphine can help relieve symptoms due to fluid in the lungs, a condition called pulmonary edema, or heart failure, for which the drug has been used for many years. Most narcotics are powerful cough suppressants. If you suffer from an irritating cough and are receiving morphine, codeine, or other opioid analgesics for pain control, you may also experience relief from coughing. Narcotics can reduce breathlessness, which is a common symptom in cancer of the lung and other cancers. Finally, narcotics' sedative effect can reduce the anxiety many people with serious illness experience, in part because pain control is achieved and in part because the narcotic has an independent effect on anxiety itself. With less anxiety, you are able to think more clearly. The depression and fear of unnecessary pain lessens or vanishes, and along with them, potentially suicidal thoughts.

As in Barbara's predicament, however, the fear that adequate doses of morphine could accelerate death can get in the way of appropriate care. It is true that high doses of morphine and other narcotics can depress respiration and may reduce blood pressure. In patients who are near death, blood pressure may already be low, or when disease has affected the lungs, the patient may be at higher risk of developing life-threatening side effects, which could accelerate death, though by only minutes or at most, a few hours. The risk of accelerating death was believed to be significant for Barbara because her emphysema had produced respiratory failure, but in fact, respiratory failure would ultimately take her, with or without morphine. Moreover, many pulmonary specialists believe that, at low doses, morphine acts on the brain rather than the lungs to reduce the *sensation* of breathlessness. Indirect evidence in emphysema patients less severely ill than Barbara suggests that opioids do impart this subjective effect. In addition, a February 1992 study in the *Journal of the American Medical Association* that looked at critically ill respirator-dependent patients in California supports the view that morphine and other sedatives do *not* accelerate death when given to ease the dying process once respirator support is discontinued. Opioid treatment in situations like Barbara's might therefore carry somewhat less of a risk than many believe.

At the end of life, when fears are raised that high narcotic doses may hasten death, most patients with severe pain (and many patients maintained on respirators) have already been receiving high doses of narcotics. Thus, they have developed tolerance to side effects, including respiratory depression and lowering of blood pressure. If the dose is not adequate to control their pain, an effective increase in dose is unlikely to produce a life-ending side effect, so that the theoretical risk of accelerating death is unlikely.

Remember, too, that administration of effective pain-relieving medicine at the end of life is subject to the same moral argument made by Father John, and the legal protections that support it. You have the right to receive maximum pain relief and comfort care, and you may use advance directives such as living wills to reinforce this right. In the words of Dr. Kathleen Foley, an internationally recognized authority on pain control, "treatment of pain is never a form of euthanasia."

Fortunately, a great deal of attention has been focused recently on the impediments to adequate pain relief, the mythology surrounding medicinal use of narcotics, and the development of new techniques to manage pain. In the past few years, a number of professional organizations have been formed that are devoted to the study of pain and the dissemination of knowledge about modern methods of pain relief (see Appendix). In addition, important information about pain control for the terminally ill and others has started to enter the curriculum of medical schools. Experts from a wide variety of the health professions—not only medicine—have entered the field. Multidisciplinary pain clinics and in-hospital pain-management consult teams have sprung up around the country. These are groups of professionals skilled in all methods of pain control, and they come from fields as diverse as medicine, psychiatry, neurology, rheumatology, nursing, physical medicine and rehabilitation, acupuncture, clinical pharmacology, psychology, and fields exploring newer forms of behavioral treatment including relaxation through biofeedback, art, music, and dance (movement) therapy. These groups apply a variety of techniques to control pain; if one technique does not work, another can be tried.

Nonpharmacological treatment of pain includes an ever increasing number of techniques. Some pains can be relieved when nerves are stimulated electrically using a method called transcutaneous electrical nerve stimulation (TENS). In acupuncture, the nerves are affected indirectly; a sterile needle is inserted beneath the skin at specified areas and this may stimulate the nervous system in such a way that pain relief occurs. Some pains that are due to "trigger points" in muscles can be relieved by simple injections. Topical treatments applied to the skin include coolant sprays or salves that may produce local pain relief when applied to the affected area and followed by massage. A new topical cream derived from the pepper plant is believed to deplete irritated nerves of "substance P," which helps to transmit the pain message to the brain. When applied to the skin, the cream may relieve pain in some conditions. Anticancer chemotherapy and radiation, by shrinking tumor, are techniques that may themselves help to relieve cancer pain. Refractory pain can often be controlled by injecting the affected nerve with anesthetics (nerve block) or severing the nerve surgically.

Pharmacologic treatment of pain goes far beyond the use of opioid analgesics; a wide variety of medications are available that can relieve pain. Often patients, even those suffering from cancer, achieve pain control with milder, nonnarcotic analgesics, including acetaminophen (Tylenol), aspirin, and nonsteroidal anti-inflammatory agents, of which ibuprofen (Motrin, Advil, and other brands) is the most widely used. In some painful conditions, nonnarcotic analgesics may actually be superior to opioids or when used in conjunction with the latter, may enhance their effect. Nonsteroidal anti-inflammatory agents, for example, may have a specific effect on bone pain in cancer that involves the bone. When cancer or other disease involves nerve fibers, pain relief can sometimes be obtained with medications that are usually not thought of as painkillers but act in that way in specific circumstances. Examples of these include antidepressants such as amitriptyline (Elavil) and anticonvulsants (medications used for epilepsy) such as phenytoin (Dilantin) and carbamazepine (Tegretol). These and other medications are used in combination with each other and with sedatives, depending on the patient's individual circumstances.

But for most types of severe pain, opioids remain the mainstay of treatment, owing to their effectiveness and safety. Although in exceptional circumstances the drugs are injected directly into the spinal canal, by subcutaneous (under the skin) injection or by intravenous drip, they are most commonly given by mouth. At home, in hospice, and in many hospitals, you are able to administer your own medications if you are physically capable of doing so. This control over pain management is essential in combating the feelings of helplessness and hopelessness people experience in the face of potentially excruciating pain. The ability to become actively involved in easing pain empowers patients and alleviates not only their discomfort but their fear of being rendered passive victims by their disease. Apparatus has been designed so that even morphine drips can be given by the patient, a technique called patient-controlled analgesia.

If you feel your pain is not being adequately addressed, you should ask your physician or local hospital or health care center about special pain-control groups that exist in your community. Hospitalized patients should ask if there is a pain specialist or pain consult team that can make an evaluation right there and give added input.

Many techniques are available for the management of pain and other disabling symptoms associated with serious illness. These are listed on the following table for quick reference. The table is intended as a summary. *Not all techniques are applicable for all patients, and some may be harmful if used by persons for whom they are not designed.* Medication, including that purchased without prescription, should always be taken under the supervision of your doctor, who will tailor the treatment to fit your individual needs. The information given in the table should reassure you that help is available; significant relief is attainable; there *are* alternatives when one method does not work.

Important Pain and Symptoms Relievers in Serious Illness
Painkillers
Opioids (narcotics) Used for Severe Pain
   hydromorphone (Dilaudid)
   levorphanol (Levo-Dromoran)
   meperidine (Demerol)
   methadone (Dolophine)
   morphine (many brands)

morphine controlled-release (MS-Contin, Oramorph-SR)
oxymorphone (Numorphan)

Opioids Used for Moderate Pain

codeine—available alone or in combination with aspirin or
acetaminophen

hydrocodone—available alone or in combination with aspirin or
acetaminophen (Vicodin, Lortab)

oxycodone—available alone (Roxicodone) or in combination
with aspirin (Percodan) or acetaminophen (Percocet, Tylox)

propoxyphene—available alone (Darvon) or in combination with
acetaminophen (Darvocet) or aspirin

Other Painkillers (nonnarcotics)

acetaminophen (Tylenol, Datril, others)

aspirin (many brands)

nonsteroidal anti-inflammatory agents (arthritis pills)
   diclofenac (Voltaren)
   fenoprofen (Nalfon)
   flurbiprofen (Ansaid)
   ibuprofen (Motrin, Nuprin, Advil, others)
   indomethacin (Indocin, others)
   ketoprofen (Orudis)
   ketorolac (Toradol)—by injection only
   meclofenamate (Meclomen)
   piroxicam (Feldene)
   naproxen (Naprosyn, Anaprox)
   sulindac (Clinoril)
   tolmetin (Tolectin)

salicylates (aspirinlike analgesics)
   choline magnesium trisalicylate (Trilisate)
   choline salicylate (Arthropan)
   diflunisal (Dolobid)
   magnesium salicylate (Doan's pills)
   salsalate (Disalcid)

Topical Agents for Localized Pain

capsaicin cream (Zostrix)

ethyl chloride coolant spray

methyl salicylate and menthol (Ben-Gay, Thera-Gesic)

Constipation
Laxatives (also called purgatives)

   bisacodyl (Dulcolax, Carter's Little Pills)
   lactulose (Chronulac)
   milk of magnesia (Haley's M-O, Phillips', other brands)
   milk of magnesia with cascara
   senna (Fletcher's Castoria, Senokot)
   stool softeners
      docusate sodium (Colace, other brands)
      docusate calcium (Surfak)
   enemas (many types available)
   suppositories
      bisacodyl
      glycerin
      docusate

Other Bowel Aids
   high-fiber foods
   methyl cellulose (Citrucel) with liquid
   polycarbophil (FiberCon, Fiberall chewable tablets) with liquid
   prune juice (contains a derivative of phenolphthalein, a potent
         laxative)
   psyllium (Metamucil, Fiberall, Correctol, Perdiem) with liquid

Diarrhea
   aluminum hydroxide (Amphojel, Basaljel); if antacid needed
         bismuth (Pepto-Bismol)
   codeine (many brands) or other narcotic
   diphenoxylate plus atropine (Lomotil)
   loperamide (Imodium)
   tincture of opium
   steroid-retention enemas for colitis due to radiation

Nausea or Vomiting (antiemetics)
   chlorpromazine (Thorazine, others)
   cyclizine (Marezine)—by injection only
   dimenhydrinate (Dramamine)
   dronabinol (THC [popularly marijuana], Marinol)
   haloperidol (Haldol)
   hydroxyzine (Atarax, Vistaril)
   lorazepam (Ativan)
   metoclopramide (Reglan)
   ondansetron (Zofran)
   perphenazine (Trilafon)

prochlorperazine (Compazine, others)
promethazine (Phenergan, others)
scopolamine skin patch (Transderm-Scōp)
thiethylperazine (Norzine, Torecan)

Itching
antihistamines
cyproheptadine (Periactin, others)
diphenhydramine (Benadryl, others)
hydroxyzine (Atarax, Vistaril)
cholestyramine (Questran) if related to liver disease, jaundice, or
kidney failure
prednisone or other corticosteroid
topical treatments
corticosteroid creams or ointments (Hytone, Kenalog, many
other brands; many strengths)
skin-lubricant creams or ointments
ultraviolet light

Cough Not Due to Infection Alone
expectorants (loosen and enable cough)
guaifenesin (Robitussin, other brands)
iodinated glycerol (Organidin, other brands)
suppressants (suppress cough)
codeine (alone or in combination cough syrups)
dextromethorphan (in combination with expectorants:
Robitussin-DM, many other brands)
morphine and other strong narcotics

Hiccups
carbamazepine (Tegretol)
chlorpromazine (Thorazine)
dexamethasone
haloperidol (Haldol)
metoclopramide (Reglan)
perphenazine (Trilafon)
other methods:
granulated sugar swallowed dry
radiation to tumor irritating phrenic nerve
injection or crushing of phrenic nerve

Mouth Pain
   in thrush (oral yeast infection)
      clotrimazole lozenge (Mycelex)
      fluconazole (Diflucan)
      ketoconazole (Nizoral)
      nystatin lozenge or mouthwash (Mycostatin)
   anesthetic mouthwash
      dyclonine (Dyclone)
      viscous lidocaine (Xylocaine, other brands)
   other soothing topical agents
      corticosteroid paste (Orabase)
      sucralfate slurry (Carafate)

Dry Mouth
   artificial saliva (Salivart)
   carboxymethylcellulose (Xerolube)
   ice chips
   iced-beverage sips (any flavor)
   lemon drops, or other sour candy (apple flavored)

Poor Appetite
   medications
      cyproheptadine (Periactin)
      dexamethasone or other corticosteroids
      megestrol (Megace)
   other techniques
      antidepressant medications (if due to depression)
      glass of alcoholic beverage prior to meals
      liberalization of diet to include preferred foods and "food
         cravings"
      liberalization of mealtime to coincide with hunger

Anxiety (anxiolytics)
   alprazolam (Xanax)
   antidepressant medication if significant depression
   buspirone (Buspar)—effect may be delayed for one to three
      weeks
   chlordiazepoxide (Librium)
   clorazepate (Tranxene)

diazepam (Valium)
halazepam (Paxipam)
hydroxyzine (Atarax, Vistaril)
lorazepam (Ativan)
meprobamate (Equanil, Miltown)
oxazepam (Serax)

Insomnia (hypnotics)
antianxiety agents (see above)
chloral hydrate (Noctec, others)
diphenhydramine (Benadryl, Nytol, Sominex, others)
flurazepam (Dalmane)
hydroxyzine (Atarax, Vistaril)
pentobarbital (Nembutal)
pyrilamine (Dormarex, others)
secobarbital (Seconal)
sedating antidepressants if depression is present
temazepam (Restoril)—onset of effect may be delayed
triazolam (Halcion)

Although many pain-control methods are used in nonmalignant pain, it is particularly important for patients with terminal illness to be aware that pain control is something to be
pursued. Patients should be informed of the possible impediments to adequate pain control and should realize that sometimes their fears can get in the way. Once we overcome our
misgivings about pain control, we will be well on our way to
overcoming many fears about death and dying.

Herman, a former nurse at a large urban hospital, was accustomed to the agonies of dying patients and had attended to
the sickest cases. He had always prided himself on being
attuned to subtle signs and symptoms. Many times he had
pried important information about discomfort or pain out of
patients who did not want to be seen as complainers. He
made sure the sleepless received their sleeping pills; that
those in pain received their morphine on time; and that anti-

nausea medications were delivered to the floor from the pharmacy *before* chemotherapy sessions began and not *after* the nausea had started. Herman appreciated that a patient's complaint about feeling weak or lacking appetite might be just as important to the patient as having severe pain. He recognized that a cough was a misery for a lung cancer patient and would hound the doctor until an effective cough suppressant was prescribed. He understood that the inability to control one's bowels could be a source of agony and shame more powerful than cancer pain itself. He attempted to ensure that these indignities were addressed by the physician, who might otherwise have concentrated on more "sophisticated" problems.

But just as Herman had done all in his power to relieve suffering, he had also been forced to stand back and watch those whose suffering seemed beyond relief. Herman had seen the worst. And now, suddenly, the worst had caught up with him. Herman had pricked his finger on a contaminated needle while caring for an AIDS patient and in this way had contracted AIDS himself. He had gone through many treatments and was beginning to lose weight. He developed lymphoma of the intestine and was afraid. After all he had done for others, it hardly seemed fair that this should happen to him.

Herman had always considered himself to be a rational person. He had long learned to live with the attitude that there was something odd about a man's going into nursing. Now those stereotypes would be perpetuated because he had developed AIDS, of all things. It hardly mattered that he had contracted it while caring for the sick. Herman agonized over the unfairness and bitter irony of it all. But the greatest of his concerns was the fear that he might suffer excessively. What if he got so sick that nothing could relieve his pain or discomfort? He had worked with many patients with cancer and AIDS and had seen some unpleasant things. One patient— with intestinal lymphoma, Herman remembered with dismay —had spent his last days with nausea and vomiting that had not responded to any medications or treatment.

Herman was now a patient at a university hospital, where care was known to be excellent and where he knew many of the staff. But Herman knew it was a teaching hospital, and he was concerned that his day-to-day care would be given by inexperienced interns and residents. Familiar with the health care system, Herman asked for, and got, the attending oncologist, who spent an hour with Herman at the end of a very busy day. Dr. Summers, who Herman always thought looked "more like my Aunt Sarah than the big boss," had a warm smile and a wealth of scientific knowledge. She explained a recently published technique called titrated intravenous barbiturates, which consisted of giving medication by vein to patients whose symptoms could not be relieved by other methods, and in effect helping them to sleep through their misery. Herman felt this was a fairly primitive approach and was somewhat taken aback. He knew that intravenous barbiturates were used for general anesthesia, and the thought of "putting someone to sleep" made him somewhat uncomfortable. He wanted to be sure it would only be used as a last resort, when he was already dying and could not gain relief from any other form of treatment. Herman also questioned whether this approach would hasten death and be illegal. Dr. Summers reassured him on both counts and explained that it was quite acceptable to her and most of her colleagues as a means to relieve suffering when all other methods had failed. Like Dr. Persico, she was able to explain this technique in a satisfactory manner to her patient, and Herman had confidence that she would act only in his best interest, in accord with his wishes and values.

In Herman's case, the technique of titrated intravenous barbiturates ended up being of mere academic interest because his symptoms never became so severe that he required it. But after thinking about it, Herman was quite relieved to know that this logical technique was actually being adopted. And yet the technique was not reported in the medical literature until 1991, when two doctors from South Carolina described successful treatment with dying patients who had not responded well to other treatments. As in Barbara's case, where morphine allowed a hopelessly ill patient to be disconnected from a respirator and die as she wished, a technique as simple as an intravenous infusion of a well-known medication can ensure a peaceful end for the terminally ill, who might otherwise have to undergo significant misery in their last days.

By producing anesthesia, the barbiturates could theoretically hasten death by minutes or even hours, if they were to dangerously lower blood pressure or depress respiration. But the technique involves a short-acting barbiturate, thiopental, the dose of which can quickly be changed (titrated), if anesthesia is perceived as too powerful. However, one cannot know when the disease itself has ended someone's life, and it is theoretically possible that the comfort provided by the anesthesia could actually *prolong* life by a short time. Most importantly, the intention is to relieve persistent suffering while nature takes its course, and the risk taken to achieve this compassionate care seems a morally acceptable one.

Control of physical symptoms is only part of the overall approach to easing the dying process. Our attitude toward pain—and toward the future—may also affect our psychological interpretation of suffering and illness. If we believe we are suffering for a purpose, such as a cure or remission, or that there may be some relief in sight, we are much more likely to put up with pain. As long as we have something to look forward to—even if it's only a reduction of our pain—then we can tolerate our suffering better. But when we lose all hope of any improvement, when we believe that there is no way to treat our pain and gain adequate relief, we may suffer anxiety and depression that can lead to thoughts of suicide and even requests for physician-assisted suicide. Herman's greatest fear was one of hopelessness. What if he was suffering and there was no way to relieve his pain? He became extremely anxious and depressed about facing the end of his life. But once he learned a medical technique was available to help him regardless of how serious his symptoms became, this knowledge helped relieve his anxiety and restore his spirits—even though the technique was never needed or used. It was Herman's perception that relief was available—that there was some hope—that allowed him to tolerate his pain without suffering as much.

One of the most important symptoms experienced by those who are seriously ill is depression. For some reason, this is not always perceived by patients as a symptom, and yet it is something that can be addressed and treated as if it were a physical problem. If a patient in pain is also suffering from clinical depression, treatment of the depression, with antidepressant medication if necessary, can help to alleviate pain because pain can become magnified in depression. Psychological techniques such as behavioral modification, counseling, distraction, and meditation may help significantly even in the absence of depression. Simple visiting and spending time with a patient in pain may provide substantial pain relief. Not only does this provide distraction from the pain but it indicates to the patient that he is not being abandoned. Your state of mind concerning your pain may be as important, if not more so, than the actual intensity of the pain itself. As long as you believe that there is some further treatment to be attempted, that the health care professional has not given up on you, you will be better able to accept your pain and minimize its impact. As your illness becomes more far-advanced, and the risk of depression increases, it is all the more important to maintain some residue of hope. Knowing that terminal pain can be relieved and its symptoms controlled, and understanding the myriad medications and treatments available for managing our end-of-life suffering, should go a long way toward reassuring each of us that our pain, and our fear of pain, can be effectively controlled.

CHAPTER FIVE

How to Recognize and Treat Clinical Depression

Sir, Thank you for your excellent leading article "The Road to Dusty Death" (October 18). Ten years ago, while clinically depressed, I attempted suicide several times, sincerely believing that death was the "only satisfactory release." I thank God that I did not have access then to any guides to supposed self-deliverance.

I am now thirty-three years of age, have been happily married for seven years, have recently completed a book-keeping training course and gained employment in this field, am an active campaigner for human rights, and have an unshakable religious faith.

Please, EXIT [a British euthanasia group], give other people a chance to have a new life in *this* world.

Yours sincerely,
Jean M. Haslam

Letter to the London *Times*, October 24, 1980
Reprinted in *The Oxford Book of Death*

Burt was a sixty-nine-year-old widower from a Chicago, Illinois, suburb. He had been a successful architect and a good tennis player who participated in tournaments at least once a year. At the age of sixty-five, Burt had sold his thirty-one-year practice and moved to a house he had designed especially for his and his wife Patricia's semiretirement, a sprawling split-level ranch house on the edge of a lake. Burt could not give up his work altogether and continued to design homes for a select group of clients, among whom he was much in demand. His idyllic new life was cut short when Patricia was diagnosed with amyotrophic lateral sclerosis (ALS), "Lou Gehrig's disease," a fatal disease characterized by progressive paralysis. Burt tended his wife faithfully for several years until she died.

Although Burt mourned the loss of his wife, he also felt relieved. He had been grieving for the five long years of her illness, and her death was, in one sense, a "release"—both for Patricia and for himself. Burt wanted to recuperate from the loss, pick up the pieces, and go on with his life. He had two loving children and four grandchildren, and as people always said, he was the youngest sixty-nine-year-old around. Except for a knee that was starting to bother him, Burt had much to look forward to.

But then one day Burt noticed blood in the toilet bowl and he was gripped by fear. The bleeding recurred several days later and then stopped. Burt was horrified that the bright red blood came from him. The first thought that came to him was cancer, but he fought to put it out of his mind. At about the same time as the bleeding incident, Burt noticed that business was slowing down. New clients stopped calling and it began to look as if he was just finishing up old jobs. Burt tried to tell himself it was all due to the economic situation, but he worried that he was getting too old to attract new clients. He was almost seventy. His knee wasn't holding up the way it used to, and he had to admit he had slowed down a bit. What if he had to give up tennis entirely? And the bleeding episode was yet another cause for concern.

Eight months after his wife's death, just when Burt had expected to be recovering from his grief, his life seemed to be falling apart. Burt began to notice pains he had never experienced before and thought he was having abdominal cramps. He was frightened. The bleeding had not recurred, but he was aware his bowels weren't working properly, a sure sign of cancer, he felt. He knew he was getting sick. He stopped playing tennis entirely. Food didn't seem to interest him any longer and he lost weight. He terminated work on the few projects he was still involved with and did not return his clients' phone calls. And he woke up every morning before dawn, tossing and turning and unable to get back to sleep. Instead, he thought about Patricia. His mind dwelled on their past life together—the good times he missed and knew they would never have again, as well as the mistakes he had made during the marriage. Had his behavior contributed to her stress and ultimately to her illness? He could not shake this thought.

Burt became increasingly withdrawn and took little interest in other people, including members of his family. Burt's daughter, Nancy, a physician, grew concerned; she suggested to her father he might be depressed and recommended a psychiatrist. But Burt, a man's man of the old school, would hear nothing of such talk. He had no use for "shrinks" and would take care of his own problems, as he always had. His mind revolved obsessively around the loss of Patricia, his diminishing career, and his failing health. Nancy still called regularly and visited whenever she could, but Burt was unresponsive and aloof. His son had long given up on him. It seemed that no one could reach him.

Then one morning Burt took his old army pistol and walked out to the lake. There seemed to be no hope anymore, no point to anything. Burt would end it quickly. He would no longer be a burden to himself or anyone else. He raised the gun to his head and fired, but as he would later admit, his aim had been purposely poor. As hopeless as things seemed, Burt was still ambivalent about ending his life. A neighbor heard the shot, came running, and found Burt sitting on the ground in despair. He had an ugly but superficial wound near his temple.

The neighbor drove Burt to the hospital emergency room. After his wound was cleaned, disinfected, and bandaged, Burt was ready to leave. But by this time Nancy had arrived and she insisted that Burt be seen by the attending psychiatrist. Nancy provided details of her father's personal and family history to Dr. Alvarez, who agreed to do an evaluation. Burt resisted at first, saying that the gun had gone off accidentally while he was cleaning it. As for the wound, he had sustained much worse physical damage while training in the army, but no one had made such a fuss about it. Dr. Alvarez, himself a former Marine captain, answered, "Your flesh wound is relatively minor and should heal quickly, but I think we need to talk about some other problems. You're up against a very powerful, deadly foe—only you can't see him yet." The doctor explained to Burt that he was suffering from major depression and needed immediate medical treatment. He persuaded Burt to stay in the hospital and start on a small dose of Prozac, an antidepressant medication.

After two weeks, Burt went home from the hospital and Nancy saw to it that he showed up for his follow-up visits with Dr. Alvarez. The psychiatrist encouraged Burt to talk about himself, his wife's death, and the life they had shared for forty years. "Tell me about yourself," Dr. Alvarez said. Burt began to express some guilt because he had felt relieved when Patricia finally died after her long illness. This led to Burt's feelings of guilt over an affair he had carried on years earlier, feelings that had also resurfaced when his wife died. In some ways he had felt responsible for her illness even though he knew he had not caused it. Delving into his past with Dr. Alvarez, Burt recalled that his grandfather had become noticeably withdrawn after his own wife's sudden death and had "died of a broken heart" six months later.

Burt began to talk about his fears of growing old and becoming incapacitated. He wanted to stay in shape but his knees were going. Eventually Burt revealed the incident involving his rectal bleeding. He was terrified that he might have cancer. He feared he would need surgery and a colostomy would have to be performed, leaving him with a "bag" to wear. Burt's voice shook as he described these fears. But he also felt as if a great weight had been lifted from him. He had never before discussed feelings of such a personal nature.

Dr. Alvarez referred Burt for a complete medical workup,

which included a colonoscopy, a long tube inserted into the rectum that provides a view of the entire length of the colon. Burt's bleeding had been caused by internal hemorrhoids, but the doctor also found a small polyp, only a quarter of an inch wide, in the intestine, which he removed during the colonoscopy. The biopsy revealed that the polyp was completely benign—there was no evidence of cancer. The doctor did recommend that Burt have a follow-up colonoscopy to screen for any new polyps that could become cancerous. Otherwise Burt need not worry about his bleeding. Nothing in his abdomen was responsible for his symptoms.

Dr. Alvarez explained that Burt's real medical problem was that he was clinically depressed. A series of losses and perceived losses, foremost among them being Burt's fear of deteriorating health, had sent Burt into a major depressive episode. Although his knee problem was real, his other "physical" symptoms were largely due to his depression. He had magnified everything, including the abdominal pain, because he felt that his body was giving out on him. Burt was afraid of growing old and weak and dying—and so he had almost killed himself.

Several other factors had converged to bring on Burt's depression and suicide attempt. He had watched his beloved wife gradually succumb to a wasting illness, and now he feared a similar fate for himself. His relief over her death had tapped into his guilt over a previous affair. He also grieved for Patricia and for the life they had shared together, which he would never again have. He now faced the last part of his life alone. And though Burt was lonely, he was no longer sure of his ability to attract and keep another woman. Burt's self-esteem had recently sustained several blows. He was losing his identity as a professional architect—as a man defined by the job he did. It had been the biggest part of his life for so long that he did not know who to be without it. Because of his knee problem—osteoarthritis, the doctor called it—Burt's tennis triumphs were over. Tennis had always allowed him to maintain a certain balance in his life. To be told that osteoarthritis was "not crippling" seemed like scant relief if it meant he could no longer play tennis. Burt's role in the family was also diminished, now that he was a grandfather in retirement. His son's business career was starting to take off, and now it was Burt's son and *his* plans for expansion that were the central topic of conversation at family gatherings. Burt could only offer advice from the sidelines. These were real changes he had to adjust to, but they had become magnified because of Burt's fears about cancer.

Dr. Alvarez emphasized that Burt should view his depression as he would view any urgent medical illness—as something that required appropriate treatment by a professional, in this case a psychiatrist. Burt was not crazy and his illness could be treated and even cured with the right combination of drugs and therapy, but he needed help. He had been on the verge of ending his life. And the real killer was not cancer or arthritis—it was, or could have been, depression.

After his colonoscopy and a few weeks of taking the new medication, Burt's mood began to improve. He slept better, his appetite gradually returned, and he again felt like going out and getting involved in new projects. He resumed work on a greenhouse that he had started building before Patricia's illness. He began to swim and found he enjoyed the exercise immensely. He called up Nancy and invited her to dinner with her entire family. Burt went shopping and prepared the meal by himself. He played with his grandson and promised to attend his next soccer game. He showed off his new greenhouse.

Between 10 and 20 million Americans—about 5 million of them over sixty-five—will suffer from an episode of depression this year. We all know what it is like to suffer disappointment or loss and to feel sadness. Most of us consider these feelings part of life and we accept them along with our portion of joy and happiness. We may wake up with a case of the blues or feel down in the dumps for a period. The majority of us snap out of these doldrums in time and regain our normal buoyancy. But for many thousands of people, these low, dispirited moods may gradually develop into what psychiatrists call a clinical depression. And clinical depression is a debilitating, oft-hidden disease that leads to immeasurable pain and suffering. It accounts for untold and unnecessary human misery: physical and emotional distress, mental confusion, economic loss, social isolation, and at an alarming rate, to death by suicide.

Depression is a factor in over 50 percent of all suicides in the United States, a remarkable fact that makes depression a deadly disease and the leading indicator of suicide. People who are depressed are far more likely to kill themselves than any other identifiable group. And people with terminal illnesses such as cancer or AIDS are at a much higher risk for depression than others in the general population. Cancer patients, for example, are twenty-five times more likely to suffer depression than others without the disease. Thus there is an important connection between terminal illness, depression, and suicide—but depression is the key that links them together into a potentially fatal combination. Contrary to popular belief, terminal illness alone, in the absence of depression, does not significantly increase the risk of suicide. A 1990 article by Drs. Thomas Mackenzie and Michael K. Popkin in the book *Suicide Over the Life Cycle* noted that "no more than 5 percent of suicides occurred in the context of terminal illness." But among the terminally ill who chose suicide, Mackenzie and Popkin found that anywhere from 70 to 100 percent were suffering from a psychiatric illness, most notably depression. Depression is the missing link, the critical, highly combustible element, that can turn our normal concerns about age and illness into desperate acts of self-destruction.

As we grow older, we become more susceptible to new illnesses and disabilities, as well as to new fears and uncertainties about our future well-being. We are also more likely to suffer other losses, in terms of our jobs, economic and social status, family position, spouses, and friends. These factors may contribute to serious depression, and depression, in more than one out of seven cases, will lead to suicide. Burt's fears about his declining health and age, combined with other stresses in his life, led to a major depressive episode and an attempt to commit suicide. Burt did not even have cancer, as he had feared, but his mental and emotional anxiety about his health brought on depression, and depression almost killed him.

Depression is a serious, potentially fatal illness that often masquerades as "a bad phase I'm going through." Most people do not recognize their depression, and because of this, they do not seek medical help. As we age, some of the common physical and mental impairments that we experience often mask depression and hide it from view. Loss of memory, physical function—and even loss of friends and family—may be regarded as "just a part of life." When these losses accumulate and depression results, we may not realize we are sick and thus we will not seek treatment.

In addition, many physicians who evaluate and treat elderly patients and others for symptoms such as insomnia or weight loss—or for unrelated complaints that may appear exaggerated—do not realize that these people are actually suffering from clinical depression. This is the real tragedy of depression because the overwhelming majority of people who suffer from this illness—at least 80 percent—can be effectively treated with the right combination of medical treatment and psychotherapy.

People who suffer a single tragic event; people who gradually grow gloomy and melancholic with the infirmities and losses caused over time; those who develop a serious or even fatal medical illness; people who have a recurring personal or family history of mood disorders; and those who, for no apparent reason, suddenly fall into deep depression—all these people can be helped. In most cases drug treatment can bring depression under control, and in many cases, it can prevent symptoms from recurring. And psychotherapy, which may also relieve depressive symptoms, can often help individuals deal with the emotional and social problems that accompany this illness. "Why can't I just get a grip on myself and control my depression? Am I a weakling? Will I always be sick and dependent on medication? Can I ever have a relationship with anyone again? Will my family have to take care of me like an invalid? Maybe I really am better off dead?" Thus it is essential for patients and their families to recognize the symptoms of depression, understand their implications, and seek help for this serious but treatable medical disorder.

The symptoms of major depression are varied. If you are clinically depressed, you may feel generally sad, hopeless, and discouraged. You may begin to have trouble sleeping and experience difficulty getting out of bed in the morning. Your appetite may be poor, leading to significant weight loss, or in some cases you might overeat and gain weight. There may be a noticeable loss of interest in life and falling off from involvement in your usual activities. The smallest task may appear difficult to complete for the depressed individual who loses his or her entire motivation for going on and is wracked by feelings of inadequacy and worthlessness. Thoughts of death may occur, and also thoughts of suicide, because a common belief among depressed people is that they would be better off dead. In the most severe cases, about 15 percent, suicide attempts are undertaken and completed.

Some important diagnostic tools can help identify depression. The patient's specific complaints and symptoms, external behavior, family history, and recent life events may all provide significant clues. In the United States, the American Psychiatric Association publishes a widely used classification system for identifying mental disorders based on standard criteria. Called the *Diagnostic and Statistical Manual of Mental Disorders* (DSM-III-R), this manual is currently in its third (III) edition, and it has been revised (R). The *DSM-III-R*'s diagnostic criteria for "major depressive episode" are summarized on the next page. These criteria help to establish the diagnosis of depression and to differentiate it from other conditions that share some features of depression and may mimic it. These conditions include such problems as grief reactions and other syndromes with depressive features milder than major depression, such as sadness, or more serious problems such as schizophrenia accompanied by depression. These criteria underscore the need for patients who experience dramatic changes in mood or behavior to seek professional help.

Diagnostic Criteria for Major Depressive Episode

Note: A "Major Depressive Syndrome" is defined as criterion A below.

A. At least five of the following symptoms have been present during the same two-week period and represent a change from previous functioning; at least one of the symtoms is either (1) depressed mood, or (2) loss of interest or pleasure. (Do not include symptoms that are clearly due to a physical condition, mood-incongruent delusions or hallucinations, incoherence, or marked loosening of associations.)

  (1) depressed mood (or can be irritable mood in children and adolescents) most of the day, nearly every day, as indicated either by subjective account or observation by others

  (2) markedly diminished interest or pleasure in all, or almost all, activities most of the day, nearly every day (as indicated either by subjective account or observation by others of apathy most of the time)

  (3) significant weight loss or weight gain when not dieting (e.g., more than 5 percent of body weight in a month), or decrease or increase in appetite nearly every day (in children, consider failure to make expected weight gains)

  (4) insomnia or hypersomnia nearly every day

  (5) psychomotor agitation or retardation nearly every day (observable by others, not merely subjective feelings of restlessness or being slowed down)

  (6) fatigue or loss of energy nearly every day

  (7) feelings of worthlessness or excessive or inappropriate guilt (which may be delusional) nearly every day (not merely self-reproach or guilt about being sick)

  (8) diminished ability to think or concentrate, or indecisiveness, nearly every day (either by subjective account or as observed by others)

  (9) recurrent thoughts of death (not just fear of dying),

recurrent suicidal ideation without a specific plan, or a
suicide attempt or a specific plan for committing suicide

B. (1) it cannot be established that an organic factor initiated and
maintained the disturbance

(2) the disturbance is not a normal reaction to the death of a
loved one (Uncomplicated Bereavement)

Note: Morbid preoccupation with worthlessness, suicidal
ideation, marked functional impairment or psychomotor
retardation, or prolonged duration suggest bereavement
complicated by Major Depression.

C. At no time during the distrubance have there been delusions or
hallucinations for as long as two weeks in the absence of
prominent mood symptoms (i.e., before the mood symptoms
developed or after they have remitted).

D. Not superimposed on Schizophrenia, Schizophreniform
Disorder, Delusional Disorder, or Psychotic Disorder NOS.

Do not be put off by the formidable-looking list of symptoms here. They represent the medical profession's effort to
create objective standards for diagnosing a serious illness that
remains elusive. There are other diagnostic tools, such as the
Beck Depression Inventory and the Geriatric Depression
Scale, that some physicians may also use. Overall, despite
some limitations, these academic guidelines have proved
helpful to both doctors and patients. As in all medical situations, your personal observations and insights, as well as common sense, must work with the accepted pool of knowledge
to help identify this illness.

The first episode of a depression may be relatively mild
and go unrecognized even by the sufferer. You may not be
aware that anything out of the ordinary has occurred. It is
difficult for anyone to determine exactly when a sad or depressed mood becomes a medical condition. The sudden disturbance in mood, appetite, or sleep, if it comes in the wake
of a specific setback or loss, such as the end of a relationship
or a job, may be related to depression, but it is hard to be

sure. Because most of us normally experience changes in mood that may be set off by a variety of factors, we may not be aware that we have been overtaken by a single, prolonged emotion that is distorting our mental and emotional life. What sets a major depressive episode apart from other feelings is that the low, depressed mood and its symptoms occur together for several weeks or months and are different from anything that came immediately before. A major depressive episode holds us in its grip like a vise and colors everything we think about and see—yet we may still not recognize it as an illness. Observers, including family, friends, or even the physician, may also misunderstand and misinterpret our change in mood and behavior. However, if the sadness persists and the loss of interest continues, there may be a serious mood disorder.

The duration of a depressive episode is unpredictable. Although untreated depression lasts an average of approximately six months, it may be shorter or longer, sometimes persisting for two years or more. Some people only become depressed during certain times of the day, or during specific seasons. It has been observed that cases of depression in general peak during the spring and fall. It is also known that suicide deaths peak in May and October.

Even when the symptoms of depression subside, your illness may not be over. The shock waves or aftereffects of a major depressive episode, like those of an earthquake, can be devastating and work to undermine an individual's sense of self-esteem. You may lose your previous level of confidence because you behaved in such a self-destructive and unpredictable manner. You can no longer trust yourself and become full of self-doubt. Or you may have resorted to drugs or alcohol to help relieve your depressive symptoms—you "self-treated" yourself—and now find you are dependent on these substances to help get you through. In addition, because you were so depressed, you may have said or done something rash that ruined a long-term personal or family relationship. Even your closest friends had never seen this side of you and failed to grasp the depths of your illness and despair. Instead they saw a cruel and unfeeling monster. If you had the misfortune to exhibit your erratic behavior at work, both your present job and future career opportunities may be jeopardized. Years of carefully laid plans and a spotless record can instantly be overturned and undone. And perhaps worst of all, your fear of a recurrence—of being once again at the mercy of such powerful and overwhelming forces—may paralyze any future action and initiative on your part. The depression, and fear of depression, now dominates and controls your life.

There is also a powerful social stigma connected with depression. A 1991 survey by the National Mental Health Association found that 43 percent of Americans believe depression is "a sign of personal or emotional weakness." Such an attitude prevails despite the overwhelming scientific evidence in the past twenty years that depression is a medical illness. Burt's response that "I can take care of my own problems" is a typical reaction, particularly among many older men. Some people believe they can "beat" the problem themselves, without resorting to outside assistance or medication. Others believe it may simply pass if they wait long enough. Depression lacks the credentials of other "real" illnesses and is still suspect as a bona fide disease. It is often referred to as the "common cold" of major psychiatric illnesses. Feelings of sadness or even depression affect so many of us at some point in our lives that we tend to underestimate true depression as a serious mental health problem. When we do become depressed, there is also a tendency to blame ourselves, and to feel shame about succumbing to such a weakness. In the 1991 National Mental Health Association survey, 30 percent of respondents said that if depression strikes in a family, they would not want their friends to know about it. Many feel guilt over this disorder and believe it is not socially acceptable. Others simply seek to deny it.

Families can be seriously and fundamentally disrupted when a member becomes clinically depressed, especially if he or she is the primary breadwinner or homemaker. They may try to care for the needs of the ill relative while carrying on with their lives as if nothing has happened. This may lead to a confusing shift in roles as well as exhaustion, anger, and shame. Efforts to reach out and "cheer up" the loved one may backfire because we cannot simply talk someone out of a serious depression. Family members may feel frustration and resentment because their best efforts seem ineffectual, while the depressed person continues to feel listless and low because he or she is helpless in the face of an overpowering disease. The family's expectation of immediate improvement may actually make things worse because it is an impossible demand that we cannot meet. Eventually the family may seek professional help and acknowledge the severity of the illness. A doctor can assist them in establishing a strategy for treatment and coping. Sometimes, when the patient is suicidal and has other acute symptoms of depression, hospitalization may even be necessary. Psychiatric hospitalization ranges from two weeks to thirty days and aims to return the patient back to the family and the community as quickly as possible. But its connotations are deeply upsetting and may further divide a family with a depressed relative.

It is particularly hard to recognize depression among older people. While most cases in those over sixty-five are recurrences of previous depressions, anywhere from 10 to 20 percent of people over sixty-five who suffer from depression have their first depressive episode in late life (called late-onset depression). Older people deny or fail to recognize that they are depressed and do not report that they are feeling sad or low-spirited. Instead, they report the chronic pain and other bodily ills such as stomach upsets or constipation that often are symptoms of late-life depression rather than of other ailments. Depression in older people may also present itself as problems with memory and concentration or lower energy and drive. These "depressive equivalents" may camouflage or mask the underlying depression and make it more difficult to diagnose. Under these circumstances, family members and health professionals should have a high index of suspicion that depression exists.

Early recognition of depression in older people is important because those who have other age-related infirmities may be more vulnerable to physical complications of depressive illness. By recognizing and treating the depression, we may prevent a further deterioration in their overall health. In addition, symptoms that mimic depression are sometimes due to unrelated but treatable problems such as thyroid disease or medication side effects, or to serious illness such as cancer. By recognizing the true cause of the symptoms, we can accurately diagnose and treat the underlying problem. Conversely, severe depression may be misdiagnosed as dementia, a common disorder in late life that doctors overdiagnose because they expect to see it; as a result the depression goes untreated and becomes worse. At other times, when depression and dementia coexist, dementia alone may be diagnosed when in fact treatment of the underlying depression (false dementia or pseudodementia) may improve the patient's confused state.

Early recognition of depression is particularly important for older people because of the increased risk of suicide in late life and because of the known link between depression and suicide. As previously mentioned, those over sixty-five have the highest rates of suicide in the U.S. population. Recently, after thirty years of decline, those rates have increased, with men over seventy showing the most significant rise and the highest rates of all. Burt's unrecognized and untreated depression was the reason for his suicide attempt. Once his depression was brought under control, Burt was able to adjust to other painful changes in his life. Treatment of depression, whether directly through antidepressant medication and psychotherapy, or indirectly through family support and other supportive services in the community, may be the best way to prevent suicide among older people.

Depression and Suicide

Although serious physical illness can lead some people to contemplate suicide, it is psychiatric illness that is largely responsible for completed suicide. In fact, over 90 percent of people who take their own lives suffer from a major psychiatric illness. A number of mental illnesses increase the suicide risk —for example, mania, schizophrenia, and personality disorders that lead to substance abuse—but the single most important mental illness directly linked to suicide is depression. Fifty percent or more of those who kill themselves are clinically depressed at the time of death. The vast majority of these suicides are committed by people with no other medical illness. Among those few who kill themselves *because* of their illness—like the three women who sought the help of Dr. Jack Kevorkian—90 percent or more suffer from clinical depression. According to Dr. Robert Steer, a psychologist at the University of Medicine and Dentistry in New Jersey who has studied depression and hopelessness, "most patients with severe diseases don't become hopeless if they are well adapted to life before their illness." People with serious illnesses such as cancer, AIDS, or multiple sclerosis rarely become suicidal unless they are depressed; whereas people without any of these diseases who are nonetheless depressed are at a higher risk for suicide than those with these diseases. The fact that *over half of all suicides are committed by people who are clinically depressed* speaks volumes about the powerful, though by no means inevitable, link between depression and suicide.

The connection between depression and suicide is so strong that "suicide ideation" or thoughts of suicide, as well as suicidal behavior, is considered one indicator for the diagnosis of major depression. In other words, if one of your symptoms is that you can't stop thinking about killing yourself, then you may be suffering from depression. In this case, once your depression is treated, suicidal thoughts and impulses should subside.

More than one out of seven depressed patients, or roughly 15 percent of Americans whose depression is *not* treated or is inadequately treated, will ultimately commit suicide whether or not they have a physical illness. A depressed patient is twenty-two to thirty-six times more likely to kill himself or herself than someone in the general population. When depression coexists with alcoholism—which alone accounts for about 25 percent of suicides—the risk is even greater. Among those with a major mood disorder, people who live alone are twice as likely to commit suicide as those who live with another person. However, it is not known if living alone predisposes a person to commit suicide (e.g., from the lack of a support system) or whether the personality types predisposed to suicide also tend to live alone.

While a majority of those who commit suicide suffer from clinical depression, depression *alone* is not a predictor of suicide. If 15 percent of those with major depressive symptoms will kill themselves, it's also true that 85 percent will not. Suicide ideation is a basic symptom of depression, but having suicidal thoughts is a far cry from acting on those thoughts, or even making a plan to activate them. Several other factors must also simultaneously be present, such as the series of physical and emotional losses experienced by Burt—the death of his wife, his bleeding and knee problems—as well as social alienation and withdrawal, a personal and family history of mood disorders, and an overriding sense of hopelessness.

Nevertheless, it is critical for close family, friends, and health care providers to be open and attentive to a depressed person's clues or mention of suicide. One problem is that a depressed individual having suicidal thoughts may feel ashamed of revealing these hidden impulses, not realizing they are a recognized component of the illness. Such feelings of shame and guilt may be reinforced when those around us dismiss our thoughts and suggest that we stop being melodramatic and pull ourselves together.

Suicidal thoughts and impulses must be taken seriously and treated as part of the person's illness. Sometimes the clues may be subtle. An older patient named David went to see his doctor about a growth on his skin. The doctor assured David the lesion would not turn to cancer. David then asked whether he should be rechecked in a week or so. The doctor said that this would not be necessary and David wouldn't need to be seen for at least six months. But David was seriously depressed and what he really needed was someone to talk to. His real problem, the depression, went unrecognized and untreated by the doctor, who thought he was being helpful about the skin lesion. David later tried to kill himself. As previously mentioned, several studies have shown that the majority of older patients who kill themselves will visit a physician in the months preceding suicide. Some, like David, may not discuss their true fears and secret intentions but instead report physical symptoms and other complaints. It takes a perceptive, caring, and highly trained physician to detect the depression or other psychiatric disturbance underlying the patient's complaint. Too often, the diagnosis is missed. At other times, the depression is recognized but inadequately treated. The result can be fatal.

The medical profession must learn to be unusually sensitive and responsive to older or terminally ill patients who visit with any kind of complaint. The slightest hint of suicidal thoughts or ideas should be seriously and openly discussed. The physician may probe and try to rule out any remote possibility of suicide by bringing up the subject himself or herself. Many if not most people who are very sick or old or unhappy have at one time or another considered the idea of suicide. Totally denying such thoughts could even be a clue that there is suicidal intent, although religious constraints or just a very well-anchored and stable personality could also be the basis of such denial. But it should certainly be explored with the patient. So should any direct admission of suicidal thinking. It is not true that people who talk constantly about killing themselves never act on their threats. Many depressed patients who commit suicide communicate their intent to others before they finally act. Studies have shown that anywhere from one-third to two-thirds of suicidal patients give advance warning about their actions, usually through explicit and concrete statements about their intent. The physician should reassure the patient that these thoughts are common and then try to determine how far they have gone. Has the patient actually felt in danger of killing himself? Has he come close? Does he have a specific plan and has he worked out all the details? The physician must encourage the patient to be as frank and open as possible. The doctor should also explain that the impulse to commit suicide can be sudden and overwhelming. The patient will feel hopelessly trapped and see no other way out. At times like these, the patient must promise to call the physician, or some other responsible party, before taking any action.

Although depressed patients may be preoccupied with death and thoughts of suicide, once their underlying depression is effectively controlled, suicidal thoughts almost invariably recede and cease to preoccupy them. Even when suicidal ideation follows the diagnosis of a serious or terminal illness, it is often a mind distorted by depression that makes the decision to seek suicide as a solution. Dr. Aaron Beck, a noted psychiatrist at the University of Pennsylvania, points out, "When people are facing death from illness, only a small percentage are suicidal. And what makes them suicidal is depression, not the physical condition." Beck suggests that among the symptoms of depression is an inability to see more than one option for solving problems that can lead patients to fixate on suicide as the only way out of their suffering. When alternative options are presented, as when Dr. Marshall explained the various therapies available to Jeanette, who had multiple sclerosis—or when depression ends and normal thinking returns—such patients may suddenly find other viable strategies for coping with their illness. Jeanette's decision to take her life eventually gave way to a more measured determination to live with multiple sclerosis and make the best of her remaining time. Treatment of depression is itself an option, as it was for Burt, and so is knowledge of the medical options for the person's illness—pain control, for example, which helped Herman, who contracted AIDS from a needle stick, adjust to his terminal illness.

The greatest risk for suicide among the seriously or terminally ill is immediately following the first diagnosis. The overwhelming sense of hopelessness when we hear the news—"I'm sorry, but you have cancer"—may lead to sudden, rash action. A mind overcome by such knowledge may feel there is no other way out. With time, the risk subsides, as people have the chance to find coping mechanisms or in some cases, to learn that there is even hope for the disease itself. The Dutch experience with euthanasia has shown that it is the threatened loss of control that drives many people to request physician-assisted suicide. Once they are assured their request will be honored—they have another option, a means of escape—most terminally ill people see their lives through to a natural end. Hope is another key element. People who maintain a degree of hopefulness about their lives are far better able to cope with tragic illness. In a study of people with paralysis from spinal cord injury, reported in the October 1991 issue of *The Journal of Personality and Social Psychology*, patients who reported more hope, compared with those having little hope, had less depression, greater mobility (despite similar levels of injury), more social contacts, and more sexual intimacy. According to Dr. Timothy Eliot, one of the authors of the study, "those with high hope were more adaptive in all realms, regardless of how long they had been injured, whether just a month or forty years." Half the cases involved men under thirty who were victims of accidents and were paralyzed for the rest of their lives. Yet despite being stricken in the prime of their lives, many of these people were able to adjust and cope with their tragic circumstances. They were severely injured but they were not depressed, and so suicide did not become a realistic option.

Some experts, such as Dr. David C. Clark, a psychiatrist who is president of the American Association for Suicidology, assert that there is no such thing as a truly "rational" suicide during depression. Dr. Clark argues that a person who is severely depressed can't ever think rationally about suicide because his or her thoughts are distorted by the depressive illness itself. "The patients who argue convincingly and intelligently on Wednesday that they want to take their lives are able, after treatment, to tell you on a Monday that they weren't themselves. They'll tell you it was the depression driving the suicide and they're grateful to you for stopping them." Others, such as geriatric psychiatrists Yeates Conwell and Eric D. Caine argue that more research and more data are needed on the concept of rational suicide so that we can "be better able to distinguish between people whose suicidal intent is clearly conceived and free of distorting mental disturbances and people who are in need of psychiatric care."

Obviously if the determination to kill oneself persists after the end of a depressive episode, other motives and factors may be playing a significant role. It would be misleading to suggest that *every* person who contemplates suicide is suffering from a psychiatric pathology such as depression. But because so many suicidal patients *are* clinically depressed, and because depression is treatable, it would be irresponsible *not* to first rule out the possibility of depression and seek medical treatment that could reverse the course of the illness. If you feel that uncontrolled mood disturbances may be contributing to your sense of hopelessness—and to thoughts of suicide— you should consult a doctor. Do not assume that these feelings are an inevitable part of your medical condition, however serious that condition might be. You may be suffering from depression, and depression, not your other illness, is responsible for your suicidal impulses. Yet depression is treatable and your suffering may be unnecessary. Help is available, in the form of medication, psychotherapy, and other techniques. But first you must recognize that a problem exists.

Causes of Mood Disorders

Although much progress has been made in the understanding of depression and mania, no one knows exactly what causes these major disruptions of mood, also known as affective disorders. Mania substitutes elation for depression and gives the person undergoing it a feeling of overinflated optimism and grandiosity that may lead to reckless acts, including suicide. People who experience the highs of a manic episode will frequently also experience the lows of depression. These people suffer from manic-depressive illness, otherwise known as bipolar disorder because the patient can at various times experience two extremes (poles) of mood—depression and mania. It is widely believed a strong genetic component is involved and that people inherit a susceptibility toward mood disorders. Both twin and adoption studies have shown there is a greater likelihood of developing either a depressive or manic episode if there is a family history of such disorders. If you have a close relative who suffered from depression (like Burt's grandfather), you are two to three times more likely to develop this disorder than someone without such a family history. However, it is not clear how large or determining a role genetic factors play as opposed to environmental influences. No specific gene responsible for depression has as yet been identified. Thus depression may develop in people who are unaware of any family history of mood disorders. Conversely, people with a family history may be untouched by these problems.

Some small evidence suggests certain families may even have a genetic predisposition to suicide. There is also evidence that biological factors contribute specifically to suicidal behavior in some people. For example, brain activity of the neurotransmitter serotonin may be lower in a subgroup of people who commit or attempt suicide, perhaps leading to a greater likelihood of violent or impulsive behavior. But further research on this complex issue is required before we can be certain of these biological factors and delineate them with precision. We are still far away from a biochemical test to predict who is at risk for suicide, and these findings remain inconclusive. However, we do know that people with a family history of suicide are at far greater risk themselves of taking their lives. The writer Ernest Hemingway, who suffered from lifelong depression, wrote many stories based on his father's suicide, which became a central, defining event for him. At the age of sixty-two, Hemingway took his own life. Later, both his brother and sister also killed themselves.

A widespread view today holds that depression is caused by a chemical imbalance in the brain, although the precise mechanisms involved have not yet been delineated. Indirect evidence suggests that people with a major depression have lower levels of certain neurochemicals, such as norepinephrine and serotonin. These neurotransmitters carry nerve impulses or messages across the gap between nerve cells and link up to many parts of the brain that control functions disturbed in depression and mania, such as mood, sleep, appetite, and sexual activity. Another hypothesis asserts that circulating levels of these hormones increase as a result of the stress that accompanies depression, blunting the responses of neurochemical receptors (binding sites) in the brain, which have been found to be abnormal in depression. The precise location of these neurochemical abnormalities could even determine whether a person tends to develop a unipolar (depressive) or bipolar (manic-depressive) mood disorder. Researchers have observed that a variety of drugs that affect mood also change the synthesis, transport, and metabolism of these neurotransmitters. Many of these drugs have been found to ameliorate dramatically the symptoms of depression and are widely used today in its treatment. (See below, under "Drug Treatment.")

Other changes in the chemistry of the body and brain have been identified as a possible cause for mood disorders. People with thyroid or adrenal problems often have symptoms similar to depressives. The hormone cortisol, which plays a critical role in the individual's response to stress, has been found to be abnormally secreted in patients suffering from depression. No one knows, however, whether the abnormal secretion of cortisol is itself a cause or an effect of depression. The chemical alterations that occur are complex, and more research is required before they can be fully understood.

Many experts believe that, for certain individuals with a

predisposition, stressful events such as separation and loss may induce neurochemical changes that lead to depression. The symptoms of grief during bereavement resemble those of depression. Traumatic life events that are experienced as loss, from the death of a loved one or divorce to the loss of a job or friendship, may trigger depression. Conversely, the success of an important psychotherapeutic technique called cognitive therapy suggests that by simply changing the negative way we *think* about the world and ourselves, we can trigger neurochemical changes and prevent or reverse depression. This approach, based on improving our basic mental outlook, has proved effective in treating some patients with depression.

Drug Treatment

There are many medications you can take and therapies you can undergo to treat depression. It all depends on your individual medical condition and psychological state, and how well you respond to the treatment. There is no one right answer or solution that works for everyone. But there is almost certainly something that can help you. Following is a summary of the most common and effective methods of treatment for depression.

Treatment of mood disorders is not only effective in reducing a patient's desire to end his life or to ask for a physician's aid in dying; it can also dramatically improve the patient's quality of life. This is true not only in the case of depressed individuals who are otherwise healthy or young. Depression can also be effectively treated when it worsens the suffering of those who are terminally ill or when it interferes with a peaceful end to a long life.

A fifty-six-year-old patient we know named Elise suffered from recurrent ovarian cancer. When she was told that her condition was most likely incurable, she became very depressed. She could not face the fact that her life was ending. Elise had always had a strong will to live, and there was no indication that she was suicidal. However, her appetite became poor, she had difficulty sleeping, and she felt fearful of the future, despite her doctor's assurances that he would not abandon her or allow her to suffer pain. Elise spoke frequently about her "depressed feeling," and it soon became apparent that this feeling alone was the greatest cause of her suffering. Elise's doctor gave her an antidepressant medication, nortriptyline, and referred her to a psychiatric social worker for supportive psychotherapy. Within a few weeks, Elise's depression and all its accompanying symptoms had subsided.

Elise's most dreaded symptom, "that depressed feeling," technically called dysphoria, is a consistent symptom of depression. When the depressed feeling lifted, the quality of Elise's remaining life improved considerably. She was once again able to enjoy the time she had left with her close-knit family and her friends. She finished work on a painting. Her depression was not the inevitable result of a terminal diagnosis but a specific and treatable medical disorder.

A wide variety of antidepressant medications are available for the treatment of depression. Antidepressants relieve the most oppressive and crippling symptoms of depression and restore patients to their previous level of functioning and mood. Nortriptyline, the drug Elise received, is an important member of a commonly used group of drugs known as tricyclic antidepressants (TCAs). Other groups of antidepressants include the monoamine oxidase inhibitors (MAOIs), and newer or "third generation" antidepressant medications including fluoxetine (Prozac), which Burt received.

With the increasing number of antidepressants available today, more and more options are available for patients suffering from depression. And there is no evidence that one antidepressant is more effective than any other. However, individual patients may respond to one medication but not to another; or they may be unable to tolerate one drug but do well with a different one. For example, the MAOIs are very well tolerated by many patients, but because they may interact in dangerous ways with certain medications and even with some nutrients, they cannot be prescribed for someone who is subject to confusion or is otherwise unreliable, unless that person lives in a supervised environment. TCAs, on the other hand, do not pose these types of risks but should be avoided by people with one variety of glaucoma called acute angle closure glaucoma; and these drugs must be used with caution in heart patients with unstable coronary artery disease or with untreated heart block. The tricyclic antidepressants may cause bothersome though less serious side effects such as dry mouth and constipation, and they may cause potentially dangerous but reversible urinary retention in elderly men with enlargement of the prostate gland. Side effects can best be managed by switching to a different class of the TCA group or to a different type of antidepressant.

The popular new antidepressant Prozac received a great deal of publicity when concern was raised over the possibility that the drug increased the risk of suicide in a subgroup of patients being treated for depression. However, this claim has never been substantiated. Presently, fluoxetine is considered a highly useful antidepressant medication, and although some patients experience nausea or nervousness when taking this drug, it is less likely to cause the side effects seen with TCAs. At low doses, it tends to be quite well tolerated by elderly patients who commonly develop TCA side effects.

All antidepressants require a *minimum* of two to three weeks before a noticeable improvement occurs, but the results are often dramatic. Insomnia fades, energy and appetite return, and there is a renewed interest in all aspects of life. Sometimes even before patients report feeling better, friends and family notice significant improvement in their appearance and behavior.

Antidepressants must be prescribed and monitored carefully by a physician experienced in their use. In this way the appropriate antidepressant can be selected with the vulnerabilities of the patient in mind, and the dose can be carefully tailored to meet the individual needs of the patient. Dose requirements may differ markedly among patients. Some patients may need to start out on a very low dose with dose increases made very gradually. Elderly patients need lower doses of antidepressants because the medication remains in their bodies longer and has a stronger and more prolonged effect. Others may require relatively high doses to achieve a therapeutic benefit. Still others may temporarily require adjunctive medical treatment with sleep medication or sedatives until the antidepressant has had a chance to take effect.

Antidepressants should be discontinued gradually, with a progressive reduction in dosage. Patients who stop taking them too soon or too suddenly after depressive symptoms abate may find that they relapse. Careful medical supervision is required at all stages of treatment. The normal length of therapy with antidepressant medication is six months to a year, but this varies with the individual patient and medication.

Doctors should not withhold antidepressant medications from their patients because they fear patients will store up a supply for a suicide attempt. Although frankly suicidal patients are generally best treated in the hospital, the best defense against suicide is to reverse depression, and the best way to achieve this is for the patient to take the medication at an appropriate dose and on a regular schedule. For the same reason, physicians should not prescribe too low a dose or withhold a refill, forcing the patient to return to the pharmacy or the doctor repeatedly. This strategy may well backfire, providing the patient with a ready excuse not to take his or her medication, which may turn out to be far more dangerous than any presumed stockpiling.

Following is a list of the antidepressants that are currently available.

AVAILABLE ANTIDEPRESSANTS

DRUG	BRAND
Tricyclic Antidepressants	
amitriptyline	Elavil, Endep, generic
desipramine	Norpramin
doxepin	Adapin, Sinequan
imipramine	Janimine, Tofranil, generic
nortriptyline	Aventyl, Pamelor
protriptyline	Vivactil
trimipramine	Surmontil
Monoamine Oxidase Inhibitors	
isocarboxazid	Marplan
phenelzine	Nardil
tranylcypromine	Parnate
Newer Antidepressants	
amoxapine	Asendin
bupropion	Wellbutrin
fluoxetine	Prozac
maprotiline	Ludiomil
trazodone	Desyrel

Another group of drugs, not usually classified among the antidepressants, are the "psychostimulants" methylphenidate (Ritalin) and amphetamine (e.g., Dexedrine). These older drugs were once used for depression. Although supplanted by other antidepressants, they are still useful in patients who cannot tolerate the others. Psychostimulants are particularly effective in increasing alertness and can help to combat lethargy in serious illness.

Electroconvulsive Therapy (ECT)

For depressed patients who do not respond to any antidepressants, or for those to whom these medications pose a danger, electroconvulsive therapy (ECT) is a recognized and highly effective form of treatment. Although rarely the first line of treatment for those suffering from depression—ECT involves electric stimulation of the brain—ECT provides relief and offers hope to many seriously depressed patients who are otherwise resistant to treatment. Negative cultural attitudes are associated with ECT, which was once called shock treatment. These attitudes persist into the present day, despite the fact that it is now given with anesthesia and muscle relaxants so the patient sleeps quietly and comfortably during the procedure. Although there is still some disagreement about the exact nature and extent of its side effects, most patients tolerate the treatment well, and many have achieved significant, even life-saving relief from ECT after all other methods had failed. If you have any questions about this technique, consult your physician and any patients who have used it.

Psychotherapy

While important advances have been made in the understanding and treatment of depression as a physiological illness, the psychological component of this disorder cannot be neglected. Depression represents a disturbance of mood, and mood is a highly personal and subjective state that influences how people view themselves and how they interact with others. Medication may help relieve some of the clinical symptoms of depression, but patients also need to understand what is happening to them and why. Psychotherapy, or simply talking about one's feelings and exploring the roots of an emotional disturbance with a trained professional, has proven invaluable in helping patients cope with depression and even in relieving symptoms. This is true for people who suffer from recurrent bouts of depression and for those whose family members and close relatives are also afflicted with the disorder; they often feel unfairly singled out and stigmatized.

When depression is linked to a terminal illness, whether real (Elise with cancer) or imagined (Burt), feelings can be especially strong and overpowering. Psychotherapy can help patients deal with immediate feelings of despair, fear, and anger arising from their illness (real or imagined) as well as to understand their susceptibility to depression and possibly to suicide. While the antidepressant Prozac helped bring Burt's depressive symptoms under control, it took him several months of talking with Dr. Alvarez to understand how his entire self-image was undermined by his fear of failing health and how this fear was tied to the death of his wife and his suicide attempt. Most experts now agree that an integrated treatment plan—one that combines drugs *and* psychotherapy —is the best approach to managing the complexities of depression.

Psychotherapy for depression may involve highly sophisticated and different treatment approaches—several "schools" have evolved—but they all begin by allowing patients to explore and express their underlying anxiety. In order to feel secure, patients need a strong and trusting relationship with a therapist: either a psychiatrist, a clinical psychologist, or a psychiatric social worker. By listening attentively and giving depressed individuals permission to describe their peculiar and often harrowing pain, the therapist validates the patients' feelings and gives them an opportunity—to cry, to blame, to complain—often denied them by family members and loved ones. Elise, normally a quiet, soft-spoken woman, was able to vent the full force of her muted anger and despair in discussions with a psychiatric social worker. Why should she succumb to ovarian cancer at such a young age? What had she done to deserve this? Depression does have specific characteristics, but each person succumbs to this illness in a different and totally individual manner. He or she needs to describe and explain it in personally appropriate terms—not to suffer in shameful silence.

The therapist recognizes that the person suffering from depression has a serious medical illness and is not just complaining. He or she is sick and needs medical help. An experienced and compassionate therapist is also able to offer empathy. In addition, patients who believe their feelings are accepted and respected will be more likely to confide in a therapist and alert him or her if they feel a depressive episode is about to recur so that preventive steps can be taken. Following his initial suicide attempt and treatment, Burt continued to see Dr. Alvarez sporadically for several years. Whenever Burt appeared after a long absence, Dr. Alvarez knew that something was up, and he was able to steer Burt through several more crises, including his internist's suggestion that he should use a cane. This depressing advice came in the wake of Burt's break-up with his forty-six-year-old girlfriend, who left him for another man closer to her age. This double crisis revived Burt's fears about aging. But with Dr. Alvarez's help, Burt returned to his regular doctor and they discussed the positive option of knee surgery. Burt was surprised and gratified when told he would be an "excellent surgical candidate."

Help for depression most often comes first in the form of prescription drugs. One of the therapist's most important tasks may be enabling the patient to accept the need for medication. Only psychiatrists or other M.D.'s may prescribe drugs, but any good therapist will help the patient see the importance of following a prescription. Having to take medication carries its own stigma and may make a depressed patient feel even more dependent and helpless. It can become a daily reminder of illness and the loss it represents. Many patients react by denying the problem altogether and refusing medication, or stopping it prematurely on the grounds that they feel better and can make it on their own. After two months, Burt felt he had made a complete recovery and did not see the need for continuing medication. Dr. Alvarez convinced Burt he had only won the battle, not the war. He also told him about Winston Churchill, the great British prime minister and wartime leader, who had suffered from depression most of his life. When medication is needed, a good therapist will help a patient understand the need for it—emphasizing that depression is a real illness—and will explain how to take the medication and handle its physical and psychological side effects.

Psychotherapy can also help patients to distinguish the signs and symptoms of emerging depression and separate them from more normal mood changes that accompany daily life. Whereas the unsuspecting patient may be slow to recognize clinical depression at first, once diagnosed, he or she may find it lurking behind every emotion. Someone with a depressive history may become oversensitive to the slightest alteration in mood and become distrustful of his or her feelings, fearing that they signal a new episode and thus fleeing from any potential emotional entanglement. Therapy may aid such a patient in gaining greater knowledge and understanding of the specific course his illness is most likely to take. For example, if he is a patient whose depression seems worse in the morning, like Burt, he can learn to separate his mood disorder from the normal ups and downs of emotional life. In addition, by examining previous patterns of behavior, patients may learn how to ride out a depressive episode and avoid embarrassing or dangerous situations. Burt, for example, no longer kept a gun in the house. Conversely, once medication relieves the symptoms of depression, patients may need to *unlearn* previous patterns of behavior, such as self-imposed solitude, used to protect against the dangers of depression. Jeanette had to reach out to her children after years of isolation once she made peace with her illness and felt confident her moods were under control. She realized how defensive her posture had been, and she went out of her way to draw the kids back into her life.

Depression often has a dramatic and pernicious effect on the patient's relations with other people, and therapy may assist in understanding the impact and minimizing the fallout on others from major depressive episodes. The depressed individual's relationship with family members and loved ones, because of its intimacy, is particularly vulnerable to such disruption. Burt's depression over his fear of cancer and declining health was so strong that it jeopardized his relationship with his daughter, Nancy, and especially his son, who seemed to be flourishing just when Burt was ailing. Sometimes even after an episode of depression has ended, the damage lingers. Former bonds must be reestablished and trust renewed. Burt invited his son to dinner and gave him an old pocketwatch, a real family heirloom, which *his* father had handed down to Burt. Harsh words spoken and cold actions taken repeatedly in the context of a major depressive episode —where a general withdrawal from life includes diminishing sexual energy and interest—may also seriously undermine a marriage. A loving but uninformed spouse may misinterpret such behavior in a personal way ("He [or she] doesn't love me") and respond accordingly. This is what happened to Elise's husband, Eric, who was kept in the dark about Elise's true condition. Sometimes bitter marital disputes that seem irreconcilable turn out to have been initiated by one partner's depression. Marital therapy involving both spouses and family therapy, where the depressed patient and members of his or her family become involved and educated together, can also be helpful.

Another approach, interpersonal psychotherapy, suggests that individuals who are depressed may scare and antagonize those around them, who respond by offering nongenuine support or avoiding the depressed person altogether. This rejection confirms the depressed individual's suspicions that he or she is not valued by others and increases feelings of insecurity and unsociability. When Jeanette's multiple sclerosis took a turn for the worse, and she became depressed, her husband did, in fact, leave her and she naturally felt rejected and abandoned. But Jeanette then assumed that everyone she knew felt the same way toward her, and she became even more aloof and unreachable to those who genuinely cared for her. Interpersonal psychotherapy seeks to break this vicious cycle by providing a stronger self-image to the depressed and teaching them how to communicate better and establish more sustaining relationships with others.

Perhaps the best known psychotherapeutic approach to depression is cognitive therapy. Cognitive (meaning "thought") therapy is based on the concept that an individual's mental outlook and thought processes may color and even determine his emotional state. Therefore, the best way to reverse a mood disorder such as depression is to alter the way a depressed person thinks. Dr. Aaron Beck, who pioneered the concept, believes that a depressed individual tends to have a negative attitude toward himself, the world, and the future. This "depressive triad" overshadows reality and governs the individual's response to everything around him: for example, that he is doomed to failure. Therefore, no matter what happens, the depressed person will impose this mindset of failure on real experiences and force them into a precast negative mold or "schema." By changing the depressed person's negative thinking, cognitive therapy seeks to break the mold and reroute the depression into a more positive channel of thought—and ultimately into an improved mood. A person who is depressed and claims that life has nothing more to offer him may be asked to think of one small thing he looks forward to during the day, for example, a favorite television show, a walk to the grocery store, a cold drink, or the mailman's daily visit. Slowly, he builds up a stock of positive images and associations so he can think about larger issues in his life in a more hopeful way. In a series of regular sessions over a period of several months, he begins to see what a distorted picture of himself and the world he normally carries. The therapist helps him replace negative thoughts and images with positive ones and to turn built-in hopelessness into built-up hope.

Dr. Beck has developed a "hopelessness scale," which measures the degree of optimism—or lack of it—that most people have. In a ten-year study published in the 1985 *Journal of American Psychiatry*, Beck showed that patients' scores on the hopelessness scale were the single best predictor of whether they would go on to attempt suicide. People who naturally have a high degree of hope, as well as those who can be taught to develop the mental habit of hopefulness, are far less likely to become depressed and turn to suicide. Other studies of patients with serious diseases such as congestive heart failure have shown that people who are more hopeful will remain involved with life despite their physical limitations and medical problems. Cognitive therapy seeks to nurture hope and so affirm the value of living.

While psychotherapeutic and drug-treatment approaches may vary from case to case, one fact remains paramount: depression is a serious, potentially life-threatening illness afflicting millions of people, but it can be effectively treated and reversed. Help can almost always be found through some combination of medical treatment, psychotherapy, and support.

Depression is a common illness, but it is hard to identify and potentially lethal. Among older people, whose suicide rates are highest, recognition of depression is complicated by coexisting health problems. Depression may often be masked, both intentionally and unintentionally. Patients and their loved ones must be educated to recognize the symptoms of depression, to understand the serious nature of the condition, and to seek prompt professional treatment.

Knowledge of the risk factors for suicide, which is closely linked to depression, is crucial. People who are very old, particularly men; people who live alone or have made a major move; those who have recently lost a spouse; people who have had a serious rift with a family member or close friend; those who have previously attempted suicide; people with chronic pain and impaired function who are concerned about their health; those with a recent diagnosis of cancer or other terminal illness; people with alcoholism; and those with other mental health problems are all at increased risk for depression and suicide. Doctors must be ever vigilant for the earliest signs of the illness and actively draw out their patients. Any significant disturbance of mood, appetite, or sleep and any suggestion of suicidal thought, previous history, or any other risk factor must be followed up and explored. With proper and compassionate care, the symptoms of depression can be brought under control and the patient's previous equilibrium restored. Suicide will no longer seem like the only way out of an impossible situation. Life will not necessarily be easy, but you will feel better and your thinking will be undistorted by mental illness.

Terminal illness alone rarely leads to suicide, but when it is accompanied by depression and hopelessness, the combination can be lethal. It is important to separate depression from terminal illness and to treat each as a medical problem in its own right. While people who are very old or sick may become depressed, their depression can usually be treated regardless of their underlying physical illness. Elise had incurable cancer and was going to die within a year. Medical science, in its current state, could not cure her disease. But it could control her depression, a serious secondary illness she developed in response to the cancer, and the most disabling and intolerable symptom she experienced. Modern treatments for depression enabled Elise to adjust to the painful changes in her life, including her cancer, and to get the most out of her remaining months. Because of its powerful connection to suicide, depression itself may threaten to mar and ultimately destroy the lives of people with serious illness, or those who are facing infirmities late in life. Treatment can improve both the quality and the quantity of such lives.

Clinical depression is not an inevitable accompaniment to the infirmities of age and illness. It is a medical disease and it can almost always be treated. Then hopelessness can be turned into hope, and thoughts of death transformed into a renewed interest and pleasure in life.

CHAPTER SIX

Nature's Anesthesia: Dying a Peaceful Death

> The art of healing comes from nature, not from the physician. Therefore the physician must start from nature, with an open mind.
>
> —Paracelsus, sixteenth-century physician

Veronica suffered from Alzheimer's disease. Now in her nineties, the disease had advanced to its very late stages. Veronica's extreme condition differed markedly from Ruth's, the woman we met in Chapter Two. Ruth still enjoyed a pleasant life despite her severe forgetfulness and her son Mark's anxiety. For seven years, Veronica lived in a nursing home, and although her daughter, Sharon, visited her regularly, Veronica no longer recognized her. Because of the marked deterioration of her brain, Veronica had lost the ability to speak, to walk, and even to feed herself. Fortunately for her, reasoned her daughter, she doesn't know what has happened to her. Fortunately for her, but not for me.

On more than one occasion Veronica developed pneumonia, a complication of Alzheimer's disease and a frequent cause of death. Antibiotics had treated the condition but did not restore the mother Sharon once knew. The most recent bout with pneumonia had led to Veronica's transfer to a nearby hospital where she was given intravenous antibiotics. By the time she was well enough to return to the nursing home, she had developed a bedsore on her backside that healed only after six weeks of diligent nursing care.

Sharon visited the nursing home as often as she could, and on the weekends she fed her mother lunches and dinners. The feeding required a great deal of patience because her mother seemed to want only small amounts at a time and would sometimes spit the food out, only to take more small spoonfuls a few minutes later. Veronica's caloric intake was not great, and she seemed to be getting scrawny, but Sharon continued to insist on a natural diet. She so vigorously rejected Dr. Roth's suggestion of inserting a feeding tube, he decided never to raise the issue again.

Many years before, Veronica had cared for her own mother, who had suffered from heart failure. Veronica was present at the bedside to see her mother quietly close her eyes for the last time. Veronica wanted to die like that, she'd said, peacefully, with her family nearby. "When the time comes, I hope you let me go quietly, nothing artificial, no fuss, no bother, no machines."

One day Sharon received a call and was told that her mother was very lethargic and feverish; she needed to be sent to the hospital. Sharon rushed to the nursing home and found her mother sleeping, breathing through her mouth, and was able to arouse her only with difficulty. Veronica's skin was moist and warm. Dr. Roth said it was likely that Veronica again had pneumonia, that pneumonia often presented itself this way in his very elderly nursing home population. Antibiotics and intravenous fluids would be required, and this could only be given in the hospital, and the sooner the better. Although people have recovered from pneumonia without antibiotics, Veronica's condition was very grave, and it was possible she would not survive without quick action.

Sharon grew horrified at the thought of sending her mother to the hospital for another extended stay. But the thought of not treating the pneumonia horrified her as well, and she felt tremendous guilt. Perhaps, though, the moment had finally come to step back and let her mother go. Perhaps the moment had been there several times already.

"Why wake my mother up with antibiotics again?" she

asked the doctor, showing some irritation. They didn't improve her quality of life before, she reasoned, and she was sleeping quietly now. Another hospitalization didn't make sense. Antibiotics didn't make sense.

Dr. Roth was well aware that a wide variety of medical illnesses, even a simple urinary tract infection, could make his patients extremely lethargic, almost peacefully so at the end of life. He had seen many debilitated patients in the nursing home become confused or lethargic from small doses of sedatives or even heart medicines that would have produced no adverse effects in a younger or more robust person. For a patient who was in the final stages of dying and had nothing but pain or fear to look forward to, such a narcotic effect might actually be desirable.

Dr. Roth remembered one elderly patient whose advanced age and brain disease caused her to be unaware that a painful and potentially fatal illness was present. This woman, disabled by a stroke, had seemed somewhat sleepy one day, and if it had not been for a low-grade fever and a mild case of diarrhea, the doctors would not have discovered that she had developed intestinal gangrene—a true abdominal catastrophe in medical terms. This condition develops when the blood supply to the intestines is cut off; death is certain without surgery to remove the dead bowel. This elderly patient did not survive the emergency surgery that took place that night, but she never had to suffer serious symptoms prior to death either. She simply felt a little tired that day and had the urge to sleep and be left alone. Roused only when the concerned staff needed to examine her to find out what was wrong, she did not even have a bellyache.

Dr. Roth's wife had died five years after being diagnosed with breast cancer. In the end, when the disease spread to her brain, she became lethargic and slipped into a coma. In an effort to save her, Dr. Roth agreed when the oncologist suggested giving his wife adriamycin, a form of anticancer chemotherapy that offered the possibility of some good effect. Dr. Roth watched apprehensively as the oncologist injected the adriamycin, and within a day, his wife was again alert. But she never left the hospital and died a month later, having suffered considerable discomfort in the meantime.

Dr. Roth considered Sharon's question, "Why wake my mother up again?" and he thought about his other patients and his wife. It was a logical question indeed. More than once he had been hit with pangs of guilt over the fact that he had allowed yet another intervention in his wife's fatal illness, an intervention that awakened her from a peaceful sleep only to let her consciously experience the discomforts of illness and the fears of dying. Had his efforts to "save" his wife been for himself and not for her? he wondered. He had brushed those thoughts out of his mind then, but they haunted him now. Medical treatment could prolong Veronica's life—wake her up—but it would not save her or restore her. On the other hand, it would be foolish not to give antibiotics; unlike anti-cancer chemotherapy, antibiotics had few side effects. But which decision was the most compassionate?

Veronica was sleeping peacefully. Her breathing was becoming more rapid and she sounded congested, but she did not budge. Soon she was completely unarousable. She was in a deep coma, nature's anesthesia.

Nature provided Sharon's mother with exactly what she had always wished for, the chance to die peacefully when the time came. We generally picture pneumonia as an illness accompanied by a deep cough, high fever, and shaking chills, but among the very elderly, particularly those with Alzheimer's disease, stroke, or other brain impairments, pneumonia paints an entirely different picture. Cough may be absent, body temperature may be only mildly elevated or even normal, and the disease may first present itself as lethargy or deep coma. Even a chest X ray may fail to reveal that pneumonia is present, and the only proof comes after death, if an autopsy is done. The reasons are unclear. Explanations for this sleeplike state can usually be found in younger or more robust people, when a spinal tap, a CAT scan of the brain, or blood test shows evidence of brain infection, brain injury, or abnormal body chemistry. But these tests generally reveal nothing in patients like Veronica, who sleep easily when seriously ill.

Most people at some time have expressed a preference to die in their sleep. Both our living and our dying would be a lot easier if we could all be assured of such a peaceful end. Ironically, because of scientific advances, more of us are living into old age, and this may bring with it chronic illness and disability as well as the increased concerns and anxieties about dying that accompany it. At any age, patients with diseases such as cancer or AIDS fear that they will die a difficult or torturous death. Most of us fear dying—the gradual deterioration—as much as we fear the actual moment of death. We are afraid of pain and suffering and the great unknown. We are terrified of losing control and being at the mercy of impersonal, purely biological forces. For some, this fear becomes so heightened that they take their lives rather than waiting for death to take them. Suicide becomes a way to terminate the fear and anxiety of living through a painful and prolonged end.

While death is never easy or benign—and we must all approach it with a measure of awe, if not with terror—we must also learn to look more closely and realistically at the dying process. What actually happens when we die? Is dying always painful and agonizing? As we saw with Veronica, despite our greatest fears death may often come peacefully, during a sleeplike state provided by nature. It does not have to be a horrible and devastating physical experience. Of course nature can be both kind and brutal—and none of our medical interventions would *ever* be necessary if nature were only kind. But more often than we realize, nature has a way of protecting us from its worst actions. Without surrendering any medical drug or technology in our arsenal, we would all benefit from greater knowledge and understanding of how the body naturally shuts down and ceases to function.

When illness produces a deep sleep from which one cannot be aroused, the person is said to be in coma. Less deep forms of coma occur when, for example, the person may become temporarily aroused by a loud voice, by being shaken vigorously, or by a painful stimulus such as pinching the skin, and such states are called stupor or deep lethargy. Whether the coma is light or deep, these sleeplike states are considered very serious from a medical standpoint. Diseases that can lead to coma include tumors and infections of the brain, overwhelming infection of any cause (sepsis), severe dehydration, life-threatening metabolic derangements (such as a severe form of hypothyroidism called myxedema) or diseases that produce imbalances in body chemistry, disturbing blood levels of nitrogen, calcium, or even water. Coma can be an outcome of liver or kidney failure. These organs function to rid the body of toxic substances; when these substances build up to a critical level, they can affect the brain and produce coma. Failure of breathing allows carbon dioxide to build up in the blood, which can produce a sleeplike state called carbon dioxide (CO_2) narcosis. Strokes, brain hemorrhage, and deprivation of oxygen during a cardiac arrest can lead to coma. Drug overdose can produce coma. Head trauma can produce coma, and if it does, the likelihood of permanent brain damage is much greater than if no coma has occurred. Thus, coma is a signal that serious, life-threatening, and even fatal disease exists.

The cause of coma must be diagnosed swiftly and appropriate action taken immediately or damage can be permanent and death can occur. Alfred was an eighty-four-year-old man who had "never had a sick day in his life." That was until his wife was unable to arouse him one morning. He was rushed to the hospital where doctors diagnosed diabetic coma. He was treated with intravenous fluids and insulin, and within twenty-four hours he was fully awake and joking with the nurses. Alfred was discharged in good health, and his diabetes was managed at home with a daily antidiabetes pill. The only clue to his illness had been the fact that he had been urinating more than usual for a few days and had been feeling a little tired. When he became comatose, it was swift diagnosis and treatment that saved Alfred's life.

Coma may need to be approached quite differently, however, among those who are terminally or hopelessly ill. Like general anesthesia for surgery, coma allows a person to sleep through pain, fear, and virtually any physical or psychological discomfort. Before initiating tests and treatments to awaken a terminally ill person from coma, one should first ask, is this what the person would want? Or is it now the time to withhold heroic measures and permit a peaceful death? Obviously the answer depends on the stage of the illness, other methods of relief available, and the preferences of the patient and his or her family. But when there is no hope of recovery and the patient's quality of life is intolerable, coma itself may come as a relief. It is *nature's* anesthesia, allowing the end to be free of pain and fear and signaling that one's time may have come. In this state, medical technology adds little or nothing to the patient's comfort. In fact, when death is imminent and medical techniques attempt to thwart nature, the effort can simply make things worse for the patient. The anticancer chemotherapy Dr. Roth's wife received when she was terminal and in a coma is a medical advance that has helped thousands of cancer patients in different circumstances. But in his wife's situation, as Dr. Roth came to realize later, the medical advance could not restore or comfort her. The compassionate choice would have been to let nature take its course.

Dr. Roth recalled another cancer patient who died about the same time as his wife. Larry, a forty-five-year-old business executive, grew more seriously ill when the disease spread to his lungs. He began to experience uncomfortable breathlessness and was admitted to the hospital, but within twenty-four hours he was comatose. Blood tests revealed hypercalcemia —the level of calcium in the bloodstream—was severely elevated—a stubborn complication of cancer that typically produces alterations in mental state. Treatment with intravenous fluids and a drug called furosemide rapidly—though temporarily—normalized the calcium level, and Larry was once more alert. He died of his disease about a month later. Hypercalcemia does not necessarily produce coma, and when it occurs earlier in cancer, or when it occurs in nonmalignant disease, aggressive treatment with any of a variety of medications may improve quality of life. However, Larry was near the end of a terminal illness, and treatment did no more than force him to experience his disease, physically and psychologically, as had happened to Dr. Roth's wife. Had Larry been allowed to remain in a coma, he would have died within days or perhaps even hours and would have experienced no pain, fear, or suffering.

Dr. Roth's wife and Larry both died in the mid-1970s, when medical advances were occurring rapidly but our understanding of their consequences lagged behind. Concepts such as "medical bioethics," "patient autonomy," and "right to die" were new, not yet tested, and not yet widely discussed. In still earlier, more innocent days of medical practice, natural death was the norm. People died at home, usually with family members nearby, and unless death was sudden or completely unexpected, the patient often lapsed into a sleeplike state, lingered for hours or days, and then expired. When technologies were introduced that prolonged life but did not always cure—intensive care units, anticancer chemotherapy, respirators, and antibiotics—patients were given the opportunity to live longer. However, in many emergencies—as Larry's and Mrs. Roth's—treatments were given *because they existed*, and not necessarily because they were *appropriate*. Medical options presented by doctors were generally accepted by patients or family members. Neither doctor nor patient spokesman typically considered that these state-of-the-art treatments could or should be avoided—that it would be wiser in the long run to avoid them than to use them.

Decisions about end-of-life treatments are highly personal. None of us wants to suffer, but on the other hand, we may want to give medical technology and our will to live, or our religious faith, every chance to work. If you or a loved one has a serious illness, it is important to discuss possible treatments in advance and to let your doctor as well as your family know what your specific values and wishes are. If you believe that every form of available treatment should be used, you have every right to request this. But you may also wish to set limits and avoid useless or burdensome treatment that you feel is inappropriate for you. Sam's case is one illustration of this.

When Sam developed AIDS, he made it clear to his friends that he did not want any kind of treatment that would merely prolong his dying. He felt so strongly about this that he put his wishes into writing, stating that if he was ever in a coma or "didn't know what was going on," no treatment should be given. He had seen a number of his friends die of AIDS, and more than one had lingered on a respirator until the moment of death. Sam went to live with his parents, who gradually grew to accept their son's disease and the social stigma it carried. Together Sam and his parents discussed his wishes to avoid treatment that might prolong his life briefly but would make dying more difficult and prolonged.

After two years of battling the disease, and several hospitalizations, Sam grew increasingly weak and thin and could no longer care for himself. He began to develop severe headaches; one day he had a seizure and became unconscious. Sam was admitted to the hospital and connected to a respirator, but he remained in a coma. His chest X ray showed that his lungs were diffusely diseased, and a CAT scan of the brain showed a mass lesion. The doctors could not be sure what the mass was but were relatively certain it was one of two brain lesions that often develop in patients with AIDS—lymphoma, a cancerous tumor, or toxoplasmosis, a parasitic infection. In both cases, medication could be given that would give Sam a fighting chance, but he had been treated several times for toxoplasmosis and had developed serious side effects from the medication. The chances of recovery from a lymphoma were slight, given Sam's overall condition.

Despite the gravity of his situation, and despite the diffuseness of his disease, Sam himself felt no pain or discomfort because he was in a coma. He had lapsed into a confused state a year before. At that time he underwent a spinal tap that revealed meningitis and had responded well to antibiotic treatment. Sam's parents had allowed the spinal tap and the treatment because his chance of recovery was good at that time and his overall condition had been different. Now, when his parents realized that his "chance" consisted of the possibility he might wake up and live for a few short weeks, but there was an equally good chance he might have to remain connected to the respirator, awake, they knew this was the kind of chance Sam did not want to take. They refused to allow additional treatment for their son. Although the doctors attending Sam were willing to withhold or stop respirator treatment in patients gasping their last breath, some were uncomfortable about withholding this kind of treatment because there was a chance Sam would have at least a temporary remission. However, one doctor acknowledged the quality of Sam's remaining life was likely to be poor—exactly what he'd wanted to avoid. Given all of the information, Sam's parents were at first very torn about what course to take, but after much discussion between themselves and with the doctors, they felt that it was best to "let Sam go." Their son's wishes were respected. He remained in a coma and died a few days later.

"Letting Sam go" was in a sense more reminiscent of a style of medicine practiced many years ago. However, it was also more modern. Although sophisticated medical treatments were avoided, a newer process was applied—that of ethical decision-making, a process sometimes forgotten during the early boom times of high-tech medicine, but recently revived because of the demands of choice imposed by new medical knowledge. Sam, his parents, and his doctors had at one time or another weighed the burdens and benefits of continued treatment. The benefit of treatment would be the possibility of prolonging life, but the burden would be the consequence of waking Sam up to experience consciously the physical and psychological pain of protracted death. Thus, Sam's great-grandparents might have died in this same way, perhaps of pneumonia, in the end probably in a sleeplike state. But no one would have had to ask the painful question of whether to treat or to let die. In those days there was no cure for pneumonia, let alone for lymphoma or toxoplasmosis. It was not until well into the 1930s, when European physicians discovered that a sulfonamide drug called Prontosil could cure previously devastating bacterial infections, that the antibiotic era was born. And since then textbooks full of new treatments have come into use.

With new treatments have come a plethora of scenarios in which life can be unnaturally prolonged. Nancy Cruzan, whose case went all the way to the U.S. Supreme Court, was a young woman seriously injured in an automobile accident. A combination of head and internal injuries deprived her brain of oxygen to the extent that she never regained consciousness. Her heart stopped beating. But instead of dying at the scene of the accident, she was revived by paramedics, who restarted her heart. Nancy Cruzan eventually recovered from coma but she entered a condition called persistent vegetative state or PVS—the most extreme form of nonfatal brain damage. PVS is a state of eyes-open unconsciousness that resembles coma in some ways—patients have no awareness of themselves or their surroundings—but unlike coma, people almost never come out of PVS. The tragedy is that people may exist in this state of limbo for a very long time without any hope of recovering if they are provided extensive nursing care and artificial feeding by tube. Ms. Cruzan lingered in this condition for seven years, until her parents won a long legal battle to have medical treatment terminated so that she could be allowed to die.

If coma may, in some cases, be nature's anesthesia, a welcome relief for patients in the final stages of an irreversible illness, then PVS is something quite unnatural. It delays the actual moment of death by suspending the patient in a state of complete unconsciousness that may drag on for years without, after a few months, offering any hope for recovery. In the words of the President's Commission for the Study of Ethical Problems in Medicine and Biomedical and Behavioral Research, which published its landmark study *Deciding to*

Forgo Life-Sustaining Treatment in 1983: "Most of what makes someone a distinctive individual is lost when the person is unconscious, especially if he or she will always remain so." Although patients in PVS cannot experience pain or suffering as we know it—they cannot experience anything because the portion of the brain controlling consciousness does not function—many people do not want to be maintained indefinitely in such a condition. When we say we would not want to be "kept alive like a vegetable," we are usually talking about PVS. In PVS, the only functioning portion of the brain is the brain stem, which governs "vegetative" functions such as breathing, digestion, and heartbeat. Beyond the fact that recovery from PVS is exceedingly unlikely, if not impossible, the President's Commission mentioned another important pitfall of continued treatment in this permanently unconscious state: "Long-term treatment commonly imposes severe financial and emotional burdens on a patient's family, people whose welfare most patients, before they lost consciousness, placed a high value on."

PVS is an example of nature—and technology—gone awry. People who become permanently vegetative have entered this state because medical advances were used to save their lives but did not succeed in restoring them to consciousness. Instead, technology is directed to maintaining them at a minimal level of existence that they are unable to appreciate. If there were some chance of recovery, or any flicker of consciousness, all the effort might be worthwhile. But after about six months, recovery is virtually unheard of. Among those who have been in PVS for between one and two years, only two or three well-documented cases of partial recovery have been reported in the entire world literature—and in these cases, residual impairment was so severe self-care was not possible. Some groups, such as the right-to-life representatives who opposed the removal of Nancy Cruzan's tube feeding, believe that even this merely biological level of existence is a sacred form of life that must be protected. The decision is ultimately a personal one and must be made and respected on an individual basis. But those who, like the overwhelming majority of Americans, would not want to be artificially kept alive if they were permanently vegetative have the legal and moral right to refuse treatment. Many of us consider such a prolonged, inert existence intolerable, even though we do not actually experience pain or any other sensation.

Without constant intervention by man, people in PVS would die. Nature, left to its own devices, does not permit prolonged states of unconsciousness such as PVS. No other inhabitant of the animal kingdom, other than man, has ever existed in such an artificial state. Fortunately, our medical and legal establishments have now recognized it is wrong to maintain someone in this state against his or her wishes. We can avoid a medical fate like Nancy Cruzan's or any other fate that we deem unacceptable by clearly stating our wishes in advance, ideally through a written document or by appointing a health care representative.

PVS is in essence the death of the cerebral hemispheres and is sometimes referred to as cerebrocortical death. However, this is not the same as total brain death, or simply "brain death." In brain death neither the cerebral cortex nor the brain stem survives. When the brain dies, no man-made technologies can maintain the body for extended periods of time.

Brain death sometimes results directly from severe brain damage, for example, major head trauma. Heartbeat soon ceases because it is controlled by the brain stem. Brain death, however, usually occurs *after* and *because* the heart stops beating. Cessation of heartbeat (cardiac arrest) is the signal that biological life is ending. But man can intervene positively to thwart nature if cardiac arrest *precedes* damage to the brain or other organs.

Bernie, a sixty-year-old electrician, was overweight. He rarely exercised, smoked heavily, and ate whatever he wanted. Although his father had died of a heart attack at age fifty-five, Bernie refused to go to a doctor for a checkup, despite the entreaties of his wife and two grown children. One day, while walking from the refrigerator to his easy chair, he developed excruciating chest pain, broke out into a cold sweat, and became very weak. His wife called an ambulance, and as Bernie was being rushed to the hospital, his heart stopped beating. Emergency medical personnel in the ambulance, using all the resources at hand, were able to restore his heartbeat. Bernie was alive and alert when he reached the hospital. He underwent emergency cardiac catheterization, received an experimental blood thinner to open the blocked coronary artery that nourished his heart, and after a two-week stay in the hospital's coronary care unit, was able to return home.

Two years later, Bernie had a new outlook on life. He would joke about the fact that he had "come back to life." He meant more than that he had been saved from death by swift medical intervention: he now had a completely different lifestyle and felt like a new man. Bernie had quit smoking, walked three miles a day, lost thirty pounds, watched his diet carefully, took a cholesterol-lowering pill every day, and saw his cardiologist regularly. He would often talk about the "mystery" of those moments when his heart had stopped beating, of which he has no recollection. He's read books about near-death experiences and thought about the "sublime" and "unearthly" experiences, most of them pleasant, some people have experienced. His cardiologist pooh-poohed the accounts, explaining that they were due to brain anoxia (deprivation of oxygen). All in all, Bernie didn't care that much about it. He was happy to be alive and well and was eager to postpone any sublime experiences as long as possible.

Bernie's new life was indeed made possible by modern medical techniques. In the ambulance, his heartbeat was restored by a nearly perfected technique called cardiopulmonary resuscitation (CPR). A variety of methods have been used over the centuries by ancient and primitive societies to restore the dying and the dead, but modern CPR did not begin until 1960 when Kouwenhoven and his colleagues published the first full report on twenty patients successfully resuscitated by closed-chest heart massage. This ground-breaking paper marked the culmination of decades of work by scientific investigators—an accumulation of anecdotal reports and experiments on animals about attempts to restore and maintain heartbeat and breathing.

Modern CPR includes techniques as simple as the one used when a knowledgeable bystander saves the life of someone who has collapsed on the street, pressing on the chest wall once every second, and breathing directly into the victim's mouth (mouth-to-mouth resuscitation). Doctors and emergency medical personnel use more sophisticated methods such as devices called defibrillators, which can sometimes restore normal heartbeat using an electric current; tubes placed into the windpipe (endotracheal intubation) so air and oxygen can be forced into the lungs mechanically; and chemicals injected into the vein to restore or maintain blood pressure and heartbeat with normal rate and rhythm. These techniques and others can be employed until—and if—the natural forces of the body take over. CPR works under the right circumstances—when the person is in reasonably good health to begin with. In these cases, nature gets a decidedly technological and lifesaving boost.

Bernie had not been in good shape, and his poor health habits contributed to his heart attack. But his heart was not permanently damaged by the sudden blockage in his coronary artery, and his brain, liver, kidneys, and other organs were still intact. Thus, following his cardiac arrest and helped by modern medicine, Bernie not only returned to his prior existence but he improved on it.

There was not such a happy outcome in Ken's situation or in Carl's.

Ken was an alcoholic. As a result of years of heavy alcohol consumption Ken developed cirrhosis of the liver, an irreversible condition. Against his doctor's firm advice, and against Ken's better judgment, he continued to use alcohol, and his disease led to a succession of serious complications. Eventually Ken's kidneys failed and he was admitted to the hospital, gravely ill. Shortly after admission he experienced cardiac arrest. CPR was instituted and he was revived. Unfortunately, Ken did not leave the hospital alive but remained under intensive care, undergoing a succession of uncomfortable procedures, and dying three weeks later.

Carl was eighty years old and handicapped by a severe stroke that left him paralyzed on his right side, unable to speak, and unable to care for himself. He lived in a nursing home where he received what his family noted was excellent care. One day he developed a fever and became lethargic. While he was being transferred to a nearby hospital, his heart stopped beating and CPR was performed. Carl never fully regained consciousness and developed a series of complications. He died in the intensive care unit, connected to a respirator.

CPR worked well for Bernie, but not for Ken or for Carl. Why? CPR does no more than restore heartbeat or respiration; it does not restore the functions of a diseased organ. When applied to people with serious neurological impairments like Carl's, or irreversible medical illness like Ken's, heartbeat may be restored temporarily. Unfortunately, most seriously ill people who are revived from a cardiac arrest never leave the hospital alive. Rather, they often spend their last days in an intensive care unit maintained on artificial life support, where they die within days or weeks. Among many patients with advanced cancer, like Larry, or those who have been seriously ill with AIDS, like Sam, CPR is almost uniformly unsuccessful. This is because the disease itself has caused the heart to stop—the disease has ended the patient's life, or tried to. If Bernie's heart attack had been more severe, damaging large portions of his heart muscle, he might not have survived. Luckily, his heart was not permanently damaged, and although one blocked coronary artery caused his heart to beat chaotically and then stop, all other systems were go. Correcting the one life-threatening problem restored his life.

In those who are seriously debilitated or terminally ill, CPR is not lifesaving. It is merely death prolonging. For this reason, patients, their families, and their doctors can make a concerted decision not to use CPR if cardiac arrest occurs and allow nature to take its course. This decision can be formalized as a do-not-resuscitate (DNR) order. Again, in the case of cardiac or cardiopulmonary arrest, nature allows the exit to be pain free, and if not completely pain free, then swift.

Thus, nature has a number of ways to make the end of life peaceful, and in a very large number of cases death can come more easily than when medicine attempts to reverse the process temporarily. This is not to say, of course, that medicine never improves on nature. Thousands of lives have been saved and people have been restored to a normal life or an acceptable quality of life by the intervention of modern medicine. Bernie's case serves to highlight this. Pain control is an important way that medicine can improve on nature in terminal illness. It provides relief to the dying who are not asleep but may be fearful or in pain. In most cases, pain management brings suffering under control while still enabling the patient to remain alert. When this cannot be achieved, medication can be provided to do what nature has failed to do—to create a restful or sleeplike state before death.

Barbara, the woman with emphysema who had respiratory failure in Chapter Four, was helped by morphine when she was being taken off the respirator. Modern medicine was called upon first to give her a chance for continued survival and then, when it failed to restore her to an existence that she could accept, to prevent her from suffering in the end. When Barbara's husband found her and called for an ambulance, she had been in a coma—the sleeplike state of CO_2 narcosis—and nature would have ensured at that point that her death was a peaceful one. Respirator treatment normalized her level of carbon dioxide so that she was alert and relatively comfortable while connected to the respirator. The adjustment in her body chemistry, normal for someone with normal lungs, was artificial for Barbara, and when the respirator was disconnected, she was forced to endure a period of uncomfortable breathlessness and intense anxiety. However, when medicine failed to restore her health, it came to her rescue in the end; morphine made her comfortable while nature did its work. But morphine would have been even more effective if Barbara had known well in advance that such comfort measures could and would be given. Comfort measures *are* available, pain *can* be relieved, and fears and anxieties *can* be allayed when nature falls short. But to achieve these ends, we need to become more involved in our treatment plans and participate in a meaningful dialogue with our physician.

We cannot know what Barbara's thoughts would have been —certainly her husband wanted to give her another chance at life. But many patients have thought these things through in advance. One thirty-year-old man had muscular dystrophy since childhood, and he knew his chances of long-term survival were slim. The muscles in his body would grow weaker so that even his breathing would be severely compromised, and he knew that a respirator would someday be required to keep him going. Though handicapped, he had a zest for life and knew he did not want life on a respirator, and he said so often in advance. When his breathing eventually failed, he slipped into a coma and died in peace. His family mourned their loss but knew that the young man had died in the manner he had envisioned.

In most of the cases discussed in this chapter, including Barbara's, nature alone, left to its own devices, would have ensured that death was peaceful. It is for this reason that many patients with serious diseases ask beforehand that such measures not be taken if they are found in unresponsive states —if they drift into a coma, if the heart suddenly stops, or if their breathing ceases. As we will see in Chapter Eight, patients at home, in hospitals, and in nursing homes have the opportunity to put these wishes into writing, and their right to have these wishes respected, even if they are not written down, is protected by law. In order for people to make informed decisions, it is not only important to know what medical interventions exist and are feasible or practical, but it is also important to know that the end of life can be made comfortable by the ways of nature and that medical interventions may sometimes interrupt a peaceful, natural process. Before accepting suggested medical treatment, it is crucial to find out whether the consequences of this treatment conform to our hopes and expectations for the end of life. We must balance any benefits treatment brings against the burdens it may impose. Is the treatment right *for us?* Is it what *we* want?

Nature is not always kind and is often even brutal. But nature can also be sensitive and compassionate. In natural illness, at the very end when death is near, people may sleep peacefully. In this way, nature can protect us from pain, from fear, and from struggling futilely against the inevitable end of life. The psychological struggle is a natural one because when we are conscious, our instinct is to preserve our life. Nature gives us the instinct to preserve life when we are healthy or when there is still life in us, but it can put those instincts to rest when our time is over.

It is important to remember that depression, too, can alter our instinct to preserve life. But depression subverts our healthy impulse toward self-preservation. It does not reduce fear, it enhances it. Depression may give us the illusion that our time is over when it is not. Treating the depression, especially when we are seriously or terminally ill, helps us to cope better with the anguish of our disease. And just as important, by getting rid of that "depressed feeling," as Elise did, we may make other aspects of the disease more endurable and our last days more meaningful.

When the end is truly near, nature has many ways of letting us give up our struggle. More often than we imagine, it produces a peaceful psychological state or a quiet sleep. This may help bring comfort to the dying and also to their loved ones, whose anguish may be lessened by knowing the last days are peaceful. As we have seen, nature can also be brutal and unpeaceful at the end of life, calling for various medical and technological interventions. Each case must be decided on its own merits, in close consultation with a physician. We must never abdicate our responsibility to obtain modern medical care and make informed decisions by adopting a sentimental view of nature. But we would do well to understand that dying is a natural process and that nature can help us along, providing a peaceful passage when our time is near.

CHAPTER SEVEN

Hospice and Comfort Care

To cure sometimes, to relieve often, to comfort always.

—Fifteenth-century French folk saying

Rachel, an active housewife with a ten-year-old son, was only thirty-five when she found a lump in her breast. She was shocked when first told she would need a mastectomy. Worse, the lymph nodes removed during the surgery indicated the cancer had already spread. Sad, but full of hope, Rachel agreed to undergo radiation and extensive chemotherapy treatments. Two years later, the cancer had spread to the bone, and she underwent another course of chemotherapy. Rachel grew fearful as pain began in her back and her doctor ordered a CAT scan of her spine to see if the tumor had recurred. Mustering as much courage and hope as she could, Rachel returned to her doctor for the results, but there was only bad news. She could receive more chemotherapy treatments, but this was not going to cure her and might make her sicker. Rachel couldn't see the point of getting sicker in a hospital, in pain, and alone. She came home in tears. "He gave me these pills," she said to her husband, tossing him a bottle of the strong painkiller Percocet. "Maybe I should take them all now. My cancer is incurable. There's nothing more to do."

But there was more to do. No, Rachel could not be cured. But yes, Rachel could be helped.

When a cure is unlikely, care does not stop. In patients who are terminally ill, care must actually accelerate and become multidimensional. New medical and human resources must be tapped. There are still ways to bring relief from pain and discomfort and to offer solace and support. The outcome can no longer be altered, but the journey can be eased.

When Rachel's cancer was first diagnosed, she felt overwhelmed. Instead of thinking about death, she concentrated her anxiety around the disfiguring surgery she had to undergo. Rachel had always taken great pride in her appearance. She was very much in love with her husband, Scott, and feared that, at the very least, she would have to undergo some form of breast reconstruction surgery to protect his feelings for her. But in her grief and fear, she had underestimated her husband. The same day she was discharged from the hospital, Scott wanted to make love to her. Rachel declined, saying the stitches were still sore, but they slept close together that night. Rachel was deeply moved by her husband's gesture of love. Scott's continuing attention to matters of intimacy eventually made her change her mind about breast reconstruction, and she and Scott grew closer than ever.

Rachel and Scott had dealt with the first phase of the ordeal, but in retrospect the solutions then were so much simpler. After the shock of the diagnosis and the trauma of surgery, life could go on much as before. Rachel was dealing with a serious illness but not a terminal one. But as her disease progressed and became clearly incurable, Rachel's life became infinitely more complex. All the fears she had managed to keep at bay now assailed her. How bad would the pain be? How long would she have to suffer? Would she be able to cope? Who would explain the new facts of her illness to her son? And how? Who would serve as wife, mother, and homemaker when she became ill? And later on? How could she face the fact that she would die and never see her son grow up? Would the medical insurance run out? Rachel's anxiety about her illness and imminent death had now reached a critical point.

Although not a religious woman, Rachel found she yearned for support of a spiritual nature. Jewish by birth, she decided to join a synagogue for the first time with Scott. Their rabbi was a warm and approachable man, and they soon confided in him about Rachel's illness and about their fears and concerns. Rabbi Baum listened and told them about the community's hospice program, a program specifically designed to offer care for people with a terminal illness like Rachel, and for their families.

Rachel had heard about the hospice. In her view, it was a place where people went to die, and she did not want to be "one of them." Although she had talked about swallowing all of her pills at once, in truth, she did not *want* to die—she wanted to live. But gradually, imperceptibly, Rachel began to accept that she was dying. Her pain grew worse and her body reminded her daily that she had a fatal illness. At that point Rachel's thinking began to change. She had new knowledge and different concerns now. But one part of her still resisted. Rachel was almost ready—but not quite—for hospice.

A "hospice" in medieval times was a way station, usually run by monks and nuns, that offered shelter and comfort to travelers. In the twentieth century, as cancer struck more people and sophisticated treatments developed, many were cured, but for many others, the experience of dying was merely prolonged. Hospices grew up, first in England in the 1960s, as places for the dying, but places where the symptoms of the dying process could be eased. Today, hospice has become more than a place; it is a concept of care. In the United States *hospice* refers to an interdisciplinary program of support for people who are dying, usually at home, but with inpatient care when needed. The hospice concept embodies pain relief, control of symptoms, and meeting the emotional needs and personal values of the patient rather than fighting death with high technology. Hospice also recognizes that family members and other caregivers may need and are deserving of care. Hospice is a way of doing things and is limited not by walls, but only by our ability to solve problems. The hospice philosophy ensures that a dying person's last days are filled with as much comfort as possible—physical, psychological, and spiritual.

The hospice approach eases dying but does not cause death. Hospice does not support the practice of active euthanasia or assisted suicide. Rather, it embodies the practice of active comfort care, emotional support, and assistance in maintaining the fullest quality of the life that remains.

The hospice program, like any good health care program, does not ignore important practical concerns—whether they are financial ones or whether they derive from personal difficulties that exist in your home. Hospice is not free, but if you have financial difficulties, the hospice social worker or another person trained in financial counseling can assist you in obtaining the care that you need. If you are covered by Medicare, your hospice benefit will cover far more care at home than it does for patients not enrolled in a certified hospice program. Other government insurance, such as Medicaid, and many private insurance policies (but not all) will also help pay for hospice. A social worker or other financial counselor identified by the hospice program or your hospital can help you to sort out the details. If you do not have any form of health care insurance, it is unlikely that care will be withheld. However, you should discuss your specific financial needs with a qualified individual. Additional and complex questions should be directed to an attorney who specializes in health care law.

If your personal and financial concerns are compounded by a difficult home situation, a hospice worker may also be able to assist with these problems. For example, there may not be an appropriate family member who can care for you, or those at home may have so many of their own problems that they are not available or are not able to be your main caregiver. The hospice social worker may be able to assist you in finding other sources of help, a safer or more secure environment, or another place to live.

Rachel's lingering resistance to her terminal illness prevented her from finding out more about hospice, but Rabbi Baum's words stayed with her. She did not make further inquiries until her son, Adam, forced the issue. Adam knew his mother had cancer, he saw she was in increasing pain and distress, and so one day he asked her directly if she was going to die. Rachel was badly shaken, but she could not withhold the truth from Adam. And if she could not keep it from him, then she could no longer deny it to herself. She returned to her doctor.

Rachel still had mixed emotions when her doctor told her he fully endorsed the hospice concept. He had overseen the care of several patients while they were enrolled in the hospice program. Dr. Bingham had not discussed this option with Rachel yet because he hadn't thought it was the right time. Rachel asked him bluntly if he had been less willing to "give up on her" than she herself had been. They spoke frankly, and Dr. Bingham told Rachel she had not misunderstood him —that neither he nor any other cancer specialist could offer her a cure. But he himself would put her in contact with the local hospice program and could still be her doctor during that time if she wished—or if not, the hospice would refer her to another doctor.

Rachel and Scott went together to speak to a representative of the local hospice program. They discovered that over 90 percent of the patients enrolled in the program remained at home, where they received all their care. Not only doctors and nurses were involved, but also a social worker, a psychologist, a physical therapist, a dietitian, a pharmacist, and a retinue of volunteers from the community. There was also a full-time chaplain, but the hospice was nondenominational, and personal clergy, such as Rabbi Baum, were often closely involved. The entire hospice team held weekly meetings to work on new problems that their patients faced—pain or other serious symptoms, depression, family problems, inadequate housing, financial problems, lack of transportation. These problems were addressed and a solution to each was somehow found. The team would expand, amend, or completely rework each patient's plan of care, if necessary. They all believed that dying was a significant part of living and were committed to providing services and a network of support to help each patient live as comfortably as possible.

The type of program offered to Rachel and her family is

available across the country. There are about 1,800 hospice programs in the United States today, and one very likely exists in or near your community. If you or your loved one would benefit from hospice care, your personal physician can make arrangements for you to be enrolled in a hospice program, and in most cases he or she can continue to serve as your personal doctor. If your physician does not mention the option of hospice to you, you should raise the issue. Perhaps the physician does not feel it is the time for hospice care, as Rachel's doctor initially felt; Rachel herself had been dubious. Generally patients enter a hospice program if their disease is incurable and they are expected to survive for six months or less, but these limits are flexible. For example, Medicare guidelines that previously limited coverage to six months have now been relaxed to allow for longer periods of care. If you are expected to survive longer than a few months and your care needs are simple, doctor, hospice program, and even you yourself may be resistant to the idea. If there is indecision or uncertainty about the prognosis—how long you will survive or even whether the disease is incurable—more attention needs to be given to these factors. Every situation is different. But in cases of terminal illness, it is never too soon to gather information and find out how you or your loved one fits into the scheme of things. Your doctor or your local hospice program can advise you and help you to decide what course of action is best for you, and when.

You can also find out about hospice programs in your community by contacting your hospital's social work department, by contacting a state or local hospice organization, or by calling a national hospice helpline (see Appendix).

What exactly does a hospice do for you? How does care differ from what is done in a hospital or nursing home? Why should you select hospice over care in a hospital, or should you?

First and foremost, hospice addresses your individual needs and physical concerns, and all efforts are made to provide care in your home so that you can remain independent and carry on with your personal activities as long as possible. If you need assistance, your family or other caregivers will be trained by hospice staff to assist you. Generally one family member or friend will be designated as the "primary caregiver" through whom the hospice team's efforts are coordinated. A hospice nurse will visit your home on a regular basis if it is difficult for you to get out and monitor your condition or supervise a home attendant or home health aide (nurse's aide). These home care workers can assist with daily activities and chores such as bathing or shopping or with tasks related to your medical needs. Either your personal physician or one employed by the hospice program will direct your medical care and may also visit you at home. The physician's treatment plan will focus on controlling your pain and managing any distressing symptoms so that you can remain as comfortable and active as possible. Social workers provide supportive counseling and assistance in obtaining a variety of services.

Rachel's hospice was located in a small but separate wing of the local hospital, but as in most hospice programs, she received the bulk of her care in the home. Inpatient beds are intended for short-term care of patients whose symptoms cannot be managed at home. Patients may also be admitted for a short-term stay if a family member or home care worker is temporarily unavailable. For example, one patient was admitted because his wife, who was his principal caregiver, had become ill herself and required hospitalization. At other times, family members are so exhausted and worn out from around-the-clock caretaking that they simply require a respite from their efforts. The hospice in your community may be like Rachel's, or it might be a free-standing unit or a separate wing of a nursing home. Each hospice program is designed around the particular needs of a community and the resources that exist there.

Because treatment takes place largely in your home, it is highly personal, and you are treated as an individual whose needs, preferences, and tastes come first. Because you are the only patient (except in the unusual circumstance where another family member also takes ill), you do not have to wait unnecessarily while a busy nursing staff attends to the needs of a ward full of other patients whose emergency treatments take precedence. In your home, you are in a familiar environment, and, unless you live alone, you are among loved ones who may themselves assist in your care, under the direction and guidance of the hospice team. However, an important part of the hospice approach ensures that if you need to become an inpatient, all efforts are made to duplicate a home-like environment in the hospice. Unlike visiting hours in hospitals, they tend to be unrestricted; children are generally allowed; and some hospices even allow your pets to visit.

As a hospice patient you are treated as part of a family unit, whether your family consists of blood relatives or close companions. You and your family are given support and comfort. If you have no family, you may form important relationships with members of the hospice team, who act as a surrogate family.

Because treatment is geared to comfort, painful treatments are avoided, unless their goal is to improve the quality of your life. However, the hospice approach does *not* mean that you are abandoned to die at home without access to medical care. You can receive any kind of treatment to control symptoms, and it will be given at home or in the hospice inpatient unit if necessary. If you have to become an inpatient for the treatment, you go home afterward. Thus, when Rachel developed pain and shortness of breath from fluid surrounding one of her lungs, she was admitted to the inpatient hospice for a palliative procedure—one that would relieve symptoms although it would not cure the disease. The fluid was withdrawn with a needle and syringe, and medication was injected into the space holding the fluid. This closed the space by producing scar tissue and preventing fluid from reentering. Although not without its risks and not without pain, the procedure helped Rachel's breathing considerably.

Most treatments given through hospice are not highly technical or invasive, but if it can improve your quality of life,

such a procedure is encouraged. Hospice patients with localized tumor pain may undergo radiation treatments for symptom control. A patient in Rachel's hospice program agreed to
have surgery when the tumor invaded her hipbone and caused
it to break—a "pathological fracture." After the fractured hip
was mended, she underwent physical therapy and was able to
walk around with the aid of a cane. She agreed to surgery
because she wanted to be physically independent as long as
she could, and without the surgery, this would not have been
possible. Although not all palliative procedures are successful,
the "aggressive" treatment that this patient had is an example
of how the hospice approach encourages and assists you not
to give up on the life that remains.

Because the emphasis is on keeping the patient comfortable, rigorous efforts are made to control pain and other disabling symptoms. It was the hospice movement, first in
England and later in the United States, that called attention
to the fact that cancer patients often received inadequate
treatment for their pain. All hospice patients are encouraged
to receive adequate doses of whatever pain medication is required—potent narcotics if necessary—and on a regular basis.
If higher doses are required, they are given. This was one of
the first things Rachel learned about hospice.

Rachel had been so worried she would die in pain she
considered hoarding her Percocet—"just in case," she would
admit later—and had skipped a few doses the first few weeks
for this purpose. As a result, her pain was much worse than it
had to be, and she tried to hide this fact. When she became
aware of the hospice attitude about pain control, she was more
forthright about her symptoms. Her doctor explained the
need for her to take her medication on a regular basis. She
could report any problems directly to him or to the hospice
nurse—if the pain control was inadequate, or if she developed any side effects, such as constipation or nausea—and
she would be treated immediately. When the new regimen
failed to control her pain, she was switched to another narcotic, Dilaudid, which "made the pain melt away," she re-

ported to her doctor. Still, she was fearful that her pain might someday increase and be uncontrollable, and she confided this concern to the hospice nurse. The nurse explained the available methods of pain control to Rachel—that potent narcotics were available not only as pills but as liquids, suppositories, and injections, and that all forms, even the intravenous form, could be given at home. In the end, Rachel was kept quite comfortable with oral narcotics, but knowing there were other forms of pain relief, and that they were available to her, gave her a feeling of control over a situation that had been making her feel increasingly helpless. Although Rachel never seriously considered suicide, others in her situation do, and Rachel herself had thought about it. There were moments when she was gripped with despair. But the skilled and sensitive care she received, and the knowledge that her fears and concerns were being directly addressed, reassured her and helped her regain a sense of control over her life. Hospice is devoted to the idea that terminal illness, which has the potential of being intolerable, need not be if the fear of pain and suffering and abandonment is addressed. The patient must be "heard" even if all his or her problems cannot be fixed.

If you are seriously or terminally ill, it is natural to think about death and not unusual to think about suicide. And when suicidal thoughts become overwhelming, a request for a premature and swift exit may be next. Many people who beg others to end their life immediately with a lethal injection or to give them enough pills for a fatal overdose do so because something crucial has not been addressed—the pain, depression, fear, hopelessness, or sense of abandonment that terminal illness may bring with it—or in other cases, because they are overwhelmed by the feeling that their disease controls them and they are completely at its mercy.

Dying often conveys a sense of helplessness and loss of control. A study of euthanasia requests in Holland shows that it is often the loss of control and feelings of dependence and helplessness that are at the basis of patients' requests for active euthanasia and assisted suicide. Hospice physicians and nurses have repeatedly pointed out that these requests are a cry for help, calling attention to some important lack in the dying person's life. In most cases, once the source of the anguish is found and addressed, the request for active death ceases. Sometimes, it is only the knowledge that euthanasia *would be* available, if the patient requested it, that reassures the patient. In rare cases, of course, no amount of pain relief or comfort care can reassure a dying patient intent on taking his or her life. But although thoughts about suicide are common, persistent requests for aid in dying are, by most accounts, very uncommon among dying hospice patients. This is undoubtedly due at least in part to the philosophy of hospice—that all aspects of suffering be addressed.

Although most hospice patients are cancer patients, it is not the specific disease you have but rather the stage of the disease you are in that determines whether you need or would benefit from hospice care. Hospice is designed for people whose disease is not expected to be cured but who select symptom control and comfort care to ease the end of life. If you accept the hospice philosophy, it does not mean you give up hope—rather, you accept the inevitability of death and now want to concentrate on achieving the best quality of life in the time available. The dying woman who agreed to have surgery on her hip realized the hope that she would be able to walk again. People with AIDS, kidney or liver failure, advanced emphysema, progressively paralytic diseases such as amyotrophic lateral sclerosis or multiple sclerosis, and people with other serious illnesses have all been helped by hospice with its emphasis on pain control and comfort care. People in the terminal stages of Alzheimer's disease and similar illnesses may also benefit from the symptom management of hospice care.

But hospice does not stop here. A fundamental aspect of hospice care is tending to the emotional and spiritual needs of the dying person and their family or loved ones. Regardless of your religion, spiritual counseling is available, and if you do not have specific religious convictions or are a nonbeliever, your needs will not be ignored. Hospice workers, particularly social workers, psychologists, and nurses, are trained to recognize emotional needs and to address them. Emotional comfort can take many forms. Rachel found a great deal of emotional support from her family. She also received support when her nurse visited. This support was not a formal psychotherapy session; rather, the nurse's training and experience enabled her to recognize Rachel's worries and to address them. Sometimes emotional support consisted of merely providing answers to Rachel's questions. At other times, Rachel would talk or even cry, and the nurse would listen.

Rachel received similar emotional support from community volunteers who brought her lunch on the days Scott was at work. This encouraged some of Rachel's friends to volunteer for hospice work as well, which lifted Rachel's spirits. Rabbi Baum visited Rachel and her family on a regular basis. Rachel found she was discussing issues of a religious nature she had never addressed before. Rachel's family also received emotional support through the hospice's bereavement program, led by a counselor specifically skilled in assisting patients and their families to deal with the emotional impact of dying. Bereavement, a recognized part of hospice programs, is available for as long as a year after the death of a loved one. As described by the National Hospice Organization, the family is an important part of the entire hospice approach: "The family members are seen both as primary caregivers and as needing care and support so that their own stresses and concerns may be addressed."

Comfort Care

The hospice approach is based on comfort care—you can think of a hospice program as a formal extension of comfort care—but you do not need to be enrolled in a hospice or even to have a specific disease to receive comfort care. The hospice approach can be used anywhere—by people who do not qualify or do not wish to enter a formal hospice program—and we call it comfort care.

Comfort care is an appropriate part of all medical and nursing practice. Certainly comfort can be given to anyone acutely or temporarily ill—for example, someone who has just had surgery and is still in pain. However, the comfort care we discuss in this chapter is more complex. It consists of the many levels of care that are given to patients who face death, whether they are in a formal hospice program or not. It may be the loving relationship that develops between a dying person and family members—enhanced by the efforts of the skilled hospice worker, who can guide the family in the best ways of seeing to the person's needs. It may be something as simple as fluffing a pillow or helping someone to stand and walk across the room, or as highly technical as surgery to repair a tumor-laden hip. It may be the decision to refuse or get rid of an uncomfortable treatment that does nothing more than prolong dying. Comfort care—whether in hospice or elsewhere—is not a specific technique. It is whatever works.

Comfort care is an active process. It brings together all available skills and uses them aggressively and creatively without resorting to high technology. It gives us a personal role to play. Comfort care—wherever it is given—cannot prevent death, but it enables patients and their loved ones to become involved and do all that is humanly possible in the face of the inevitable.

You do not have to have a terminal illness such as advanced cancer to be the recipient of comfort care. Many who become helpless because of chronic illness and severe impairments can benefit as well. Sometimes comfort care can involve *not* doing something, such as avoiding unwanted life-sustaining treatment. It can mean letting individuals die in the manner they want, without forcing them to undergo treatment they don't want. Louis is a case in point.

Louis had a severe stroke that left him paralyzed and unable to communicate, comprehend, or swallow. After a three-month hospitalization and a stormy course, he was left completely helpless, fed by a tube implanted in his abdomen. He was seventy-nine years old and it was clear he would not recover. But now he was trapped. Louis had always dreaded this fate, and his children knew he did not want to be maintained indefinitely with tubes. He had often expressed a desire to "die with dignity"—in his own home if possible. He had watched his wife linger for a month in an intensive care unit, maintained on artificial life support, "on every kind of machine you could imagine." He had vowed never to end like this.

Louis's body was being artificially maintained, but the focus was more on preserving physiologic function than on care. Initially, a nasogastric feeding tube was inserted through his nostrils and connected to a bag of artificial liquid nutrients hung above the bed so the substance could drip directly into his stomach. When he tried to pull the tube out with his good arm, his hand was tied to the bedrails with a restraint. Later, the doctor recommended replacing the nasogastric tube with a gastrostomy tube (G-tube), which would be placed directly through the skin of the abdomen into the stomach. Without a nasogastric tube in his throat it would be easier for Louis to swallow, and perhaps after a while he could eat normally again. At that time the G-tube could easily be pulled out, and the gastrostomy would close up and heal on its own. Melanie knew her father would not want to be "cut," but reluctantly agreed to the procedure. Louis did not improve. After another three months and no improvement, it appeared that his fate was sealed.

Now the family insisted that the feeding tube be removed so Louis could live out his last days naturally. Melanie was dismayed but not surprised when the physician refused, but she was taken aback when he stated his reason—he did not believe in "starving people to death." Still, he said he would not stand in the way if she insisted on taking her father home.

Melanie discussed the question of "starvation" with her own physician, who reassured her this was a misleading term. People who were starving were those who were hungry, people who craved food but had none available. People with significant brain damage such as Louis lacked the healthy appetite or drives of a normal person who was not ill. For centuries, people near the end of life have stopped eating and have died without feeding tubes. A severe stroke victim such as Louis would be completely unaware that dehydration was occurring, and he would quietly lapse into a sleeplike state before he died. He would die painlessly, quietly, and with the dignity that he desired.

So Melanie brought her father home for the last time, where he could live his last days in comfort and die in peace. His death would be a natural one, but his dying would not be a passive abandonment to nature with his caregivers uninvolved. He would be free of tubes and would never see the inside of the intensive care units that he feared. Instead, he would receive *intensive comfort care*. His last days would seem a relief in contrast to what he might otherwise have faced.

At home, Melanie rented a hospital bed, which Medicare would pay for. She had it set up in the living room since there was no extra bedroom. The hospital social worker arranged for Louis to be enrolled in a home care program, providing frequent nurse visits and a physician who would make house calls. In response to Melanie's concern about "starving" her father, the home care physician explained that, if anything, Louis would be more comfortable without artificial feeding than with it. There would no longer be a tube instilling an artificial substance into a stomach that could not "complain" when it was full. If Louis could taste or appreciate food and drink at all, natural food could now be given—in small amounts if that was all he would take—but by mouth, and according to whether or not he was hungry. If his intake was inadequate, it would be because his body did not desire it. Tube feeding did not contribute to his comfort, and avoiding it would not produce discomfort.

Melanie's living room became an intensive comfort unit. Louis was cleaned, touched, comforted, visited, and offered small amounts of cool, thick liquids such as ice cream or milk shakes. He took in very little food, but it was more than he had eaten in the hospital—perhaps because his stomach was not constantly full from the tube feedings, perhaps because Melanie's food was tastier, or perhaps because he sensed the familiarity of his surroundings. On days that he ate and drank little, his lips would become dry, so they were moistened with soothing lemon-flavored glycerin swabs and with ice chips. A home health aide assisted the family with Louis's care, and he was given a sponge bath and a shave daily. Melanie recalled that her father had loved Mozart's music, and so she would play her father's favorite sonatas softly during the day on the off chance that he could hear and appreciate it.

Louis survived for several months after he left the hospital, far longer than the doctors had predicted. He was able to take in just enough nourishment by mouth with the repeated, around-the-clock feedings of his family and other caretakers. He was a person again—a very special one to those who loved him—and he received personal care. His last days were made as comfortable as possible and he died at home from pneumonia, surrounded by his family. He died the way he wanted, free of tubes. Melanie had placed some old photographs on his bedside table, in the hopes they might give her father some pleasure. She was not sure he could take them in—he seemed to exist in a different world—but a few days before he died, Louis lifted his hand and grazed one of the frames. It was the old black-and-white shot of Louis and Melanie at the beach, a favorite of them both. Melanie could not tell if she was dreaming, but she thought she saw a faint smile at the corner of his mouth. He seemed to be thanking her, or so she imagined, and tears of gratitude came to her eyes.

Comfort care is not only for the dying. It also benefits those whose pain comes from the loss and from watching the loved one die. Whether or not Louis fully appreciated his daily shave—Melanie was convinced he did—his grooming was a comfort to his daughter and the family. Playing Mozart sonatas was a beautiful tribute that Louis may or may not have heard, but the music comforted Melanie. It made her father's presence more palpable. Even if he himself was completely unaware, Louis's dignity remained intact. And if some small part of him was still sentient, then Louis knew he had received the best and most loving care.

Maye was also the recipient of comfort care. She resided in a nursing home and had close family who lived nearby, as well as a second "family" consisting of a large, caring nursing staff.

Maye was eighty-three years old and had longstanding diabetes. She was disabled from a series of strokes that had left her bedridden and helpless. She had been blind for many years, and now she had advanced dementia and was unable to speak or take care of any of her needs. Her right leg had been amputated above the knee when she developed gangrene, and now, two years later, she had gangrene of her other leg. Without amputation of her left leg, Maye would not survive for more than a few weeks. But the amputation carried its own risks and might prove too much for Maye. She had almost died from the first amputation and had been forced to return to the hospital for a second operation when the site of the amputation had not healed well. The surgeon had to cut higher that time. It had taken Maye several months to recover. She developed a large bedsore and had several bouts of pneumonia. Her survival had been a day-by-day battle.

Maye's son and daughter were asked once again to sign consent forms for surgery. But they did not feel another amputation was the best course for their mother, whose quality of life was so poor already and would only become worse. They did not want to put her through such an ordeal again. It seemed too cruel. And for what? Even if she somehow recovered from the amputation, it was unlikely Maye would survive the year. Her body was riddled with vascular disease. She was already blind, mute, and helpless. How much indignity could a human being take? They knew Maye would never agree to this procedure if she could speak for herself. None of them would have wanted it for themselves. On the other hand, they felt by not permitting the amputation they would be guilty of causing their mother's death. After much discussion among themselves, with Maye's doctor, and with their minister, they decided it would be best to let nature take its course.

Their decision created some consternation in the nursing home. Previously, any patient requiring amputation was sent swiftly to the nearby hospital and surgery was performed. A team conference was held, including the doctor, nursing staff, and social worker. One nurse argued that amputation would relieve the pain Maye might be suffering. Her colleague responded that strong painkillers could have the same effect, without putting Maye through the trauma of surgery. The social worker, a young man who was usually soft-spoken, said bluntly that he would not put his dog, let alone a loved one, through such indignities. "Stop carving her up and let her die in peace," he pleaded. A nurse's aide, who had worked in the nursing home for ten years, stated simply that it was immoral to "just let her die"; and although she agreed with people's right to their beliefs, she herself could not accept this decision. The nursing home's medical director, a physician, emphasized that the family had the right to decide for the patient because they were most likely to have known how she would have felt. The nursing supervisor agreed and stated forcefully that it was the nursing home's responsibility to come up with an appropriate *alternative* care plan.

The alternative to amputation was comfort care. The team of professionals put their heads together and agreed it was best to respect the family's wishes for the patient while recognizing the misgivings of anyone uncomfortable with the decision. The staff member who could not accept the treatment plan was not required to do anything that violated her beliefs. If she wished, she could temporarily work on another floor with other patients. Meanwhile, Maye would get the best treatment available and everything would be done to make her as comfortable as possible.

Although Maye now slept most of the time, she would awaken and appear to experience pain when the dressings on her leg were changed. Thus, she was given strong pain medication around the clock. This would ensure her comfort at all times. She also tolerated the dressing changes better, and the necessary antiseptics could be used, reducing odors.

Maye herself became less and less aware of her surroundings, but her family was comforted to see the devoted care she was receiving. They sat by the bedside, held her hand, brushed her hair, and said their good-byes. Maye's "second family," the nursing staff, had grown attached to her in the four years she had lived there, and it had been hard for them to let go. But those who were initially uncertain about the decision grew to see there was more than one way of doing things. It was clear that Maye's last days were ones of dignity and not indifferent abandonment. She was surrounded by two families. They did not *fail* to amputate—they *succeeded* in giving the most comfortable and humane care available.

Comfort care and hospice offer what many consider the most enlightened and compassionate form of treatment available today to dying patients and their families. Because hospice was designed specifically for those with terminal illness, it treats the patient as a total person with individual needs and preferences, family relationships, and a life that is worthy of respect and the best care possible. Hospice care for dying patients involves emotional support and physical comfort. The patient is always the center of focus, and his or her pain and distressing symptoms are aggressively treated, but invasive procedures are generally avoided. The challenge is to help make the patient's remaining life as comfortable and rewarding as possible. The family is an integral part of this approach, both as primary caregivers and as loved ones who need care and assistance and counseling in confronting their impending loss. When possible, care is provided at home or in familiar surroundings. Comfort care and hospice have helped transform the experience of terminal illness for thousands of people.

If you or a loved one are faced with tragic illness, you

should inquire about the hospice option. The choice is never an easy one—it must meet your physical, emotional, and financial needs—but it may help you face the end of life with greater courage and comfort. And always remember that comfort care is an approach that can be used anywhere—in hospice, hospital, nursing home, or your home.

CHAPTER EIGHT

How to Safeguard Your Legal Rights: Living Wills and Durable Powers of Attorney for Health Care

Jacqueline was a forty-five-year-old English teacher and mother of two living in the suburbs when she became concerned about some aches and pains in her joints. Her sister, Teresa, had died at age thirty-two of kidney failure after an eleven-year bout with lupus. Now Jacqueline feared that she, too, had contracted the disease.

She made an appointment for a blood test to screen for lupus. The test came back positive. Jacqueline was devastated, but Dr. Paterson said the positive result did not necessarily mean she had the disease, or that she would ever become sick from it if she did have it. Most cases of lupus occur in women in their twenties or thirties, not Jacqueline's age. Family members of people with lupus often have positive test results yet seldom develop the disease itself. But although Dr. Paterson thought it "unlikely" Jacqueline had lupus, he could not completely rule it out either. They would have to keep a close watch over her symptoms.

Jacqueline was sure she had lupus and would die a painful death like her sister. She did not want to become a dialysis patient, as Teresa had been for the last two years of her life. Teresa was completely dependent on regular hemodialysis treatments that left her weak and nauseated. She was constantly getting infections and was maintained on high doses of prednisone, a corticosteroid, with some serious side effects.

Toward the end stages of her illness, Teresa had discussed suicide with Jacqueline. She had no plan to kill herself, but wanted to know that Jacqueline would help her if she could no longer tolerate her condition. Jacqueline had been horrified at the suggestion. She hugged her sister and swore she would do anything to ease her suffering—but not *that*.

Now Jacqueline wondered how much pain and suffering she herself could tolerate or whether she too would consider suicide if she became seriously ill. But suicide was still not an acceptable option to her. Jacqueline thought about her family, her husband, Richard, and her children, Yvonne and Jeremy, whom she loved so much. What would happen to them if she died? She read up on various catastrophic health insurance options and considered them all. It certainly made sense to do something now, before she became too ill to act. She thought about filling out a living will to make sure she was not hooked up to some machine. But as the months wore on and new symptoms did not appear, Jacqueline gradually forgot about her concerns. She did not fill out a living will, although she still thought it was a good idea. Dr. Paterson believed she had passed the danger point and was in reasonably good health, although he would continue to monitor her condition. Richard took her on a second honeymoon and they had a splendid time.

About a year after her first positive test result, Jacqueline was driving back from school when a large truck, an eighteen-wheeler, careened out of control and collided with her car. The impact shattered the door and window on the driver's side and crushed Jacqueline's body. Her spleen was ruptured, causing severe internal bleeding, and she suffered cardiac arrest. By the time an ambulance arrived, Jacqueline's brain had been deprived of oxygen for a crucial ten minutes, and although paramedics managed to revive her heart, she remained unconscious.

Jacqueline was rushed to the hospital, where emergency surgery was performed to stop the bleeding. She was treated in the intensive care unit and maintained on a respirator to help her breathe. Medications and fluid were given through her veins. After two weeks, a nasogastric tube was inserted through her nose so she could receive complete nutrition and hydration. Two months later, Jacqueline no longer required a respirator, but she had still not regained consciousness. Her nasogastric feeding tube was replaced with a gastrostomy tube, a more practical method of providing long-term artificial nutrition and hydration. After three months had elapsed, she was diagnosed as being in a persistent vegetative state (PVS). She had sustained severe brain damage that had left her in a condition of chronic unconsciousness with virtually no chance of recovery.

Jacqueline's husband, Richard, a successful lawyer, and her two children, Yvonne and Jeremy, never lost a sense of shock when they saw Jacqueline lying unconscious in the hospital bed encircled by tubes and machines. It was hard to believe such a vibrant woman could so suddenly be turned into an empty shell. The one hopeful sign was that her eyes occasionally opened and stared blankly out at the room. They seemed to be gazing around but did not show the slightest flicker of recognition or awareness. The family called in an outside expert, a renowned neurologist, who confirmed the diagnosis of PVS. The eye movements, he said, were random and not conscious or sustained, owing to the fact that while Jacqueline's cerebral cortex—the higher part of the brain, responsible for thinking and awareness—no longer functioned, the lower part of the brain—the brain stem, which controls vegetative functions—was intact. Due to her age and apparent good health, Jacqueline might survive for another ten or even twenty years if her body was maintained by tube feeding and meticulous nursing care. But there was almost no chance that she would ever regain consciousness. Even if a miracle occurred and she did resurface, she would certainly be brain damaged. However, just to be sure, the neurologist suggested they could wait another eight weeks to see if there were any signs of improvement. If, as he suspected, Jacqueline's diagnosis remained unchanged after that time, then he considered her fate sealed.

Ten more weeks elapsed and Jacqueline showed no improvement. By this time, she had been transferred to a long-term care facility because the hospital, an acute care center, could not keep a bed in the ICU tied up for so long for a nonemergency case. Jacqueline, who had not regained consciousness since her accident and who could not see, hear, feel, or understand anything, was deemed "stable" because machines had taken over her vital functions and were running smoothly.

Richard did not want his wife transferred to a nursing home. Jacqueline had told him repeatedly that if she were ever in this kind of situation—so physically and mentally maimed that she was "like a vegetable"—she would never, under any circumstances, want to be kept alive by artificial means, including tube feeding, which she dreaded. It was her worst nightmare, and yet she had never filled out a living will. Some barrier prevented her from writing down her wishes until it was too late. Her children, too, had often heard her discussing the subject and agreed this would be the last thing their mother would want. Nevertheless, Yvonne now pleaded with her father to "give Mom a little more time" and let Jacqueline go into the nursing home.

In deference to his daughter, who had still not accepted her mother's tragedy, Richard reluctantly agreed to the transfer. But after the transfer, he wrote the nursing home's medical director, informing him that if there was still no change in his wife's condition three months from now, then he wanted the tube feeding withdrawn in accordance with his wife's wishes. Richard also authorized a do-not-resuscitate order (DNR) so that Jacqueline would not be revived if she suffered another cardiac arrest. And he requested that no antibiotics or drugs be given if she developed a life-threatening infection.

Despite Richard's instructions, Jacqueline was given antibiotics on several occasions. When Richard confronted the medical director, he was told antibiotics were considered ordinary care and it would be illegal to withhold them. Richard, who knew the law, responded that it was not illegal to stop antibiotics for someone who was hopelessly ill, but he held his anger in check. More than six months had already passed and he now requested to have all life support terminated, in keeping with his wife's wishes. The medical director responded that withdrawing such treatment went against the policy and philosophy of the nursing home. This, too, would be against the law. Did Richard really want to starve his wife to death? The nursing home could not authorize such action.

Richard became furious. He asked sarcastically whether the nursing home was more interested in preserving Jacqueline's life, which was one long humiliation, or in the high reimbursement rate it was receiving for her care. Richard had successfully sued the owner of the truck that hit Jacqueline —it was an open-and-shut case of negligence—and so a third-party insurance was covering his wife's medical bills. As a result, the nursing home was being paid at a much higher rate than it received from the Medicaid patients who made up more than 50 percent of the population. Because Jacqueline's unconscious existence might be prolonged for years by tube feeding, the nursing home had a lucrative, long-term source of income for a minimal expenditure of effort. All these reasons, as Richard well knew, made Jacqueline an ideal patient for the nursing home from a financial point of view.

Richard was in a bind. Despite often having talked about a living will, Jacqueline had never gotten around to filling one out. As a result, there was now no written evidence of her wishes. Nor had she appointed a health care agent to speak for her. Either of these documents would have instantly clarified matters and made it much harder for the nursing home to ignore Jacqueline's treatment preferences. However, in the absence of any written instruction from the patient, the nursing home was making the decision for Jacqueline based on *its* interpretation of her best interests. It didn't seem to matter that Richard, her husband of twenty-two years, was in a far better position than the nursing home to know what his wife would want. It rankled Richard that Jacqueline, who had spoken about living wills in connection with her lupus, was now the victim of an accident and without an advance directive. Why hadn't she acted when she had the chance?

But Richard, himself a lawyer, knew he had rights. There was common law—the right of self-determination—that protected Jacqueline's body from outside interference. And following the Cruzan case, the U.S. Supreme Court had affirmed that individuals were constitutionally protected from unwanted treatment. Richard began collecting affidavits from Jacqueline's family, close friends, and colleagues—he made one out himself—testifying how she had often said she would not want to be sustained on life support if she could not recover her former quality of life. The evidence of her strong feelings on the right to refuse treatment was overwhelming. Richard prepared his documentation and approached the nursing home lawyers, ready to take them to court. The lawyers realized he had a strong case and was not about to be scared off. They informed the nursing home that court costs and legal fees would be expensive—at least $10,000—and that Richard would win the case anyway. And now Richard was threatening to stop payment of his wife's nursing home treatment, requiring even more litigation and expense. After consulting with the medical director and the administration, the nursing home lawyers agreed there was sufficient evidence to justify taking Jacqueline off life support. Eight months after her accident, Jacqueline was allowed to die, and Richard had the small but not insignificant satisfaction of knowing he had carried out her final wishes.

The tragic accident that befell Jacqueline, and the predicament confronted by her husband, Richard, concerning her care, illustrate an increasingly common and complex problem that millions of us face today. In the event of an injury or illness that leads to physical or mental incapacity, we or our loved ones may be unable to indicate what kind of medical care we want. As a result, we may receive unwanted or inappropriate medical treatment—such as the tube feeding Jacqueline wished to avoid. This happened to Jacqueline even though she had a medical reason to write down her wishes in advance, and even though she had very strong feelings about life support. But she procrastinated and failed to act. By similarly procrastinating, many of us may lose control over our bodies and our medical fate. Not only may our treatment wishes be ignored when we can no longer speak for ourselves, but even family members and loved ones may be frustrated in trying to intervene on our behalf, despite knowing exactly what kind of care we would want or not want. This is an awful but increasingly common fate, as we saw with Jacqueline's family. External factors may become more decisive than our own treatment choices: the modern hospital environment where all human and technological effort is expended to *avoid* death; the personal beliefs or qualms of individual medical personnel or family members; institutional policies and state laws and regulations regarding life-sustaining treatment, such as Missouri's prohibition against removing tube feeding; and financial incentives, as in Jacqueline's case, where reimbursement rates and methods may influence the institution's actions.

All these forces may converge to take control of our bodies away from us and leave us suspended indefinitely in a helpless state. And our fear of such a frightening scenario may lead us to consider extreme, preemptive measures, even suicide, in an effort to prevent such a situation from ever developing. But while assisted suicide is illegal and deeply disturbing—Jacqueline refused to help her sister commit suicide and rejected it as an option for herself—there are ways we can act within the law to protect ourselves and retain legal control over end-of-life decisions. The best protection is to plan ahead and fill out an advance directive such as a living will or durable power of attorney for health care. Jacqueline had reasons to fill out these documents at least a year before her accident. If you are facing a serious illness, you can protect yourself legally with an advance directive. And your loved ones, even if they are healthy, can protect themselves as well. A living will allows you to put your wishes about life-sustaining care in writing. A durable power of attorney for health care lets you appoint another person to speak on your behalf.

We are all aware that modern technology may keep our bodies "alive" even when we are unconscious with no hope of recovery. Because biomedical developments allow us to postpone and negotiate the timing of death, human choice and human responsibility now enter into the end-of-life equation in an unprecedented way. Choices are involved, whether we like it or not, and filling out an advance directive has become a fundamental way to assert our legal right to influence the course of our medical treatment. Legally binding decisions about initiating life support, withholding it, or withdrawing it are being made every day in health care institutions across the country. Almost anyone who is terminally ill, or who cares for a dying family member or loved one, will confront this kind of decision. Those of us who evade the issue and do nothing will run the risk of ceding our decision-making authority to another person not of our choosing: a doctor, nurse, lawyer, or hospital administrator. Indecisiveness in end-of-life matters is really a decision to let others decide for you.

As long as we are conscious and have the capacity to make our own decisions—in legal terms, as long as we are "competent"—we can speak for ourselves and give explicit directions about our care. Under the law of "informed consent," no treatment can be given to us until we have understood its implications and agreed to it. However, even when we are able to make decisions, treatment wishes are not always understood or even articulated clearly. Many doctors are reluctant to broach the issue of life support and may wait until someone is seriously ill, when he or she may be in no condition to appreciate all the nuances and options available. At that stage, the unsettling emotional effects of a terminal illness and various technologies and medications administered simultaneously may make it difficult for us to remain clearheaded and fully rational.

Complex decisions about end-of-life treatment demand

time for the natural give-and-take of discussion and debate. It is important for you to discuss these matters with your physician and your family well in advance of a crisis requiring hospitalization. Learn how your doctor feels about living wills and life-sustaining care *before* it becomes a personal issue. One way to initiate discussion is to bring in an advance directive and ask for help in filling it out. Make sure your physician understands how strongly you feel about the subject. Most doctors welcome the opportunity for dialogue once the subject has been initiated and appreciate specific guidance from patients.

A 1989 survey in the *Journal of the American Medical Association* found that an overwhelming majority of physicians endorsed the use of living wills and felt they made it easier to reach the best treatment decision. Doctors also praised advance directives for improving communication and trust between themselves and their patients. Living wills laws contain an important "immunity clause" that protects a physician from any civil or criminal liability for agreeing to withhold or withdraw treatment in accord with your wishes. So a doctor need not fear prosecution for following your instructions. There is a greater risk of legal liability for the physician if he or she *refuses* to follow your directions, or to transfer you to another physician who will. Nevertheless, if you know beforehand that your doctor has strong reservations about honoring living wills, *even after you have expressed your feelings*, you might consider switching doctors.

The most serious problem arises when you become "incompetent" and lose the ability to make decisions on your own. The brain may lose this capacity as a result of sudden, traumatic injury, such as Jacqueline's, or from a stroke or dementia. It is also common in the final stages of terminal illness when confusion or coma can set in. Other serious diseases—heart disease, cancer, AIDS, Alzheimer's—may impair decisional capacity or lead to a terminal period of incompetence: an interval preceding death when we are unconscious or semiconscious and lack the ability to understand or communicate our preferences. In such cases, the decision about our care may be taken out of our hands and made by others. And in most instances, the determination by a health care facility will be to continue life-prolonging treatment unless we have clearly indicated otherwise. Thus we may find ourselves, or our loved ones, unwitting "prisoners of technology," our minds gone and our body functions taken over by machines. Trapped in a kind of medical purgatory, we may languish indefinitely, maintained in the very condition we wanted to avoid. We may also bring great emotional anguish to those who love us, forcing them to make life-and-death decisions under extreme stress, decisions that are really *ours* to make. And in some instances, we may impose undue financial hardship on our families, who may feel compelled out of guilt or a false sense of duty to pay for treatment that can do us no good and that we don't even want.

Although most people use living wills to *refuse* unwanted treatment, you may also *request* to have specific forms of treatment administered to you in your will. It may also be used to stipulate that you want treatment limited to all measures that will give you maximum comfort care and pain control. It is important to remember that doctors are trained to preserve life and will do everything in their power to keep you alive unless you are able to say no or have explicitly refused treatment in advance in a legally binding manner. Even then, a living will can *only* be used to refuse life support systems if they are all that is keeping you alive. It cannot be used to obtain assistance with suicide, or to ask for any form of active euthanasia where death is intentionally hastened by a lethal injection.

When you are dying of an incurable or irreversible condition, you may refuse medical treatments that you would have wanted when you still had a fighting chance for improvement. The most commonly refused treatments in a living will are: *cardiopulmonary resuscitation (CPR)*, usually ineffective in terminally ill patients; *mechanical respiration*, which may prolong the existence of a hopelessly ill patient without offering any chance for recovery; *tube feeding*, which may maintain a purely vegetative existence for an indefinite period; *antibiotics*, which may cure a secondary infection without affecting the underlying disease, and so make a dying patient more aware of his discomfort; and *dialysis*, which may delay death by doing the blood-cleansing work of the kidneys, without improving the chances of recovery from the terminal illness.

Other treatments patients might refuse in their living wills include: *surgical procedures* that may be used to relieve pain when other methods of pain medication might be just as effective; *invasive diagnostic tests* that may cause discomfort or even side effects without any counterbalancing advantage; *intravenous (IV) lines* inserted into veins in the arm or neck that may be useful for receiving fluids, blood, or medication but may also cause pain and discomfort, so that patients try to pull them out; *chemotherapy and/or radiation*, which may improve comfort in some patients but may also become burdensome when incurable cancer recurs despite repeated treatments; *blood transfusions*, which may provide some comfort but may also require invasive IV lines or result in acute hepatitis or transfusion reactions. Because these last four treatments, used selectively, can increase comfort in certain cases, some people recommend that you insert a clause in your living will such as, "I wish to avoid these treatments if they merely prolong the dying process but would accept them if there is no better way to increase my comfort." To understand what treatments might apply to your particular case, carefully discuss your living will with your doctor.

Whatever the living will in your state looks like, you can always add personal instructions to the standard form. Any written expression of your wishes will be legally significant. Although it's generally best to keep it simple, you may attach an extra sheet of paper if necessary. If you prefer to die at home, or to remain at home as long as you receive comfort care, you may indicate these preferences here.

Once written, you should sign and date your living will in the presence of two witnesses who also sign. In most states, the witnesses cannot be beneficiaries of your estate. Then you should give copies of your living will to your spouse, close friends, doctor, lawyer, religious adviser, or anyone else who could come forward on your behalf. Don't stash it away in a safety deposit box, where it can do no one any good. You should also keep a card in your wallet indicating that you have an advance directive and explaining where it can be found. Make sure you explain your feelings about life-sustaining treatment to all family members beforehand so they don't suddenly object once you are incapacitated. Dissenting family members can complicate matters—even if you have an advance directive—and you want to keep things as simple and uncomplicated as possible. Try to explain your position to your family and help them understand why this is important to you. Even if they don't agree with you, make sure your family knows how strongly you feel. *This is your decision to make*. If one member is particularly disapproving despite your efforts, you might bring the subject up in front of the whole family and make them promise to follow your instructions over his or her opposition. Always be as open and explicit as possible, so there can be no doubt about your wishes.

By exercising your legal right to fill out a living will or appoint a durable power of attorney for health care, you need not worry that you are forsaking your moral or religious beliefs. The main current of opinion among the major religious groups in the United States—Catholicism, Judaism, and Protestantism—supports the moral right of an individual to refuse extraordinary medical treatment. Although some segments within the Roman Catholic Church argue that life-sustaining treatment must always be given, in mainstream Catholic tradition, life is considered a basic and fundamental value but not an absolute one. Hence it is not absolutely necessary in each and every case to provide artificial sustenance, especially if further treatment would be too burdensome for the patient. As Pope John Paul II publicly stated in "Declaration on Euthanasia": "When inevitable death is imminent in spite of the means used, it is permitted in conscience to take a decision to refuse forms of treatment that would only secure a precarious and burdensome prolongation of life.''

Certain strictly orthodox Jewish groups also oppose removal of life support under any circumstances because of the sacredness of life, arguing that life does not belong to man because the Creator has given it and only He can take it away. However, mainstream Judaism believes this view must be tempered with reason and compassion. As stated by the Central Conference of American Rabbis: "The conclusion from the spirit of Jewish law is that while you may not do anything to hasten death, you may, under special circumstances of suffering and helplessness, allow death to come." Among the wide range of Protestant churches and denominations, there is almost universal sanction for the right to die with dignity and refuse unwanted medical interventions. The determining factor in Protestantism, as in Catholicism and Judaism, is the deeply moral view that human life does not consist merely of physical existence but is also a spiritual condition. Nevertheless, if you have any questions or doubts, it is a good idea to discuss your feelings and views about living wills with your religious or spiritual adviser. If you want your religious adviser —priest, rabbi, or minister—consulted about your treatment, you may state this in your living will.

Although they vary in some important particulars, living wills are recognized in every state. Living-will legislation, first passed in California in 1976, now exists in forty-five states and the District of Columbia. Most other states have court decisions that recognize living wills. Outside of statutes and case law, both the common law of informed consent and the Constitution as interpreted in the Cruzan case protect the right of patients to be free of unwanted treatment as expressed in a living will.

State laws, or statutes, vary widely. For example, some state forms still do not allow you to refuse certain treatments, such as tube feeding, even though the courts have overruled this. In other states, the living will only goes into effect once you are in a "terminal condition" but does not include permanent unconsciousness. Nevertheless, it is important to fill out the appropriate form for your state if one exists. You may also, in addition to your state form, fill out a generic living will, such as the one pioneered by Choice in Dying (formerly the Society for the Right to Die and Concern for Dying), whose address appears in the Appendix. This general living will covers a wider range of medical situations and treatments than most state forms and avoids some of their limitations and ambiguities. If you live in a state without living-will legislation, the generic form is ideal.

If you have a living will in one state and become ill or injured in another, your living will will almost certainly be honored. This is what happened in the case of Anna Zodin, a vegetative patient in a Georgia hospital who only had a Texas living will. The Georgia court ruled that Mrs. Zodin's wishes were clear and should be honored regardless of where her living will was executed. The important point is to have some *written* record that provides evidence of your wishes. Having such legal proof will make it much easier to protect your treatment wishes without a prolonged battle. It will enable your rights to be vindicated if the only recourse is to go to court because it is universally recognized that a living will constitutes clear and convincing evidence of your wishes.

Another way to protect your treatment rights, less well known but just as important as a living will, is a durable power of attorney for health care (DPAHC). This document, also called a medical power of attorney or health care proxy, allows you to appoint another person, usually called an agent or proxy, to make health care decisions for you in any situation where you can no longer make them yourself. It enables you to delegate responsibility for medical decision-making to a selected individual who is legally empowered to speak on your behalf. In cases of incapacity or incompetence, the health care agent represents your interests and ensures that your wishes are carried out.

A general "durable power of attorney" is "durable" because it remains in effect or endures past your incapacity. Traditionally, such laws were used to grant someone else control over money or property. The durable power of attorney *for health care* gives another person the right to make decisions specifically concerning your health care but *not* about your money or property unless you request that these two powers be combined. To date, forty-three states and the District of Columbia have passed some form of durable power of attorney for health care law or have statutes that through court decisions, attorney general's opinions, or other statutes have been interpreted to give agents the right to make medical decisions. In the other states, you may, with the help of a local attorney, draw up a general durable power of attorney statute that includes health care decisions. To find out the law in your state, you can contact your state department of health, senior resource center, local chapter of the American Association of Retired Persons (AARP), any hospital or nursing home, a lawyer, or Choice in Dying.

In most states, the durable power of attorney for health care becomes effective in a wider range of situations than a living will. In addition to terminal conditions, when a health care agent would decide about such issues as removing life support, a DPAHC applies to any form of unconsciousness and to all situations where you might temporarily be unable to make medical choices *even though full recovery is likely*. By appointing a spokesperson, rather than listing your treatment preferences on paper, the DPAHC may also be a more assertive and forceful way of making your case at the bedside in end-of-life situations. Another advantage is that your health care agent can be more responsive and adapt to new, unexpected medical situations not foreseen in your living will.

The DPAHC may confer very broad powers on your appointed agent. In most states, he or she can make all decisions about your medical and surgical care, including end-of-life treatment. Your agent can interpret your living will, control access to your medical records, hire or fire medical personnel, grant releases, obtain court authorization, and even control expenditure of funds for your care. However, you can choose to limit your agent's authority with regard to any of these powers by simply writing down the terms or conditions of his or her appointment. A health care agent only has as much power as you are willing to grant.

The person you appoint as your health care agent must be someone you have complete trust in—a person willing and able to take on a serious responsibility. Many people choose their spouse, if they have one, or a close friend or family member. If you have several grown children, settle on one as your agent to avoid potential conflict or disagreement. You can always list them in order of priority, so that if one dies or is unavailable, a second takes over. You can also choose someone outside your family, such as a companion if you live in an unmarried relationship. Some people choose like-minded friends over family members because they share the same views about medical treatment and would not feel so burdened in carrying out specific end-of-life wishes. Family members cannot overrule a health care agent unless they can prove he or she acted against your wishes, which is not easy to do and requires a court order. If you choose your physician to act as your agent, then he or she cannot also be your attending doctor if and when you lack capacity. You must decide on one or the other.

Whomever you select, it is important that you enter into a full and frank discussion with them concerning your feelings about treatment. Some people use the DPAHC as an excuse for passing on responsibility to another person, assuming their agent will "take care of it." You need to know how you feel before you can expect someone else to act on your behalf. Without guidance from you, this responsibility can be a great burden. You should discuss treatment options with a physician or other knowledgeable health professional to make sure you understand the medical aspects of each situation and how decisions might be made for you. Also speak to family members, close friends, or advisers whose opinion you respect. Then tell your agent exactly how you feel. Although your general philosophy and feelings about terminal care are the most important, it is helpful to be explicit about tube feeding because it remains controversial. (Some states require you to check off a box on the form regarding tube feeding so there is no question about your wishes.) You should discuss your views on a wide range of medical treatment, not just terminal care, because the DPAHC applies to all health care decisions when you are incapacitated, not just end-of-life treatment. Carefully discuss what kind of quality of life would be, or not be, acceptable to you. Make sure your agent understands exactly where you stand and is willing to advocate on your behalf. Your health care agent should be someone responsible and assertive, ready to stand in for you and take on the powers that be if they should try to frustrate your treatment wishes.

Your DPAHC form should be signed and witnessed by two adults, neither of whom is your agent or backup agent. A copy of your DPAHC should be given to your physician, your agent, and any backup agents. They should also have a copy of your living will, if you have one. Keep a copy of your DPAHC with your living will and the name of your agent and contact information in your wallet, purse, or other conspicuous place.

Whenever possible, people should fill out both a living will and a durable power of attorney for health care. The two documents complement one another and provide maximum protection together. Anyone can write out a living will. The forms are available free or for a minimal charge from state health departments and are increasingly distributed by doctors, clinics, in senior centers, and in other resources listed in the Appendix. The services of a lawyer are not required. The DPAHC is available from the same sources, although in some states—where the general durable power of attorney has not been applied to health care—the help of a local attorney is advisable.

Keep in mind, however, that while the DPAHC is an excellent document, it does not work for everyone. Many people have no one to appoint as their agent. They may be living alone after the death of a spouse or loved one or may have lost touch with close relatives and friends. Others may not want to "burden" their loved ones with such a difficult task. Some people may not want to give up what they perceive as their right to make decisions to another person. And sometimes, the agent of choice is unwilling to take on the responsibility. For such people, a living will is even more critical because it is the only way to express treatment decisions.

Living wills and durable powers of attorney for health care were given a big boost when Congress recently passed a new bill called the Patient Self Determination Act (PSDA). The PSDA, which went into effect in December 1991, should help ensure greater protection for patients' rights in end-of-life decision-making. The bill mandates that all health care providers receiving Medicare or Medicaid must inform patients upon admission about their right to accept or refuse treatment and to fill out advance directives such as living wills. This makes it far more likely that you will be hearing about living wills and DPAHCs as a routine matter in the health care setting, whether you asked about them or not. Do not be surprised or frightened if this happens. It is now a federal law to supply this information, and it is intended to educate and alert you to your legal rights.

The Patient Self Determination Act also stipulates that the health care institution must record on your medical chart whether you have an advance directive. This practice should greatly assist responsible record-keeping. Any hospital, nursing home, hospice, or HMO that does not honor living wills must inform patients in writing about its policy; and it must follow the state law about what to do in the event of a conflict. It is a good idea to find out about your institution's procedures and policies toward advance directives ahead of time, so that you will know what you are up against in the event of incapacity.

The PSDA legislation is significant, but it does not guarantee an overnight change in deep-rooted attitudes. For example, nursing home physicians may still tend to transfer a dying patient to a hospital for some forms of high-technology care that may prolong life even if the patient would prefer to die peacefully. Not only do many nursing homes lack high-tech equipment, but they are sensitive to their reputations and prefer not to be associated with death in the public mind. Nursing home patients can indicate in a living will that if they are dying with little hope of recovery, they do not wish to be transferred to a hospital unless treatment received there would make them more comfortable.

Even if you have made out an advance directive, you may still run into difficulty in the health care setting. The most frequent problem is that health care providers may not know you have a living will or they may not be able to locate it. Even with the PSDA requirement about medical charts, if you are suddenly injured or fall ill, there may be no record of your advance directive. That is why it is so important to make copies of your documents for your immediate family and your family doctor.

Other problems include using old or outdated forms. Initial and date the forms periodically to show they still represent your views. Also be aware that the law in some states has changed, and it is always best to try to obtain the latest forms. If you move to a different state, use the new state's form. Consult your physician if you have any questions.

Some doctors or lawyers who object to removing life-sustaining treatment may claim that your state does not have living-will legislation, or that the laws are too limited. You can respond that there is both common law and constitutional law in *every* state protecting your right to refuse treatment.

An overwhelming number of Americans now approve of living wills and durable powers of attorney for health care, and more are signing them every year—but the majority of us, about 80 percent, still have no advance directive. Like Jacqueline, we may support advance directives in principle, but we hesitate to fill them out in practice, even when we have good medical reason to do so. While these documents will greatly increase compliance with our treatment wishes, all of us still have the right to refuse unwanted life-sustaining care, even if we haven't filled out an advance directive. But it is that much more difficult—though by no means impossible—to protect our rights without these documents. After all, neither Karen Ann Quinlan nor Nancy Cruzan had a living will and their wishes were eventually honored—although at tremendous cost to their families. Jacqueline, thanks in large part to her husband, Richard, was also able to die a natural death. But her family had to fight and struggle that much harder on her behalf. When you don't have an advance directive, it may simply take more time, money, determination, and resourcefulness to protect yourself or your loved ones.

One form of protection that exists for patients and families in about thirteen states is known as "surrogate decision-making" provisions. These laws stipulate that if a patient who cannot speak for himself or herself has neither a living will or a DPAHC, the authority to make end-of-life decisions automatically goes to the next of kin. Assuming there is no evidence of bad faith, the right of the patient's family to make treatment decisions for the patient is protected by law. It has frequently been pointed out that had Nancy Cruzan been injured in Arkansas, a neighboring state, rather than in Missouri, her family would not have had to wait over seven years to withdraw her tube feeding because Arkansas is one of the states with a surrogate decision-making law. Nancy Cruzan's family would therefore immediately have been recognized as the natural spokesperson for her wishes. (In other states that don't have such a strict and narrow standard of evidence as Missouri, her wishes would have been honored even without this law.) Surrogate (or "substitute") decision-making laws provide a list of which people have priority to make decisions for the patient, including: the legal guardian, spouse, adult children, parents, siblings, physician. However, if you disapproved of this list for whatever reason—you live in an unmarried relationship, you've fought with your family—it would be even more important to fill out an advance directive.

When a patient is incapacitated and unable to make decisions, but does not have a living will or durable power of attorney for health care, and there are no laws specifying who should act as decision-maker, several things may happen. If the doctor has previously spoken to the patient and knows his or her wishes, the physician may simply follow those wishes. That is ideal, but it is not guaranteed, especially if a family member objects. Remember how Jacqueline's daughter, Yvonne, pleaded with her father to let Jacqueline remain on life support? Yvonne even pointed out that her mother had never filled out a living will as proof her feelings were unclear. It is difficult to ignore the conflicting claims of another family member, especially if there is no documentation that disproves it. If the patient's wishes are not known to the doctor, and there is no advance directive to provide guidance, the doctor will usually seek out a family member who may be knowledgeable about the patient's views. Often, the patient's relative or close friend may be asked to provide proof of the patient's wishes. The highest standard of proof is known as "clear and convincing evidence." This may include a written statement from the patient, or it may involve gathering testimony from several people who knew the patient and can attest to her preferences, as Richard did for Jacqueline.

The next standard of proof, widely accepted by many physicians, lawyers, and institutions, is called "substituted judgment." If there is no clear, written evidence of the patient's wishes, the family may make a judgment based on its knowledge of what the patient "would have wanted." Assuming a close relationship between patient and family member, in which general values and beliefs are known regardless of specific choices, a close relative may "substitute" for the patient and make the decision he or she would most likely have made. Gut instincts about how the patient would want to be treated can be followed. Surrogate decision-making laws, discussed above, are based on the premise that no one is in a better position than close family members to know what the patient would want.

Occasionally a situation arises where there are no friends or family, and no other evidence of a dying patient's wishes. The patient may be an older person with no surviving relatives or close friends, may live in a different part of the world from family, or may be estranged from any relatives he or she does have. An elderly woman living alone in Nevada who had never married and had outlived her siblings was placed in this predicament when she went into a permanent coma after being hit by a car and was placed on life support. No friends or relatives came forth to supply any information about her wishes. Another instance might involve a mentally retarded person who is similarly injured but was never capable of making any decisions. How do health care workers know whether to maintain or withdraw treatment? The standard used here is referred to as "best interest." The doctor or other health professional may act according to his perception of what the patient's "best interest" would be. Such judgments depend on generally accepted or "objective" standards of value that society as a whole endorses—such as a very burdensome treatment without much chance of success, which would not be in the "best interest" of the patient.

If someone you know is suddenly incapacitated by injury or illness, you may be called upon to represent their wishes even if they never appointed you. Your first task would be to determine their exact medical condition and prognosis. Then you would have to decide what they would have wanted to do in such a situation. Using the three standards of proof mentioned above, you should first seek any evidence of their wishes, such as a written statement or what they said to you. Then try to put yourself in their shoes and decide how they would have acted. Did they ever tell you how they felt about a relative or friend in an end-of-life situation, or did they have a reaction to a famous case? If you can't make an informed choice based on your judgment of their feelings, then consider what is in their best interest from an objective point of view.

Always try to establish and maintain a good relationship with the attending doctor. Most conflicts can be resolved at the bedside if you are patient and calm enough. By drawing on your personal knowledge of the patient, you should try to convince the physician if you feel his or her objections are not valid. The physician is your most important potential ally, and you should make every effort to win him or her over to your position. You should also speak to the nursing staff, who may have information that can prove useful. If they are agreeable, both doctors and nurses can help you by conveying the medical argument on your behalf to others who may oppose you.

If you still run into opposition from health care providers, you have several recourses. You should seek out a patient representative or social worker who is familiar with the structure of the hospital and can intervene on your behalf or can direct you to someone else who can assist you further in negotiating your way through the bureaucracy. If none of this is successful, you may wish to ask the hospital ethics committee to take up your case or to convene an ad hoc group if one does not already exist. The ethics committee consists of health care professionals, lawyers, ethicists, and clergy who can highlight the key issues in end-of-life decision-making from both the patient's and the hospital's point of view. They usually provide an excellent forum for reconciling differences. If there is a lawyer on the ethics committee, find out if he or she is an outside attorney who does not primarily represent the hospital's interests.

Another source of appeal is the hospital administration. In most cases you will deal with a risk manager, a pragmatic person whose job it is to protect the hospital from any liability. Legal matters regarding state law, policies, and regulations can be resolved at this level if care is used. The issue of money can also be persuasive with the risk manager, as it was in Jacqueline's case. You can refer to the Elbaum case in New York State, where a court upheld the right of Mr. Elbaum to refuse to pay for his wife's unwanted treatment. The nursing home, which insisted on life support against the family's objection, was left with an unpaid $100,000 bill. In the Bartling case in California, a man was awarded $160,000 in attorney's fees because the hospital made him go to court to uphold his right to refuse treatment. The risk manager will usually respond to a knowledgeable argument based on any financial loss the institution might incur. Like Richard, it is also important that you show your determination to pursue matters to their conclusion.

If you encounter difficulty in treatment refusal matters, you can even go so far as to engage a lawyer experienced with right-to-die cases to petition the state court for a hearing. However, this may be a costly and time-consuming step and should only be undertaken in extreme circumstances. It could take years to resolve a legal battle. On the other hand, if health care providers know that you are consulting a lawyer, they will generally be more responsive to your arguments. Richard's legal background and lawyerly profile served him well in his dealings with the nursing home. The issue of cost must be faced squarely. It is one thing to scrape together all one's resources in an effort to save the life of a loved one or to give them a few more years or even months of reasonable existence. But when, as in Jacqueline's case, the patient is permanently unconscious and can derive no benefit from further treatment—treatment that the patient herself rejected— then it becomes necessary to question why we should risk serious financial loss or even bankruptcy for unwanted and futile medical care. And make no mistake about it, the costs of life-prolonging care can be extravagant.

For example, Jacqueline's tube-fed vegetative existence in the nursing home was billed at the rate of $55,000 per year. Assuming that she might have been sustained for ten more years in an unconscious state, the total bill would have exceeded half a million dollars! Because Richard had successfully sued the trucking company responsible for Jacqueline's tragic accident, he did not have to pay for Jacqueline's treatment. However, had Richard lost his lawsuit, he would have been personally responsible for the full amount. Like most of us, he had no nursing home or long-term-care insurance. And

Jacqueline would not qualify for Medicaid because her husband was well off. So Richard would have had to pay $55,000 a year out of his pocket. It would be unrealistic for someone even as successful as Richard to be able to sustain this kind of expense for long. He might have had to divorce Jacqueline —a suggestion made by one of his lawyer colleagues before Richard won his lawsuit—in order to free himself from financial liability for Jacqueline's care. Richard found even the thought of such an act deeply upsetting. On the other hand, it might have come down to a question of trading off his feelings of loyalty to his beloved wife for the financial security and well-being of his children. Fortunately Richard was spared from making such an agonizing choice.

Jacqueline's tube feeding was expensive, but so are other other life-sustaining technologies. According to the 1987 congressional report from the Office of Technology Assessment, called "Life-Sustaining Technologies and the Elderly," the cost of hemodialysis averaged $25,000 per year, and mechanical ventilation, or a respirator such as Barbara had, was billed anywhere between $21,000 and $216,000 per year. These costs are significantly higher today because the congressional figures were based on data from 1985. In addition, a stay in the intensive care unit of a hospital, where Jacqueline first went, averages about $2,500 a day. And many private insurance policies will only cover 80 percent of this charge, leaving a substantial amount that patients must pay. Again, it bears repeating that we are talking about the high cost of life-sustaining technologies that are futile because they can have no effect on the underlying condition of the patient. Whether Richard paid $10 or $10,000,000, this money would not have changed Jacqueline's prognosis or improved the quality of her life in any way. But it could have had a catastrophic effect on Richard's life and the future of his children. Thus there would have been a double tragedy: the prolonged, artificially sustained "life" of a loved one who is irreversibly ill and beyond all human contact, receiving treatment against her wishes; and potential economic disaster for her loving but helpless family. You need to plan ahead and protect yourself and your loved ones from a similar fate.

The bottom line is that all of us have the fundamental right, insofar as possible, to determine our medical fate, which includes the right to refuse life-sustaining treatment. There is a powerful legal, medical, and ethical consensus regarding this right. To protect ourselves and our loved ones from receiving futile and unwanted treatment at the end of our lives, and from paying the often exorbitant costs of this high-technology care, we should all execute a living will and wherever possible, a durable power of attorney for health care.

It is important to remember that *even if we do not have these documents, we still have the rights they uphold*. But living wills and DPAHCs simplify the process of getting the law to work for us and strengthen our position at the end of our lives. They give us back control over our bodies—over what can and can't be done to us. And they enlist everyone else around us—from the health care institution to the doctor, nurse, social worker, friend, or family member—as part of the support team responsible for making sure our wishes are carried out. Jacqueline's ambivalence prevented her from filling out a living will—and cost her and her family dearly. We cannot afford this ambivalence, emotionally or financially. But we can protect ourselves and our families with these two vital documents.

CHAPTER NINE

Financial Planning for Your Health Care: How to Protect Yourself and Your Family

At age sixty-eight, after working hard all his life, Ralph retired from running his own hardware store. He had savings of $165,000. He owned his own home, had low overhead, and received a modest income from social security. He looked forward to a pleasant retirement and a chance to pursue his hobby, rebuilding old cars. Then when he was seventy-one, Ralph's wife, Annette, developed Alzheimer's disease. Ralph had his own medical problems, including a back condition that flared up now and then. One day while trying to help his wife out of the bathtub, he injured his back severely. Ralph needed help, but a home attendant for Annette would not be covered by Medicare. Eventually, when Ralph could no longer care for Annette, she had to enter a nursing home. The annual bill for Annette's nursing home care was nearly $40,000. After three years, Ralph's entire savings were eaten up.

Annette now qualified for Medicaid benefits, but not before Ralph's nest egg was destroyed. He was impoverished. Along with the bank account he had labored so hard to accumulate, Ralph lost his pride and sense of independence. A hard working, self-reliant man who had always paid his own way and supported his family, Ralph now faced the possibility of living on government handouts and borrowing money from his children. He was ashamed. When his chronic back problem grew worse, and pressure on his spine caused weakness in his legs, Ralph was almost ready to kill himself. He had never been suicidal or even depressed, but his economic humiliation, coupled with some health problems and his wife's deteriorating condition, made him feel it was not worth struggling any longer. Why had he worked so hard if it could all be so easily taken away from him?

Medicaid is the closest thing we have to national health insurance for long-term care, but in the words of health economist James Knickman, "it has one unfortunate feature—a deductible equal to your life savings." Clearly, financial planning for your health care is just as important as having an advance directive. Not only do you need to prepare for the cost of unexpected health problems, but you need to protect your loved ones for whom your assets are intended.

As we age, there is a growing likelihood that we will need assistance in our daily living. If we continue to live at home, we may need to hire a housekeeper or health care worker to help us. While most people over sixty-five years of age are able to carry on their activities without assistance, the older we get the more help we are likely to need. For those of us who reach the age of eighty-five, the vast majority, nearly 80 percent, will *not* spend our last days in a nursing home. However, a larger proportion will obtain nursing home care at least temporarily. A recent study estimated that for people who turned sixty-five in 1990, 43 percent will spend at least some time in a nursing home in the future, a higher projection than previous studies have made. There are many alternatives to nursing home care, but most are costly. And many of us do not live near children or other close family members who could assist us. For those of us who do, we may be reluctant or unwilling to depend on them for help. For those of us who will require nursing home care, someone must bear the cost.

How can we be sure we will get help? If we require assistance at home or in a nursing home, who will pay? What if we have a catastrophic illness and need to spend months in a hospital—who pays? Is a nursing home the only alternative? How will we be able to take care of ourselves if our mental abilities fail, as in Alzheimer's disease, or if we develop a physical disability?

How can we qualify for Medicaid and still leave money to our children? Should we buy long-term-care health insurance for our later years?

In the previous chapter, we discussed extreme end-of-life situations, such as Jacqueline's, where medical treatment can do nothing for patients who are past the point of recovery—yet the costs for this unwanted treatment are enormous. There are other situations, however, where both health care and social support *are* needed for us as we grow old, but paying for these services can also be financially debilitating unless we plan ahead. The need to be prepared financially and to set up a plan of care for our later years has become so acute that it has even spawned a new name: *life planning*. Just as estate planning is a way for us to dispose of our property and other assets through a will and to keep inheritance taxes to a minimum, life planning involves planning for a better quality of life as we age through wise management of our affairs.

This chapter addresses the practical side of health care for you or your loved ones when you are old or seriously ill: how to plan ahead and ensure financial security for the end of life. These issues are as important as any covered in this book, yet many of us feel awkward or guilty about discussing them. When the life of someone we love is at stake, it may seem selfish or disrespectful to be thinking about money or the amount of time and emotion we have to invest in their care. And when it comes to ourselves and our mortality, be it through illness, injury, or old age, most of us simply prefer not to think about the subject at all. When we do, we almost all agree we wouldn't want to be a burden to others and leave it at that.

Yet it is precisely for these reasons that we need to plan

ahead and prepare ourselves *now* for such eventualities. After all, our economic situation determines the context of much of our lives: where we are born, live, go to school, marry, work, raise our children, take our vacations, retire. It is only natural and fitting then that these same considerations should inform the end of our lives: where we grow old or sick and finally die, and the kind of legacy we leave behind us. Just as we need to plan for purchasing a first home, paying our children's college tuition, or retiring comfortably, so we need to act responsibly and prepare financially for our last years and the loved ones we will leave behind. If we do not, the one thing we can be sure of is that these realities will overtake us when we are at our most naked and vulnerable. And they may prove tragically costly, in both human and financial terms.

Hospitalization

In 1965, Medicare, the federal health insurance for the elderly, promised to solve some of the burdens that older Americans and people with certain disabilities would face. Because of Medicare, Ralph, like many of his contemporaries, assumed he was fully covered when his wife became seriously ill. Medicare Part A provides insurance for hospitalization, and Part B covers insurance for outpatient care, including doctor's visits. For most people, Medicare coverage exists automatically—you will receive your Medicare card as soon as you turn sixty-five and start to receive your social security benefits. But you will have to pay a monthly premium—about $30—in order to receive Part B coverage. Also, not everyone over the age of sixty-five qualifies for Medicare Part A or Part B. Only people who have themselves, or through their spouses, contributed to the social security system during their work years will qualify. If you are one of the few older people who may have to apply for these benefits, you should contact a social worker, senior resource center, or local agency on aging. The *Medicare Handbook* is available from the United States Department of Health and Human Services (see Appendix). This book discusses in easily understandable language all the things that Medicare does and does not cover.

When you retire, make sure that your company's health insurance policy can be continued so that you are not left without private insurance coverage. Some large companies will continue to provide coverage, but in most cases you will have to pay for it yourself. Most importantly, make sure that you are still insured. Before you leave your job, schedule an appointment with an experienced person in the department of personnel or benefits to find out what coverage is available to you after retirement, how much you will have to pay, and what you will need if you are already eligible for Medicare.

Medicare provides generous hospitalization benefits, but there are important limitations you should know about so you can plan ahead. Medicare will pay a significant proportion of your bill if you become ill and need to be hospitalized. However, unless you have private health insurance to pay for the amount or "gap" that Medicare does not cover, you could still be stuck with a large bill. For example, under Medicare today, you are required to pay a deductible of nearly $660 for your hospitalization and a copayment of $163 per day for a hospitalization that lasts more than two months and $326 per day for the next three to five months. Fortunately the average hospitalization is only six days, and for people over sixty-five the average stay is still only nine days.

About 90 percent of older Americans purchase insurance to cover these "gaps" in Medicare coverage. "Medigap" insurance can be purchased from a private insurance agent, but exercise care and be prepared to comparison shop. You can get a pamphlet explaining more about supplemental insurance, "Guide to Health Insurance for People with Medicare," by calling the Medicare Hotline (see Appendix). If you belong to a prepaid health plan such as a health maintenance organization (HMO) that accepts Medicare, Medigap insurance is usually not needed to cover hospitalization received through that plan. Before you purchase Medigap insurance, check to see what the hospitalization coverage through your prepaid plan is.

Medicare recipients who are slightly above the poverty line and do not quite qualify for Medicaid benefits are eligible to receive a "Qualified Medicare Beneficiary Benefit." This Medicare benefit covers the copayment and deductible for hospitalization and physician's outpatient services, as well as the monthly premium you must pay in order to receive Part B coverage. Families USA Foundation, a Washington-based advocacy group, calls this "the secret benefit" because presently the government does not publicize it. You may need to contact your local welfare office or Public Department of Social Services (*even though you are not a welfare recipient*) to apply for this benefit. A qualified social worker or health care attorney in your community may have additional information about applying. Do not hesitate to look into this benefit if you think you qualify. This benefit is similar to the coverage that you would receive if you purchased Medigap insurance privately.

If you are a veteran, you will probably be fully covered for any and all hospitalization costs as long as you obtain care in the Veterans Administration hospital system. However, if you wish to obtain some or all of your care elsewhere, you should be aware of the same insurance options as a nonveteran.

Medicare will not cover more than a maximum of 150 days in the hospital, and it will not cover everything even during this time. In the event of "catastrophic illness" that requires a hospitalization lasting for several months, there is a chance that neither Medicare nor private hospitalization insurance will provide adequate coverage. It is important to emphasize that only about 2 percent of Americans actually fall prey to a catastrophic illness that requires such prolonged hospitalization. Nevertheless, if you are one of the unfortunate few, these costs can be exorbitant. If you have private health insurance, read your policy carefully to determine the extent of your coverage. You may have extended hospitalization benefits, or you may be able to purchase this coverage, either through your employer—at a reduced rate—or on your own. If a health insurance policy premium (whether for ordinary or for catastrophic coverage) is too expensive, you can lower your annual premium by taking a higher deductible—e.g., you are responsible for the first $1,000 or more of hospitalization in case you need it, but if you don't, your premiums are more affordable. Once again, the average hospital stay for people of all ages is brief, and even those with a terminal illness—including those whom we have met in this book—rarely require five months of hospitalization. In the vast majority of cases, Medicare coverage with Medigap insurance is adequate if you are sixty-five or older. The same is true if you are under sixty-five and have full hospitalization insurance. If your income and assets are so low that you qualify for Medicaid, hospitalizations are fully covered, no matter how long they last.

Home Care

As we grow older, many of us become less proficient in caring for our needs. At some point we may need help with activities of daily living. Ideally we can get services delivered to our home, where the disruption to our lives is reduced and we can continue to function in a familiar and supportive environment. This is especially true if a family member or close friend can act as a primary caregiver and assist in our care.

Many services are available at home, including hospice care, discussed in Chapter Seven. Other services include homemaker assistance such as help with shopping, meal preparation, or other chores; home health care such as nursing, physical, and occupational therapy; or personal care such as assistance with bathing, feeding, or dressing. A variety of private organizations and public agencies provide home care. "Visiting nurse associations" now exist in most localities. Many hospitals also provide home health care, as do an increasing number of commercial for-profit agencies. If you want to check the references of a home health care group, the two main accrediting organizations are the Joint Commission on the Accreditation of Health Care Organizations (JCAHCO) and the National League for Nursing (see Appendix). Also, if a home care agency participates in Medicare, that means it has passed governmental inspection in order to be qualified. Other community services such as adult day-care centers and home-delivered meals (Meals on Wheels) may also be available, depending on where you live. You can get more information from your area agency on aging, senior resource center, or family service agency. Religious organizations such as Catholic Charities or Jewish community centers are particularly helpful and provide nondenominational care. You can also make inquiries through your hospital's department of social work, or your state's Department of Social Services or Department of Human Services.

Unfortunately, Medicare pays for home care services only in a limited number of circumstances. Medicare will cover part of the cost of durable medical equipment prescribed by a physician, such as a wheelchair, walker, or hospital bed. It will also cover intermittent nurse visits, physical and other forms of therapy, but only if you have an illness requiring skilled nursing or restorative physical or speech therapy, and only for a limited time—namely, as you recover from an acute illness. For example, Medicare will cover the cost of a visiting nurse if you were recently hospitalized for severe diabetes and now require assistance in learning to monitor your blood sugar and to take your insulin. It will pay for a physical therapist, visiting nurse, and home health aide if you are recovering from a hip fracture and require physical therapy or nursing care for a pressure sore on your skin. However, if you or a loved one have Alzheimer's disease but are otherwise healthy, or if you had a stroke but are not expected to recover further, Medicare will *not* pay for any services that you might need, unless an additional problem occurred. It is important to know that Medicare does not cover the cost of most medications that you take on a regular basis, nor does it cover meals delivered to your home, or homemaker services. And while Medicare covers visits to the doctor at any time, it presently pays such a small amount for a doctor's home visit (less than it pays for other skilled services) that most doctors will not take the time required to make routine home visits. Although Medicare patients enrolled in hospice programs receive generous benefits, most people requiring long-term care at home (i.e., not for illness, but for "custodial care") will have to find other means. You should check with a qualified social worker to find out if your condition entitles you to Medicare benefits at home and if there is a home health agency in your community that provides these services and is approved by Medicare. If you are a veteran, you may be eligible and covered for an array of home care services.

Most private insurance policies do not cover home care. However, this may be negotiable. According to Ernest Morgan, author of *Dealing Creatively with Death*, "Some insurance companies will cover home care services not mentioned in the policy—if you can demonstrate that they will save money by avoiding hospital or nursing home care." On the whole, though, neither standard private insurance nor Medicare will cover home care services. But you may discover a wealth of "informal support" that will help you to remain at home—the kindness of family, friends, neighbors, religious organizations, or other volunteers. This kind of care can be very significant, if it is properly planned and supervised. For example, another man in Ralph's situation provided his spare bedroom to a middle-aged widow rent-free, in exchange for her help in caring for his wife, who suffered from Alzheimer's disease. In this way, he not only saved several years of nursing-home bills, but he provided his wife with a familiar and more supportive environment. Such personal arrangements, combined with a resourceful use of community services, may enable you or your loved ones to receive care at home for extended periods of time. They would have been of immeasurable help to Ralph, who owned his own home and had several unused bedrooms. Ralph could easily have accommodated a live-in helper.

Ralph could also have exercised an option that has become attractive to many people who own their own home—a reverse annuity mortgage. In this arrangement, a homeowner negotiates with the bank to receive a fixed dollar amount per month (say, $1,000) with the house as collateral. When you die, the bank is paid from your assets or from the sale of your house. One obvious disadvantage of this approach is that it may prevent your heirs from inheriting your home. Another option you may choose is to sell your house at market value to a person who agrees to rent it to you until your death. This arrangement may provide you with a large amount of capital to meet your needs but obviously the house is no longer part of your estate. Some people may also feel uncomfortable with the idea of giving up ownership and living as a tenant in their former home. But if you decide this arrangement is right for you, make sure to consult a qualified attorney before signing a contract.

Nursing Homes

When the wide variety of outpatient and community services are inadequate for your care needs, or when your family can no longer bear the physical and emotional cost of caring for you at home, a nursing home may be the best solution. The thought of going to a nursing home fills many of us with fear and dread. Yet there are many fine nursing homes in the country, and due to close governmental supervision, they are getting better. However, before choosing a nursing home, you or a family member should do some research. Ask for personal references from your friends, your physician, or a qualified social worker. You should also visit and ask for a tour of the facility. Make an effort to talk with other residents or family members to get their frank opinion about the quality of the staff and the overall quality of life of the residents. Find out what activities and amenities are offered. The American Association of Homes for the Aging (AAHA) and the American Association of Retired Persons (AARP) provide useful information about many nursing homes nationally (see Appendix). The People's Medical Society publishes *How to Evaluate and Select a Nursing Home*, which can answer many of your questions.

Nursing homes are designed for people who need assistance in their activities of daily living and who may also have medical needs. In a nursing home, nursing and medical care is provided on-site, unless you develop a sudden illness that would require temporary hospitalization. Meals are provided in your room, or in a communal dining room, and friends and family can generally bring food in from the outside. If you need assistance in bathing and dressing, this will be provided. Many levels of care are provided in nursing homes, depending on the type that is appropriate for you. The nursing home may devote a separate wing or floor to those requiring the greatest amount of assistance, for example, those with severe Alzheimer's disease, and another wing for those who are fairly independent, for example, people with severe arthritis who have difficulty walking or getting in and out of the bathtub, but can dress, do their own hand laundry, and feed themselves. All nursing homes provide around-the-clock skilled nursing care, and have a medical director who is a physician and who directs other doctors providing care to patients. Simple medical care that does not require daily physician presence is usually provided in the nursing home itself, and a doctor is available on call to provide medical treatment of simple illness, such as a mild infection or a slight worsening of a diabetic condition. But if you become seriously ill and require medical care of a sophisticated nature—for example, a surgical procedure or treatment with intravenous antibiotics —you may be offered care at a nearby hospital. If this happens, Medicare may pay for part of your nursing home care on your return, for up to one hundred days, if, for example, you now required skilled nursing care or rehabilitation because of the illness for which you were hospitalized.

However, and contrary to popular belief, Medicare does *not* normally pay for routine nursing home care. Medicare Part B will cover a doctor's essential nursing home visits, as though you were living in your own home. But it pays for other facets of nursing home care only if you are suffering from a disease that requires a high level of daily skilled nursing care, *and* if you were admitted directly from a hospital where you were being treated for that condition. Once your medical condition has stabilized, the care that you receive is no longer considered "skilled"—despite the fact that skill is involved in providing daily assistance to people—and Medicare will no longer pay.

Most standard medical-insurance policies do not pay for nursing home care either. Nursing home care averages about $30,000 per year, and in some parts of the country this cost can be three times as high. It is easy to determine how fast your savings will be depleted at that rate. If your annual income is near or below the poverty level, the government does offer you another option—Medicaid, which is health insurance for the poor. Presently, if your personal income and your total savings, including stocks and bonds (but usually *not* including your home), are below a level specified by the state where you live, you may qualify for Medicaid. This type of insurance is managed by a partnership of the federal government and the government of your particular state, and *benefits and specific criteria to qualify vary, depending on where you live.* Medicaid, more generous to patients than Medicare, covers practically any type of medical expense, including hospitalization, medical equipment, medications, and nursing home expenses. Because your children are not legally responsible to pay for your health care, you may still qualify for this type of insurance even if your children are financially comfortable. If your spouse is living, however, he or she may be held responsible for a large proportion of these costs, and his or her savings may be eaten away while your care is being paid for—which is what happened to Ralph when his wife became ill. Fortunately, Medicaid regulations have changed in recent years to protect a portion of the resources of the "healthy" spouse, who, like Ralph, may himself or herself be elderly and not in perfect health. You should consult a qualified professional, such as a specialized health care lawyer, an identified individual in your local agency on aging or senior resource center, or a social worker, to find out the dollar amount of asset protection in your state.

Remember that Medicaid does not kick in automatically, even if you fall below the required income level. A large number of the elderly poor are not covered by Medicaid, although most would certainly be considered "medically needy" and would qualify. You *have to apply* for Medicaid; the process may take several months of diligent effort and may lead to some aggravation, but it is well worth it in the end. If you or a loved one is likely to qualify, it is important to look into this immediately.

No one wants to live at the poverty level, but if your financial situation places you even only slightly above that level, you are on your own when it comes to health care costs beyond the limited amount that Medicare pays for. Therefore, it is really important for you to plan ahead. You may wish to consider some of the long-term-care insurance policies that have become available in the event you or a loved one may need nursing home or home care. Long-term-care insurance policies may end up being of major help to you, but *they vary greatly in their benefits, they are very expensive, and they are not always cost-effective.* The older you are when you buy such a policy, the more expensive it will be. If you wait until you are seventy-five, the policy will most likely cost you $3,000 or more per year. If you or a close family member is currently employed, check to see if such a policy is available through work; however, while it may be cheaper than if you purchase it directly through an insurance agent, group coverage may have other drawbacks that you should look into. Some careful arithmetic will tell you whether the policy you are investigating is a good investment at your age and in your current state of health. But it is important to ask specific questions: Is there inflation protection? How much of the daily bill will still be left for you to pay? Are home care benefits included? What restrictions are there on the benefits? For example, will you be covered only if you are admitted to the nursing home directly from a hospital, or will it cover you under *all* circumstances? What diseases are *not* covered? For example, some insurance policies may not cover care for Alzheimer's disease, and because many people with this condition will eventually receive nursing home care, in most cases it would not be wise to purchase a policy that excluded that disease.

Long-term-care insurance policies may be useful if your income is high because you are not likely to spend down to a level where you would qualify for Medicaid. These policies might be less important if you have limited means and would qualify for Medicaid after a few months of living in a nursing home. However, there is no general rule that applies in all cases.

There are other creative ways to gather the resources to pay for long-term care, whether in a nursing home or your own home. Some insurance companies offer you the option to trade in your life insurance policy for long-term health care. For example, you may be able to cash in your life insurance benefits to pay for your care if a physician has certified that you have less than six months to live, or if you have been a resident in a nursing home for more than six months and are considered highly unlikely ever to leave. You can inquire about this type of option from your state's Department of Insurance or your insurance agent. And depending on where you live, you may be able to "spend down" to the Medicaid level; there may be ways to do this and still protect your assets for your heirs. Many of these options are discussed below.

An Alternative: Life Care Communities

In recent years alternative housing and community services for senior citizens have proliferated. Nearly every community has a local office on aging or senior resource center that can provide information about existing choices. Retirement communities, "congregate housing" with assistance on-site and "life care" communities are some of the newer concepts in residential alternatives that are growing in popularity.

"Life care" (also called continuing care or total care) communities are an important option for people who want to be near health care services late in life. In a life care community, you may have to pay a substantial amount of money up front in exchange for membership in the community, where you take possession of a private home or apartment and live independently. In addition to the entrance fee, which may be partly refundable, there is a monthly fee. The community offers a variety of services, including medical care, meals, and activities. Depending on the specific community, there may also be sponsored tours, beauty treatments, storage facilities, a game room, and a variety of other offerings. In this setting, you have the opportunity to prepare and eat your meals in your own home and enjoy as much privacy as you desire, or you can take one or more meals in a dining room with other residents in a pleasant social setting. Medical care is available on-site and is paid for by the cost of joining, no matter how long you live or what the extent of your future medical care may turn out to be. If you become ill, direct meal service to your home may be available. However, your home is your castle; you can invite guests and family members as you wish. If you require assistance with your daily living, you may be permitted to hire an outside caregiver to assist you if that is your preference or if the organization's assistance is not sufficient. Or you can be admitted to an infirmary on-site, which is licensed as a nursing home, and receive needed care there. Because the infirmary is located within the community, you will receive visitors who live close by, and of course, your family members are permitted to visit. Although a life care community can be costly, once you buy into the community by paying an entrance fee, there are few extra charges above and beyond your monthly maintenance charges and extra food or other services that you wish to purchase on your own. Most important, you will have the security of knowing that long-term care is guaranteed.

Life care communities are sprouting up all across the country, and it is likely that one is near you. The extent of the included services varies, depending on the community, and it is important to find out what the charges are, what is included, what is extra, and what type of medical care is included in the cost. Is medical care available or nearby twenty-four hours a day? Is there a nurse on-site at all times? Is there an infirmary or nursing home on-site and is care there included in the cost? Most life care communities will not accept you once you are seriously ill or can no longer fend for yourself—or might only accept you for a higher fee—although if this happens *after* you join, care will be provided. So you need to plan ahead and not wait until the last possible moment. To find out about life care communities, you should contact a social worker or senior resource center in your community. To find out about life care communities in another part of the country where you might want to live, you should contact the AAHA, which has information on nonprofit housing around the country and is updating its *National Continuing Care Directory*, which lists life care communities along with the services they provide and the costs. The AARP may also be able to provide information. These organizations are listed in the Appendix.

Spending Down for Long-term Care

Life care communities are an excellent solution for many people who want to feel physically secure in late life. However, the amount of money required up front—$30,000 to $100,000 or more, depending on the types of services, whether it is for-profit or nonprofit, and the geographic location—may be more than you can afford. Many people are not affluent enough for the life care solution and are not poor enough to qualify for Medicaid, which would offer the coverage you seek if you needed nursing home care. If you, like many middle-income people, feel caught in the middle, there may still be a solution available—"spending down" in order to qualify for Medicaid benefits if you should ever need them.

If your resources are eaten up by home care or nursing home costs, you may find yourself among the "medically needy" who qualify for Medicaid benefits. However, you may feel that if you have worked hard all your life and saved your money for retirement, for health care, and for your loved ones, you should not have your life savings eaten away because of a devastating illness. Rather, you yourself should be able to receive the benefit of the tax dollars you have provided during your working years. There is presently no national health insurance that covers people caught "in the middle." For this reason, growing numbers of people have found ways to spend down *prior* to becoming ill. In this way, they can protect their assets for their heirs.

One way to make sure that something is left for your loved ones in the event that you become seriously ill, is to start transferring your assets to them ahead of time. Many people do this in order to reduce the size of their estate and thereby protect their heirs from having to pay excessive amounts of inheritance tax. However, transfer of assets can also protect your legacy from being depleted if you suffer an unexpected but devastating illness. Presently you are allowed to give a major gift to someone as part of the spend-down process. However, not everyone is comfortable with the idea of giving up personal control of their assets. There is always the chance you will *not* become ill and may want to keep the money for yourself. If you give your money to your child, he or she may spend it or even die before you do.

One way to retain some control of your assets is to set up an "irrevocable trust." In this type of arrangement you assign any amount of money to another trusted individual, usually a family member. The gift is "irrevocable," which means that it can never be returned to you, although you will be able to receive interest income from the trust as long as you are alive. If you have given away enough of your assets, you may be able to qualify for Medicaid if and when you should need it. During the time that you are covered by Medicaid, you cannot receive income from the trust; rather that income will go directly to Medicaid. However, the government cannot take the principal from the trustee because it now belongs to the trustee, and not to you. Even with an irrevocable trust some people may feel uncomfortable because they themselves are no longer in charge of their assets. An alternative in this case might be to set up a convertible trust, which allows you to retain control of your assets while you are well but which converts to an irrevocable trust as soon as you enter a nursing home.

In most cases, you do not have to give up your home in order to qualify for Medicaid, regardless of how much it is presently worth. In some situations, the house may still go to your heirs after your death. But you should know that you have to wait for up to thirty months after transferring any assets at all before you can receive benefits from Medicaid. Therefore, it is important for you to plan these things in advance. They cannot be done at the last minute, and they cannot be done if you are mentally incompetent. Therefore if you or a loved one have an illness that may eventually lead to incompetence, you must act soon. Because it is difficult for someone who is ill to admit they may *ever* become incompetent, you may have to assist them in planning ahead.

It is important to remember that the fifty states vary greatly in the details of their Medicaid regulations. If you wish to transfer your assets for *any* reason, it is essential that you do this in conjunction with a reputable attorney, particularly one who specializes in trusts and estates, in health care law, or in "elder law," and who fully understands the regulations in your state. You can find such an attorney by contacting the Alzheimer's Association in your area (see Appendix), or your local bar association.

Other Ways to Cut Your Health Care Costs

There are other things that you should be aware of if you are ill. Medication can be very expensive. If you are in your seventies or older, it is possible that your doctor has prescribed one or more medications for you to take on a daily basis, and it is not unusual for monthly medication bills to total $100 or much more. Medicare pays little or nothing for medication. Medicaid, on the other hand, does pay for most if not all the medication your doctor prescribes. It is important for you to check to see what prescription costs are covered by your health insurance. If you or a family member are employed, you should find out if your health care benefits include a prescription program. Company pension plans may still provide health insurance after retirement, and prescriptions may be covered. If you are not covered, ask your pharmacist how much the prescription will cost *before* you purchase it. In many cases you will be able to purchase a cheaper generic brand of the same medication at a considerable savings. In other cases, your physician may be able to prescribe an alternative drug for the same ailment but at a much lower cost. One patient paid $45 per month for her blood-pressure medication (captopril), but when she complained to her doctor, he switched her to another one that fortunately was just as effective for her (hydrochlorothiazide), and it cost only $1.99. Physicians are usually unaware of specific prescription costs. Make sure you inform your doctor if you experience "sticker shock" at the drugstore! There may be a cost-saving alternative.

Cost containment is possible if you have a common disease that requires commonly prescribed medication or simple techniques. However, if you are being treated for a rare or complicated illness, or a procedure such as a transplant that requires expensive medication, costs can be prohibitive. You should find out in advance if your insurance policy covers the costs of your disease or the medications that you will require. If you do not already have insurance coverage, it may be difficult to obtain it. In many states there is an insurance "pool" that covers the person who is at high risk of getting sick—for example, someone with a history of a heart attack or who has been treated for cancer of an internal organ in the past. In some states, Blue Cross and Blue Shield plans are "open" and will insure all comers, regardless of age or diagnosis. Costs may be higher if you are a "high risk" patient, and you may have to wait longer for your policy to come through than in other situations. If you already have a serious illness but are not insured, you should check with your state's department of health or with the state's insurance department to find out what kind of coverage is available.

If you have a serious illness and find that your insurance coverage is inadequate, it is important to remember that *being uninsured does not mean that you will be unserved*. Health care is presently available to everyone. Most if not all hospitals will care for you in an emergency even if you have no health insurance and if there is no immediate or practical alternative. They will do this either for humane reasons or in order to protect themselves from liability. Unfortunately, since the beginning of government-funded health care in 1965, the American health professions' commitment to provide a portion of its time to "charity" cases has gradually lessened. If your means are limited, you may need to be very creative in nonemergency situations. Diseases that are undergoing active research can often be treated in special clinics at teaching hospitals. Many public and university hospitals are teaching hospitals, in which part of your care is given by M.D.'s who are not students but are still receiving training—interns, residents, and specialty fellows. It is often possible to find an excellent doctor among these young people, and their supervisors are often highly skilled and well-known specialists. If your care is being provided by one of these doctors-in-training, you should make sure that he or she has adequate supervision. If you are dissatisfied with your care, ask to switch to another doctor, and if this fails, speak to the hospital's patient representative. If you wish, you can ask to be seen by the attending physician. Costs may be lower in teaching institutions, and excellent, up-to-date care is generally given. Remember that many people travel great distances to receive care in private teaching hospitals. Usually the same doctors give or supervise care to patients in less expensive rooms or in a nearby public teaching hospital.

Many patients with cancer, AIDS, and diseases requiring transplants or other sophisticated treatments can receive care as part of a scientific study. You should ask your primary care doctor or specialist if studies are being undertaken near you. If you are enrolled in a scientific trial testing a new medication or technique, it is likely that you will not be charged at all. Often, additional care only peripherally related to the scientific study is given at no extra charge, officially or unofficially. For example, a patient receiving an experimental medication for AIDS may be receiving this through a clinic in a public hospital but will be able to receive other medications at the same pharmacy at low cost. Likewise, when the patient visits the doctor conducting the study, he or she may be able to address other medical questions related to the disease. The doctor, nurse, or other health care professional may often help you even if the visit was not intended for that reason. Don't hesitate to ask for this kind of help. You may be pleasantly surprised.

Diseases that are undergoing active research and for which care may be available include cancer, AIDS, Alzheimer's disease, multiple sclerosis, kidney, heart, or liver failure requiring transplants, lupus, diabetes, and many, many others. To find out about specialty clinics and research protocols near you, you should check with national or local organizations interested in these diseases, with a medical school in your area, or with government-funded research bodies such as the National Institutes of Health or the Centers for Disease Control (see Appendix). Always ask about cost in advance.

The best insurance of all is to get good preventive care. Although there is never any guarantee, a dollar of prevention may be worth thousands in health care costs. Margot, the retiree with an odd-looking spot on her forearm in Chapter Two, hesitated to visit her doctor sooner because she was afraid of what the doctor would find. But others in her situation put off a doctor's visit because they fear the cost. One man delayed visiting the doctor because he was afraid he would not be able to afford the doctor's fee. Tragically, he waited so long that, like Margot, his cancer spread throughout his body and became incurable. He was uninsured and his health care costs were so great that his family suffered serious financial loss. Don't ever hesitate to check up on something that might be curable. Go to the doctor; pay now or you may pay much more later—you might pay with your life and the happiness of your loved ones.

Remember that in order to get the best health care for yourself and your family, you need to plan for your financial needs. Just as advance directives help you assert your legal right to control your body, financial planning enables you to control the quantity and quality of the care you receive. Many of the fears and anxieties you may have about growing old or sick can be allayed by wise management of your affairs. You need to plan carefully and shrewdly for your later years and to consult with experts in the field. By establishing financial security for your long-term and terminal care, you can maintain control over your life and ensure that you continue to receive the best care available without jeopardizing the lives of others. You can also protect your assets for your loved ones and leave behind the legacy that you want.

CHAPTER TEN

Expressing Your Feelings about Death: Coming to Terms with the Emotional Pain

Do not go gentle into that good night,
Old age should burn and rave at close of day;
Rage, rage against the dying of the light.

—Dylan Thomas

Intellectually, each of us knows he or she will die. But the news that death is imminent—that our time has actually run out—is almost impossible to assimilate. We can only take it in, if at all, a little bit at a time. The mind resists contemplating its own extinction. Psychiatrists have long pointed out that it is impossible for our unconscious to accept the actual ending of our life. When we think of our dying, we must attribute it to some external, evil force. As Elizabeth Kubler-Ross writes in her pioneering work *On Death and Dying:* "In simple terms, in our unconscious mind we can only be killed; it is inconceivable to die of a natural cause or of old age. Therefore death itself is associated with a bad act, a frightening happening, something that in itself calls for retribution and punishment." An unexpected diagnosis of a fatal illness is met with initial disbelief. "This could never happen to me." It is hard to accept that we can die from something inside ourselves. When we see death, if we see it at all, it comes to us from outside. "I'm only twenty-two. Why would anyone do this to me?" Jeanette cried when she first learned she had multiple sclerosis.

Our initial resistance to the news of a serious or terminal diagnosis—"No, not me. It cannot be true"—serves an important purpose. Denial is a useful mechanism because it allows us time to mobilize other defenses and sustain hope. By denying that death is waiting just around the corner, you can recover from the shock and go on with your life.

When Sam recovered from his first bout of AIDS-related pneumonia, his vast relief turned to high hopes that bordered on omnipotence. "They'll find a cure and I'll beat this disease, I know I will!" Sam exclaimed. By denying, or only partially accepting, his grim medical fate, Sam was able to carry on with his life and concentrate on its more hopeful aspects. He finished the first draft of a play and undertook several new projects in his last years. Of course, denial can also be excessive and counterproductive. Burt initially exaggerated and then hid from the true importance of his rectal bleeding. "Oh, God, it's cancer. No, there's nothing wrong with me. I'm A-okay," Burt tried to convince himself. By jumping to the wrong conclusion and then suppressing his fears about the bleeding, Burt caused himself great harm. If he had visited the doctor and undergone a thorough medical examination, instead of denying his anxiety and depression, his problems could have been solved much sooner.

Rachel, too, was in a state of shock and denial when she first heard she had breast cancer at the age of thirty-five. Her husband, Scott, watched her struggle with the news and went through his own process of denial. "One minute she was this healthy, happy wife and mother. Then suddenly her whole world was turned upside down. What would you do? Rachel went to another doctor for a second opinion and even agreed to extra tests. She thought if she just went to bed and forgot about the cancer, when she woke up in the morning, it would be gone. I remember how she would first open her eyes at dawn and adjust to the new light. She was begging for a reprieve, for a new beginning. So was I." When she could no longer deny she had cancer, Rachel concentrated her energies on undergoing treatment and being cured. "For two years, she held on to the hope that she would beat her illness and return to being the wife and mother she had been. We just tried to go on with our lives and do all the same things we used to do. Other women had recovered so why not Rachel?" Denial allowed Rachel to hope, and hope gave her a fighting chance to reverse her illness. When the doctor took away any further hope, Rachel came home in tears. "She told me the cancer was incurable, there was nothing more they could do. Then she went to bed and pretended to forget all about it. She didn't breathe a word to Adam, our son, or even to her parents. Whenever I tried to bring it up, she changed the subject. I knew she was in pain, physical as well as emotional, but she just kept it all bottled up inside her."

You can pretend at one moment that your death is not imminent, and then the next moment have an overpowering need to talk about it. Denial and acceptance coexist in an uneasy alliance, especially in the beginning. If a loved one or a health professional approaches at the wrong moment, you may ignore them or change the subject altogether. But eventually you are overcome by the need to share your thoughts and feelings about dying. "One night when we were watching television," said Scott, "Rachel suddenly turned the set off and turned to me: 'You realize I'm going to die. There's not much time left and there's so much we have to talk about.' " Scott was hit hard but relieved because he, too, needed to talk about Rachel's situation and what it was doing to their lives. Coming to terms with the emotional pain of dying is as important for the loved one as it is for the terminally ill person.

You may need to deal with a tremendous amount of anger, rage, and grief when you learn you are dying. Your life is about to be taken from you and you cannot understand why. What have you done to deserve this? A terminal diagnosis may unleash powerful, primitive feelings that you cannot control. "Why me?" Herman cried, overwhelmed by the injustice that he, who had helped so many and struggled to overcome the stereotype of being a male nurse, had developed AIDS from a needle stick. "So many healthy people take their life for granted. Why were they spared? Why was I singled out?" This sense of unfairness can seem especially pronounced when illness claims us at a high point in our lives, as with Dr. Quill's patient Diane, who had overcome many struggles and attained a new level of satisfaction in her life when she learned she had leukemia, or with Sam, whose work was just beginning to win recognition when he developed AIDS. But a serious or terminal diagnosis is *always unfair.* You've been told your life will come to an abrupt and unexpected end—through no act or fault of your own. When told she had the same disease that crippled her mother, Jeanette's reaction was: "What did I ever do to deserve multiple sclerosis! Don't I have the same right as everyone else to a normal life?" Jeanette shouted at Dr. Marshall. And neither Dr. Marshall nor anyone else could fully answer Jeanette's accusation. The most Dr. Marshall could do was listen sympathetically and allow Jeanette to express her outrage and bitterness before pointing to what she still had to live for. Jeanette needed to share her feelings and be understood, to know that someone besides herself recognized the unjustness of her fate.

You may burn with such resentment at a terminal diagnosis that you fantasize about trading places with someone else, offering them as a replacement or "sacrifice" for you. Even people whom you care about may be the targets of your ire and desperation. "Why should I die while my lover, who gave me AIDS, remains healthy and lives?" Sam thought at one point during his illness. And Barbara could not help wondering why her sister, also a lifelong smoker, had never developed the same problems with emphysema. "She was always the lucky one. Why couldn't this have happened to *her?*" Such thoughts, however unpleasant, can be a natural, transitory response to dying. They indicate how much we still value life and how desperate we are to find some way of saving ourselves, even at the expense of someone we love.

You might also want to blame others when you first hear

you are dying. The need to displace your grief, guilt, and anger may tempt you to seek human targets. Sometimes your closest relationships may come under fire. Blame may take many different forms, but its aim is usually the same: to find some explanation and excuse—and even a temporary escape —for a seemingly irrational fate. Jeanette was furious upon learning of her diagnosis. "It's *her* fault!" she cried, "My mother has given me multiple sclerosis." Dr. Marshall had carefully explained that multiple sclerosis was not simply passed on from one member of the family to the other. But it was only when Jeanette began reaching out to her daughter —who feared *she* would inherit multiple sclerosis from Jeanette—that she started to understand her ambivalence toward her own mother.

Burt's wife, Patricia, who developed ALS, at first blamed her husband's infidelity for creating the stress that led to her illness. "If he hadn't been fooling around behind my back, I could have beaten this thing. But now I just don't have the heart to go on." Patricia was so overwhelmed by the devastating news of her illness that she had to focus her rage on someone. Sam also had a target: "If the government spent more money on AIDS research—if it were an establishment disease, like polio—we'd have a cure in no time," he said bitterly. The issue of blame can become an especially complex and difficult one for many AIDS patients and chronic alcoholics where their lifestyle and habits could have played a significant role in their illness.

All of these people desperately needed to find something or someone to blame for their illness. They eventually moved beyond the blaming phase, but the accusations served as a temporary refuge for their anger, guilt, and despair before they accepted their dying. But sometimes it also caused real friction and left a mark on loved ones. Burt carried his wife's bitterness with him long after she died, and as he came to realize later, it contributed to his depression and attempted suicide. "I guess I always believed there was a kernel of truth in what she said. Maybe if I hadn't cheated on her, she wouldn't have got sick and died," he told Dr. Alvarez. "But ALS is a degenerative disease with no known psychological component. Her illness had nothing to do with your infidelity," Dr. Alvarez said. Burt was only partially convinced. "Well, both things hurt her and made her unhappy, didn't they?"

It is not uncommon to blame yourself instead of others and become convinced you are responsible for your illness. This is one way you may have of making sense out of a seemingly senseless fate and trying to rationalize the irrational. Even patients with Alzheimer's disease may appear to go through this process of rationalization. When Ruth began to have signs of Alzheimer's disease, she could grasp the fact that her mind was not as clear as it once was. "I'm so stupid," she would say at such times to her son, Mark. "It's because I dropped out of college to get married. I never finished my education and my mind has become too undisciplined." Mark did not accept this explanation, but it made Ruth feel better, as if her illness were related to the internal logic of her life.

A feeling of self-blame may be especially intense when someone you love has committed suicide. Because it is a voluntary and intentional act—and thus preventable, at least in theory—suicide taps into our deepest feelings of guilt and self-recrimination. "I didn't see the warning signs," Simone said of her husband's self-imposed death. "Harry was my responsibility, but I wasn't there when he needed me. Now I'm paying for my sins with cancer," the usually stoic Simone told herself. She had never resolved her guilt over Harry's death, and now it found a convenient spot to lodge. By blaming herself, Simone also maintained the illusion of control over a random, impersonal fate. She was not merely a victim, but an agent of her unhappiness. "If I had taken better care of Harry, I would never have gotten so sick." If it was Simone's fault, then at least her illness made some sense in terms of cause and effect. The need to seek explanations, even at your own expense, can be very tempting.

As we draw closer to death, we tend to review our lives and

draw up a kind of balance sheet. In the early phases especially, we may be overcome by a sense of failure and unfulfilled goals. We all harbor dreams and aspirations. Knowing that our allotted time is over makes us think about how much we have left undone. There is no more tomorrow, and hence no possibility of further achievement. "Scott and I can never have another child, as we planned," Rachel grieved. "And I won't live to see my son, Adam, grow up to be a man." Sam had hoped to see his play produced theatrically. "They'll have to discover my work after I die," he tried to console himself, but he was tormented by the sadness and loss of missed opportunities. And Jeanette, on track to be a vice president of her advertising company when her deteriorating condition led to her dismissal, was openly bitter. "I worked many years and long hours for this promotion. I earned it and now they've taken it away from me. My entire career has gone down the drain."

Sometimes a person confronted with a degenerative or terminal illness may veer from total denial to a sudden desire to bring death on directly, ahead of schedule. New York psychiatrist Jim Strain has described this impulse as a desire to "leave at intermission rather than stay through the last act." And so, most people facing imminent death have at one time or another considered suicide. It is one of the few options we have and seemingly one of the only ways to assert our control over an increasingly helpless situation. Individuals with terminal illness represent only a small fraction of suicides, and the majority of older people who kill themselves are not terminally ill. But thoughts of suicide are common when you are seriously ill or infirm.

Often, thinking about suicide, rather than acting upon it, serves as a useful outlet. It allows you to express and explore your anxiety about death and to give vent to sheer terror and despair. Scott watched his wife, Rachel, confront this abyss. "For a while Rachel just panicked. She realized she was going to die and there was nothing she could do about it. Nothing. So she started hoarding pills. It gave her a feeling of having some control over her death. And she was really scared about the pain. She didn't want to suffer." Eventually, Rachel came to terms with the fact she was dying. "The biggest thing was getting her fear of pain under control. Once she understood there was enough medication to relieve her pain, and that she could have it whenever she needed it, Rachel calmed down. She was able to think clearly and be herself. She talked with Rabbi Baum and he made her feel better about living her life right through to the end. To be honest, I think there was another reason that held her back from suicide. She was worried about the effect it would have on me and especially on Adam. She didn't want him growing up thinking his mother had abandoned him. She wanted to leave behind a positive memory of herself."

Sam did not have the same network of support as Rachel. His mother was perhaps his closest friend, and she notes, "Sam thought of life as a play you had to rehearse for. So when he found out he was dying of AIDS, the first thing he did was to get a special vial of pills. He got them through this friend, a chemist. Sam carried that bottle around with him wherever he went. It was his way of being prepared. At first I was going to throw the pills out, but I knew he could replace them. Those pills were his security blanket. As long as he knew they were there, he didn't need to use them. Sam wanted to live, not die. But he had suffered so much from his disease and he needed peace of mind. That's what those pills gave him. The courage to fight on."

Many physicians and other health experts caution that putting pills in the hands of suicidal patients is like handing them a loaded gun. It is a dangerous and potentially lethal "security blanket" that might not be necessary if people were more aware of other alternatives such as pain control, comfort care, treatment of depression, support groups. However, the security that Sam gained from knowing he had a way out in his possession was reassuring to him and points out how the fear of losing control can override all other considerations and renders us *more* susceptible, rather than less, to suicidal impulses. This is particularly true for those who suffer devastating diseases. Nevertheless, you should be fully aware of the dangers involved in keeping a private supply of drugs, or any other potentially deadly method close at hand. Even for those who feel especially strongly about the issue of control and who, like Sam, are not clinically depressed, this is a dangerous path to take because the temptation to use pills could become overwhelming in a moment of weakness. There are "safer" security blankets that Sam only later became aware of, such as the clear, written instructions about his care left for his parents. "He made us swear not to let him end hooked up to machines," Sam's mother said. "I believe that was his greatest fear. Not even the pain so much as the humiliation of being helpless. But he was brave in those final months because he knew he'd done everything possible and covered all the bases. And we were right there for him."

Feeling suicidal means you are in crisis, uncertain whether to live or die. Your conflict appears irreconcilable, and suicide seems like the only way to resolve it. The situation is dangerous but your very uncertainty also provides an opening: the opportunity for being convinced there is hope and you should carry on with your life. Jeanette sought Dr. Marshall's help in taking her life but was rebuffed. "I just turned her request down cold. Said no, I won't do it. I didn't become a physician to help people die. My job is to help people live. And Jeanette still had so much to live for." Dr. Marshall's faith and stubbornness helped Jeanette find new meaning in a life drastically impaired by disability but a life that still possessed much value. "The most important thing I did for Jeanette was help her get past the pain so she could see she still had choices to make. When she first came to me, she was truly despairing. She sounded clear and definite about her decision to die, but she was frightened, angry, confused, completely disorganized inside herself. Her self-esteem was gone. She felt worthless and inadequate and she couldn't think straight. So suicide seemed like an appealing way out. It was really her fantasy, the one solution she could come up with." People who are depressed often become fixated on suicide because they lose the ability to consider other options. But Jeanette had other reasons, according to Dr. Marshall. "Threatening suicide was also a way of making a strong personal statement and getting my attention. It was a form of manipulation and a call for help. The idea of taking her own life gave back some control to Jeanette. It was a way of turning the tables on her disease—and on me. Now *I* had a problem—a patient who wanted, or thought she wanted, to die—and all my efforts and professional skills were called on to prevent this from happening."

Dr. Marshall, who had established a strong bond with Jeanette across the years, was able to guide her past her feelings of self-destruction. "I asked her, 'Why?' Why did she have those feelings and why were they so intense? I recognized her pain, but I suggested we both examine what caused it. I broke it down into a set of problems we could sort out and discuss. And I got Jeanette involved in the process so she had to use her skills and resources. I asked her, 'Under what conditions would you want to continue living?' She had to think about that one." Even with Dr. Marshall's expert help, Jeanette's course was not an easy one. "Of course, none of this happened overnight. At first Jeanette was angry with me for refusing to help her carry out her plan. She told me I was fired, she would find another doctor who was willing to assist her. I told her that was her right but suggested she was running away from her problems. That was out of character for the person I had come to know and respect over the years. I said she could call me anytime, day or night. We still had a lot of work to do, but I was confident we could get out of this mess together. Jeanette stormed out of my office, acting like a betrayed friend. I didn't see or hear from her for several weeks, although I called her myself several times."

Eventually Jeanette returned to see Dr. Marshall. He seemed to have a sense of hopefulness about her situation, even if she did not. "The most important thing we had to do was get her back in touch with the important people in her life. Her despair made her feel alone and isolated. I had to show her there was a whole group of people who cared about her, for whom her illness was a matter of great concern. She was not alone."

When you are feeling most desolate and despairing, it is crucial to make reconnections with other people. Sometimes, if you are especially alienated, your doctor can be your first point of contact. After you establish a bond with the physician, he or she can lead you back to other important, long-term relationships. Dr. Marshall identified Jeanette's children as a source of conflict and hope. He sent her to a psychiatrist. "She was clinically depressed and required medication. But she also needed someone to talk to. Jeanette was a product of the Midwest, and we're not always so good at encouraging openness of expression out here. So I sent her for professional counseling. And it helped, in part because she had her back to the wall. So suddenly Jeanette was talking about her tragic illness, the breakup of her marriage, her estranged children, and her upbringing. She was coming to terms with so much in her painful history. And she realized how much she loved her children and how her illness had driven them apart. She made a very conscious effort to get close to them again. This was not an easy thing for her to do—they resisted her at first —but then slowly it began to change. And this was a beautiful thing to see. Because through all of the personal agonies, Jeanette and her children found each other, really for the first time. And I believe this helped Jeanette face what lay ahead in her life—a life she had written off prematurely."

Suicide was an idea that took hold of Rachel, Sam, and Jeanette—in varying degrees of intensity—but in each case it was rejected in favor of carrying on with their lives. It wasn't the desire to die but other concerns—fear of pain, helplessness, humiliation, loneliness—that motivated their search for some kind of solution. Once underlying problems were addressed, suicide ceased to be the only way out of their predicaments. Burt's anxiety and depression led him to actually attempt suicide. He survived by a combination of luck and his own ambivalence. But he might easily have made a second attempt had Dr. Alvarez not treated him for depression and helped him sort out his feelings and separate them from real events. "Burt was scared to hell of deteriorating physically. He was losing everything—his wife, his career, his health, his identity. Then he saw blood and he was sure he had cancer. He imagined himself with a colostomy. He couldn't take that. The more he tried to suppress it, the worse it got."

It is dangerous to keep your thoughts and fears about dying to yourself. Fueled by anxiety or depression, they can take on a frightening reality of their own. Phantoms and figments of imagination may appear overwhelmingly real. You need a reality check. It can be as simple as the medical examination Burt needed in order to learn he did *not* have cancer. Or it may come in the form of pain medication, which Rachel learned she could have whenever she needed it. Ventilating your feelings and fears and sharing them with another—be it a family member, close friend, or health professional—may also relieve some of the pain and anxiety you have been shouldering alone. Once a trusting bond or relationship has been formed, and your concerns are out on the table, you may have the clarity and peace of mind necessary to weigh different options and explore the sources of your despair. You may be able to step back and gain perspective on your crisis. Situations that looked hopeless may not seem so uniformly bleak. You may even find some small, modest source of hope and undertake a new plan of action. But you must first establish a connection with another person and begin to engage. You need to talk things out and get beyond the pain and distress that seem to engulf you.

Being aware of your responsibilities to other people can help you find reasons for living. There is always someone who depends on you and for whom your premature death would be a great blow—be it your spouse, children, parents, siblings, or other friends and loved ones. It could even be a physician, nurse, or nurse's aide who has grown attached to you while providing care. You should consider what impact your death will have on these people. When your life appears to have little value to you, it may still be very important to others whom you care about. Even caring for a pet can become an important, life-affirming responsibility. In her later years, Tess adopted a wirehaired terrier, and this dog accompanied her everywhere. "I couldn't imagine life without Rusty. And I know he couldn't live without me. When I went in for my hip operation, I think I worried more about Rusty than about myself. It forced me to work harder at getting better and not giving up."

The impact of a suicide on a loved one goes beyond the premature and tragic loss of life. It may open up a wound far more painful and slower to heal than even normal grief. The aftermath of suicide may be devastating. Because it is a conscious and deliberate act, a choosing of death over life, suicide implies a failure of some kind on the part of survivors. Each person reproaches himself or herself for not doing enough to prevent the act. Suicide also carries the suggestion of humiliation and betrayal, because the loved one ran out on us without saying good-bye and because he or she did not think we were worth sticking around for. In addition, there is a powerful social stigma connected to suicide: survivors may not get the same support and sympathy that other bereaved family members might receive after a natural or accidental death.

If the person who commits suicide is a family member, there is a statistically greater likelihood that someone close will follow in his or her footsteps. Whether this is due to genetic or cultural factors, such as the breaking of a taboo within the family, remains unclear. But the aftereffects of a family suicide are profoundly unsettling and leave a trail of guilt, anger, resentment, and sorrow that may take years, or even more than a generation, to eradicate. Simone was shocked when she learned of her husband's suicide. "I never dreamed he was capable of such a thing. How could I have missed it? We were living together, I saw him every day, and I thought I understood him. After he died, I got sick and took to my bed. I couldn't stop thinking about him blowing his

brains out. For a few months I felt like I wanted to kill myself, too—out of loyalty or desperation, I don't know which.
Of course it's against my religion, so I was afraid. And my
family stood by me. They were a real help. But I still think
about what he did today. So do my children. We are all
haunted by it. I get flashbacks. It's something you never
really get over. I still don't understand why he did it."

Suicide happens with such suddenness that it prevents us
from preparing emotionally for the death of a loved one.
Grieving, like dying, normally progresses from initial shock
and denial to gradual acceptance and recovery. If someone
you love is given a serious diagnosis, your grief begins long
before death, as it did for Mark when he learned Ruth had
Alzheimer's disease. "I guess I know that Mom is not going
to get better so I'm trying to concentrate on keeping her
happy and safe. But I can feel myself disengaging because I
know that I'm losing her. I feel I have to brace myself for the
inevitable." This process, known as anticipatory grieving, is
crucial in helping you prepare to cope with the loss of someone you love. In Mark's case it was more helpful to him than
Ruth, because his mother's illness prevented her from a full
understanding of the situation. Mark had already "lost" the
mother he knew, even though Ruth was still alive and not
physically ill. In other cases, such as Rachel and Scott's, this
early grieving provides time to make your peace with the
loved one and to settle any outstanding issues that remain
unresolved between you. When this period of adjustment is
abbreviated, through suicide or sudden death, anticipatory
grieving is short-circuited, and it is much harder for loved
ones to deal with the overwhelming shock of death. Richard
and his children, Yvonne and Jeremy, were caught totally
unprepared when Jacqueline was tragically injured in a car
accident. "We never even told the kids about her worries
about lupus because we believed she was out of the woods.
Then suddenly she had this freak accident. It all happened
so fast. We never had a chance to say good-bye. I kept dreaming she'd come out of the coma so I could tell her how much

I loved her. The kids felt the same way. We all have this unfinished business with her." This sense of incompleteness —of severed lines of communication that can never be re-opened—can be a source of great pain and sorrow when you are suddenly threatened with the loss of someone you love.

There are many issues to confront when you are the one caring for someone who is seriously ill or dying. One difficulty, especially when care is provided at home, is the sheer quantity of work involved. In many cases this can be physically as well as emotionally exhausting, and very time-consuming. Family members may be reluctant to admit that caretaking is an ordeal because of guilty feelings that they, rather than the dying person, are experiencing distress. The respite care provided under the hospice system is one way of acknowledging the need to give family members a break during critical periods. During Patricia's illness, Burt characteristically insisted on doing all the work himself, without any support. By the time Patricia died, he was at the end of his tether and suffering from fatigue. He was also feeling a good deal of suppressed resentment because she had taken up so much of his time and energy. Consequently, he experienced a deep sense of relief at her death. This release and a sudden anticipation of freedom ultimately burdened him with guilt that fed into his depression.

When Veronica's Alzheimer's disease began to progress, Sharon moved her mother into her home. Sharon thought she would be able to handle her mother by herself. "I never realized what 'around-the-clock' care meant. It means twenty-four hours a day, without a break. I was getting so worn down taking care of Mom, it was affecting my whole life. First my neighbors watched her, but that didn't work for very long. I had to miss a lot of days at work so I went part-time. It got expensive when I had to hire someone to help out. When the constant strain started affecting my marriage as well, I knew I was in trouble. Mother was becoming more difficult every day, and my husband, who had been so wonderful about everything, put his foot down. He said I was neglecting him and the kids. He was right. I hated putting her in a nursing home, but I had no choice."

The stress of caring for a seriously ill relative can also ignite old feuds and bitter family feelings among the caretakers. All the normal tensions of a crisis situation—issues of blame and responsibility, love and hate, rivalry, resentment, fear, anger, power, money—are heightened because the stakes are the ultimate ones of life and death. As they watched their son die, Sam's parents felt they had failed him in some fundamental way. No matter what they told themselves, they couldn't shake the feeling they were somehow responsible for letting their child die. Sam's mother lashed out at his father, blaming him for driving her "baby" away. This drove a wedge between them that only disappeared gradually when shared grief drew them back together.

Ralph, whose wife had Alzheimer's disease, had two children: one, Susan, lived forty-five minutes away in the suburbs, while the other, Rita, was two thousand miles away at the other end of the country. While Susan often drove in to visit her father or help with the housekeeping and other chores, Rita was constantly critical of Susan's efforts. "Dad called me up the other night and said it was really cold in the house, his heating wasn't working. He was worried about Mom, but he couldn't leave her to go out and get the part he needed. And he didn't want to bother Susan because she had her cooking class that night. I couldn't believe it. My sister, who lives virtually around the corner, is too busy to help my parents. It gets me so angry, sometimes I think all she's interested in is inheriting their money, if there's any left." Rita was well aware of Susan's efforts on behalf of their parents, but the physical distance left her fearful and frustrated. The sisters had not fought since childhood but now found themselves in frequent battles over their parents' predicament. "I know Susan's done a lot already, her husband and kids feel neglected, but Mom may not be around much longer. I'm really worried about her and what will happen to Dad after she dies. They're so close. Maybe I should put my house on the market and move back east so I can be there too."

You need to be prepared for struggles of this kind with other family members as you divide caretaking responsibilities. At the same time, caring for a loved one at the end of life can also be an emotionally rich experience. Rachel received excellent hospice care at home, both from the visiting nurse and support staff. She was kept comfortable in a familiar environment, surrounded by the people she loved. Scott and Adam were under great strain, but they also had an opportunity to form many close and powerful connections with Rachel, and with each other, before she died. "I don't believe we were ever as close a family as during those last days. Adam and I got to know each other in a new way. My son was a great comfort to me and surprisingly strong and brave. Rachel was dying and this was the worst, the most awful tragedy. But it was also a strangely calm and beautiful period. I can't explain it, but we all felt the same thing together."

Toward the end, during the last few months or weeks of life, you may become more aware of increasing isolation, particularly in a health care institution. This is true both for the dying person and the loved one who must watch over them. As the clock ticks and the illness progresses toward its inevitable conclusion, your internal isolation may be mirrored in your external surroundings. Barbara's husband, Tom, grieved silently for his dying wife, when only the respirator stood between her and death. "Every night when it was time for me to leave the intensive care unit, I felt like crying. I'd watch the medical staff finish their shifts and leave. They were going home—so was I—but not Barbara. She was never leaving." Barbara's isolation was especially painful because she was physically cut off from those around her. "Barbara was attached to the respirator with tubes down her mouth and throat. Her chest would heave whenever the machine pumped air, then sink back. She looked half-automated. Her body had been taken over by technology. Any passing orderly had more control over her breathing than she did. They could just change the number of breaths per minute on the dial and she would respond like a windup doll. It was awful." In the midst of her growing isolation, Tom's presence meant even more to Barbara. "Even though she could not speak, I knew from her eyes how much Barbara looked forward to my visits. I came as often as they would let me—I often slept in the ICU waiting room—and she would just drink me in. I reminded her that she was still a person, someone temporarily in a bad state. I knew who she *really* was."

Even after they have moved beyond initial denial and accepted they will die, terminally ill patients often hold on to some fantasy or slender hope of recovery. Right until the end, Rachel spent many hours planning and talking about her son's bar mitzvah, which was two years away. "I want a big affair, with all my uncles and aunts and cousins. Rabbi Baum will officiate. And Adam will wear a three-piece suit." By suppressing the constant knowledge that she was near death, Rachel was able to turn her mind to happier thoughts and daydreams. She fantasized that she would go into remission and survive after all, even though she knew this was unlikely. Such dreams and wishes allow us to maintain our link with the world and help overcome our sense of isolation and despair. By imagining herself in a pretty evening dress at her son's bar mitzvah, Rachel could feel, fleetingly at least, that she was her old self and still had a role to play. She was not yet ready to surrender completely and give up hope. In order to go on, she had to believe there was still some small possibility of improvement, however remote and farfetched.

Just as dying people may dream of a cure, so may loved ones fantasize about taking their place and "saving" them. You may be overcome with notions of heroism and self-sacrifice when someone you love is dying. George would have done anything to save his wife, Vera, including substituting himself for her on the deathbed. "I owe her everything," he lamented. And Sam's mother, torn by guilt and helplessness at watching her child die, was ready to sacrifice her life for his. "Please, God, don't take my baby before me," she prayed. "Let me die in place of him." While such fantasies are usually harmless and allow us to express our profound sadness and attachment to a dying person, they may lead to reckless or irrational acts, even suicide, in an effort to "prevent" such a calamity from befalling or to "punish" ourselves. "I don't know how I can face life without my father," Melanie cried in despair when she first learned of Louis's stroke. The imminent loss of a loved one can set off a potentially violent chain of events. You must try to maintain some perspective on your grief and share your sadness, anger, or guilt with other people.

When you are terminally ill and get closer to death, you may feel the need to settle accounts with your loved ones. You may want to talk about practical or financial matters, such as your property will, funeral plans, or the children's care and education. Sam drew up special plans for his death and left his mother a sum of money to carry them out. "I want all my friends—here's the list—to come to a big party after I'm dead. Read this speech to them, and then I want you to give away all my possessions to the people I've designated." Tess left everything to her children, except for a small bequest to the University of Pennsylvania, her husband Alan's alma mater. "He really loved that university. I wanted to do something nice for them and to keep Alan's memory alive." Making final arrangements and setting your affairs in order may provide a satisfying sense of completion, of having dispatched your obligations. This applies to your emotional relationships as well.

As you approach your death, you are forced to examine your life and distinguish what matters from what does not—and who matters most to you. You must be honest because there is so little time left. Some personal relationships may now be unimportant, while others take on new meaning. There is usually at least one special person, a close friend or family member, whom you may want to see or talk to. It could be someone you live with or a person from your past you have not seen for years—even someone you had a falling out with.

You have an opportunity to uncover your deepest feelings and to acknowledge them in a new way. Jeanette had one surprising last wish: "I want to see my ex-husband. I know we haven't spoken for years, since our marriage broke apart. And he didn't behave very well then. But I still think about him a lot." Sam's illness forced him back to his parents' home and a partial reconciliation with them, especially his father. In some ways, they were able to make up for many lost years and establish an intimacy that had seemed gone forever. "I didn't expect my father to take me in now, when I'm so sick. He didn't approve of my lifestyle. But it was nice to be back home, treated like a kid again." Sam's father realized he could no longer indulge his prejudices if he wanted to help his son. "I still don't approve. But maybe I was a little harsh and unforgiving. He is still my son."

The need to come to terms with our feelings about death —both for the dying person and the loved one—may be complicated both by cultural constraints and by the way we normally express our emotions. Our society does not generally encourage us to explore and express our feelings in public. We tend to be embarrassed by direct displays of emotion. With his "strong and silent" male ethos, Burt was not one given to excessive self-scrutiny or self-expression. "Feelings are something you keep to yourself unless they serve a purpose or unless you are in an extraordinary situation. I may have some feelings, but I'm not going to let them all hang out." When he went fishing with his son, Burt spoke easily about sports or politics or business but not about his inner life. This masculine reserve made it far more difficult for Burt to acknowledge his immense sense of loss at his wife Patricia's death or his fears about his failing health. Burt's painful feelings were so intense yet unacknowledged that it took a life-threatening situation to get him the help he needed.

Jeanette was not used to analyzing her feelings, let alone talking about them with someone else. "At first, I resented the psychiatrist asking me all these questions. He seemed to be very nosy, and I had a good mind to walk out." But

Jeanette's illness and her need for understanding overcame her reticence. Eventually she was able to become more emotionally accessible to her children. "Mom was like a different person. She would actually ask me how I felt and then she would listen to my answer. And she told me all this neat stuff about herself I never knew before. One day she told us both that she loved us. It seems hard to believe, but she hadn't used those words with us since we were little kids. We just cried and cried."

During the final weeks and days of your life, you may reach a point when you can no longer deny the reality that is closing in around you. It is a time of resigned introspection, when you prepare for separation from the world. You review your life and tally up the losses, the people and the places you love and will never see again. You may not want other people to cheer you up or tell you to think of "one more positive thing." You may want to be alone with your thoughts and may often find visitors an intrusion. If you speak, you may want to know that you are being heard, but you may need little in the way of verbal response. A touch of the hand or a look may do just as well.

Some people achieve this acceptance and gradual separation more easily than others. Ninety-two-year-old Tess, who had lived through and weathered so many sorrows and joys, was able to think about her death as an almost natural next step in her life. Although she had a few disappointments and regrets—a talent for music she never developed, a charming widower she had turned down—she accepted the fact that she might have only a short time left and was at peace. Still articulate and coherent, she observed, "I really can't complain. I've lived, loved, married, had children, made friends, traveled, and even had something to leave behind for my kids. My life is almost complete. Of course I don't want to die, although it doesn't scare me like it used to, but I am prepared."

There are other people who struggle more before they achieve an acceptance of death. Joan, a friend of Tess's who was also in her nineties but less robust, began to express fears about dying in more subtle ways. She developed trouble walking on her own and would ask her daughter daily, "Will I be well enough to go to the park tomorrow?" Joan seemed to become emotionally more dependent each day, and her daughter was afraid to go on a long-needed vacation for fear her mother would deteriorate rapidly.

A prolonged terminal illness may complicate your relationship with a loved one. Sometimes, especially between spouses, instead of detachment there is an intensification of feeling. It becomes that much harder to disengage. The hold each has on the other becomes more pronounced. Burt's love for Patricia, itself compounded by his guilt over a past affair, made it harder for *her* to leave him behind. And Burt, although he appeared to recover fairly quickly after her death, actually experienced a delayed reaction to his grief. Burt's daughter, Nancy, watched her parents' efforts to say good-bye: "My father took such good care of my mother that she felt it was a betrayal to leave him. Even after she made her own peace with dying, she was worried about *him*. Dad kept hoping some miracle might save her. He didn't want her to die. In the end, when she was hospitalized and placed on a respirator, he wanted to bring her home, respirator and all. He just couldn't let go. Neither of them knew how to say good-bye. There was all this stuff still between them. It was terrible because Mom was suffering but Dad wouldn't release her. And she always needed his approval to do things. In the end, she died without his permission."

Modern medicine can anesthetize physical pain but not emotional pain. The knowledge that you or someone you love is dying—that you must leave the world and all the people you love behind, or must say farewell to someone who is dying—is painful and agonizing. But to avoid this suffering by denying a large part of ourselves and our feelings places us and our loved ones at great risk, as we saw with Burt. By facing the reality of old age or debility or terminal illness, we are able to more fully live our lives and enhance the lives of those we love.

We must learn to acknowledge the full range of our emotions—fear, terror, regret, loss, bitterness, anger, guilt, resentment, love, and hate—when confronting end-of-life situations. And we need to understand the options and alternatives that are available to help us deal with such feelings. While thoughts of suicide are common—a response to the confusion, ignorance, and fear surrounding death and dying in America today—suicide is not a solution but almost always an escape from these problems. It is a surrender to the fantasy of control and an attempt to avoid a quality of life we fear may be unacceptable. When we are faced with terminal illness or the knowledge that death is not far off, we need to go to the root of the problems that plague us: anxiety about our health and mortality, social isolation, depression, fear of pain, helplessness, or humiliation. Each of these concerns, as we have seen, can be dealt with in a responsible and caring way. But we all need to speak up and seek appropriate care and treatment from doctors, nurses, therapists, social support groups, family members, and others who can help us. If help is not forthcoming, look elsewhere. Positive choices and resources are available for you and your loved ones. You must communicate and talk about your feelings and concerns. You should explore different options. You need to make plans—legal, financial, social—and be prepared in advance. You must take a more active role in your end-of-life affairs.

As we live longer with more chronic diseases, and as medical progress and technology allow us to postpone death, we need to find better ways to live out the end of our lives. Great progress has already been made. We are healthier than we have ever been, and disability, on average, occurs later in life. But at some point, death must come. We need to be better informed and prepared to meet it. Life is the most precious possession we have, and we should fight for life while we can —"Do not go gentle"—but we also need to look upon death with greater clarity, understanding and, when it becomes inevitable, final acceptance. Even in terminal illness, we and our families can still survive the final passages with dignity and hope.

Appendix: Resources

Aging

American Association of Retired Persons (AARP)
601 E Street, NW
Washington, DC 20049
202-872-4700
(for people over fifty years of age, working or retired)

Families USA Foundation
1334 G Street, NW
Washington, DC 20005
202-628-3030

Legal Counsel for the Elderly
American Bar Association
1909 K Street, NW
Washington, DC 20036
202-833-6720

National Association of Area Agencies on Aging
600 Maryland Avenue, SW, Room 208
Washington, DC 20024
202-484-7520

United Seniors Health Cooperative
(publication on health-care housing and financial planning)
1331 H Street, NW, Suite 500
Washington, DC 20005
202-393-6222

Widowed Person's Service
AARP
1909 K Street, NW
Washington, DC 20036
Pamphlet: "On Being Alone"

Bioethics

The Hastings Center (National Bioethics Center)
225 Elm Road
Briarcliff Manor, NY 10510

Conditions/Illnesses

Centers for Disease Control
1600 Clifton Road, NE
Atlanta, GA 30333
404-639-3311

Make Today Count
168 Panoramic
Camdenton, MO 65065
314-346-6644

National Health Information Center
Office of Disease Prevention and Promotion
U.S. Department of Human Services
P.O. Box 1133
Washington, DC 20013-1133
800-336-4797

St. Francis Center
5417 Sherier Place, NW
Washington, DC 20016
202-363-8500
(nonprofit, nonsectarian)

AIDS

AIDS ARC Switchboard
San Francisco AIDS Foundation
Box 6182
San Francisco, CA 94101
415-861-7309

American Social Health Association
P.O. Box 13827
Research Triangle Park, NC 27709
800-227-8922 (National STD Hotline)
800-342-AIDS (National AIDS Hotline)
800-344-SIDA (Spanish)
800-AIDS-TTY (Hearing Impaired)

Gay Men's Health Crisis (GMHC) (services all people)
129 W. Twentieth Street
New York, NY 10011
212-807-6664
212-807-7517 (for educational materials)

National AIDS Hotline
Centers for Disease Control
Atlanta, GA 30333
800-342-AIDS
800-344-SIDA (Spanish)
800-AIDS-TTY (Hearing Impaired)

ALZHEIMER'S DISEASE

Alzheimer's Association
919 N. Michigan Avenue
Suite 1000
Chicago, IL 60611
800-272-3900

AMYOTROPHIC LATERAL SCLEROSIS

Amyotrophic Lateral Sclerosis (ALS) Society
21021 Ventura Boulevard
Suite 321
Woodland Hills, CA 91364
818-990-2151

ARTHRITIS

Arthritis Foundation
1314 Spring Street, NW
Atlanta, GA 30309
800-283-7800

BRAIN AND NERVOUS SYSTEM

American Paralysis Association
P.O. Box 187
Short Hills, NJ 07078
800-225-0292

National Stroke Association
300 E. Hampden Avenue, Suite 240
Englewood, CO 80110
303-762-9922

CANCER

American Cancer Society
1599 Clifton Road, NE
Atlanta, GA 30329
404-320-3333
800-ACS-2345

Cancer Information Service (CIS)
Office of Cancer Communications, NCI, NIH
Building 31, Room 10A24
9000 Rockville Pike
Bethesda, MD 20892
800-4-CANCER (in various states and regions)
800-524-1234 (within Hawaii)
800-638-6070 (within Alaska)

DIABETES

American Diabetes Association
P.O. Box 25757
1660 Duke Street
Alexandria, VA 22314
800-ADA-DISC x363

HEARING LOSS

Better Hearing Institute
Box 1840
Washington, DC 20013
800-424-8576
Hearing Helpline: 800-533-8811

Occupational Hearing Service
P.O. Box 1880
Media, PA 19063
Dial a Hearing Screen Test
800-345-3277 (within Pennsylvania)
800-222-3277

Self Help for Hard of Hearing People, Inc.
7800 Wisconsin Avenue
Bethesda, MD 20814
301-657-2248

HEART

American Heart Association
7320 Greenville Avenue
Dallas, TX 75231
214-373-6300

HUNTINGTON'S DISEASE

Huntington's Disease Society of America
140 W. Twenty-second Street, Sixth Floor
New York, NY 10011-2420
800-345-4372

KIDNEY

National Kidney Foundation
30 E. Thirty-third Street
New York, NY 10016
212-889-2210

LEUKEMIA

National Leukemia Association
585 Stewart Avenue, Suite 536
Garden City, NY 11530
516-222-1944

LIVER

American Liver Foundation
1425 Pompton Avenue
Cedar Grove, NJ 07009
201-857-2626

LUPUS

American Lupus Society
2617 E. Columbus Avenue
Spokane, WA 99207
800-331-1802

MENTAL HEALTH

American Mental Health Counselors Association (AMHCA)
5999 Stevenson Avenue
Alexandria, VA 22304
800-326-2642

American Psychiatric Association
1400 K Street, NW
Washington, DC 20005
202-682-6000

National Foundation for Depressive Illness
245 Seventh Avenue
New York, NY 10001
800-248-4344

National Institutes of Mental Health
5600 Fishers Lane
Rockville, MD 20857
301-443-3673

National Mental Health Association
1021 Prince Street
Alexandria, VA 22314
703-684-7722

MULTIPLE SCLEROSIS

National Multiple Sclerosis Society
733 Third Avenue, Sixth Floor
New York, NY 10017
212-986-3240
800-624-8236

PAIN

American Pain Society
(professional organization)
5700 Old Orchard Road, First Floor
Skokie, IL 60077-1024
708-966-5595

PARKINSON'S DISEASE

American Parkinson's Disease Association
116 John Street, Suite 417
New York, NY 10038

Parkinson's Education Program USA
1800 Park Newport, #302
Newport Beach, CA 90046
800-344-7872

RECONSTRUCTIVE SURGERY

Plastic Surgery Educational Foundation
444 E. Algonquin Road
Arlington Heights, IL 60005
312-228-9900

RESPIRATORY

American Lung Association
1740 Broadway
New York, NY 10019
212-315-8700

TRANSPLANT

American Council on Transplantation
P.O. Box 1709
Alexandria, VA 22313-1709
800-ACT-GIVE

Health Resources and Services Administration
Division of Organ Transplantation
5600 Fishers Lane
Rockville, MD 20857

VISION LOSS

American Council of the Blind (ACB)
1010 Vermont Avenue, NW, Suite 1100
Washington, DC 20005
800-424-8666 (National Legislative Hotline)

American Foundation for the Blind
15 W. Sixteenth Street
New York, NY 10011
212-620-2000
800-232-5463

The Lighthouse National Center for Vision and Aging
800 Second Avenue
New York, NY 10017
212-808-0077
800-334-5497 (Hotline)

National Eye Care Project (free eye exams for the elderly)
P.O. Box 9688
San Francisco, CA 94101-9688
800-222-EYES

National Library Services for the Blind and Physically
  Handicapped
Library of Congress
1291 Taylor Street, NW
Washington, DC 20542
800-424-8567

Consumer Groups

American Health Decisions (National Coalition of Citizens
  Groups)
c/o Oregon Health Decisions
921 SW Washington Street
Suite 713
Portland, OR 97205

Compassion Book Service
216 Via Monte
Walnut Creek, CA 94598
415-933-0830

Consumer Health Information Resource Institute
3030 Baltimore
Kansas City, MO 64108
800-821-6671

Consumer Product Safety Commission (CPSC)
Washington, DC 20207
800-638-2772 (Product Safety Line)
800-638-8270 (TTY National)
800-492-8104 (TTY Maryland)

Family Pharmaceuticals of America
966 Houston Northcutt Boulevard
Mt. Pleasant, SC 29465-1288
800-922-3444

Medic Alert Foundation
2323 Colorado
Turlock, CA 95381-1009
800-ID-ALERT
800-344-3226

National Health Information Center
P.O. Box 1133
Washington, DC 20013-1133
800-336-4797

National Library of Medicine
8600 Rockville Pike
Bethesda, MD 20894
800-638-8480

People's Medical Society
462 Walnut Street
Allentown, PA 18102
800-624-8773

Directories

Directory of Medical Specialists
Published by:
Marquis Who's Who
MacMillan Directory Division
3002 Glenview Road
Willmette, IL 60091
708-441-2364
(comprehensive: available in libraries)

Medical Health Information Directory
Published by:
Gale Research, Inc.
835 Penobscott Building
Detroit, MI 48226-4094
(comprehensive: available in libraries)

Health Hotlines
Published by:
National Library of Medicine
Building 38A, Room 3N-305
8600 Rockville Pike
Bethesda, MD 20894
301-496-1131

A two-hundred-page free booklet published by the U.S.
Department of Health and Human Services' National Library of
Medicine lists all health-related organizations that have toll-free
(800) numbers.

Health Care Coverage and Financial Planning

American College of Trust and Estate Counsel
2716 Ocean Park Boulevard
Suite 1080
Santa Monica, CA 90405
213-450-2033

American Counsel of Life Insurance
1001 Pennsylvania Avenue, NW
Washington, DC 20004-2599
202-624-2000
800-942-4242

Consumer Information Center
Department 59
Pueblo, CO 81009
(write for literature)

Medicaid
(Contact your state or local welfare, social service, or public health
agency)

Medicare
U.S. Department of Health and Human Services
HCFA
6325 Security Boulevard
Baltimore, MD 21207

Medicare Hotline 800-638-6833

Health Care Institutions/Programs

Joint Commission on Accreditation of Health Care Organizations
875 N. Michigan Avenue
Chicago, IL 60611
312-280-8374

NURSING HOMES

American Association of Homes for the Aging
901 E Street, Suite 500
Washington, DC 20004

American Health Care Association
1201 L Street, NW
Washington, DC 20005

The National Citizens Coalition on Nursing Home Reform
1424 Sixteenth Street, NW
Washington, DC 20036
202-797-0657

HEALTH MAINTENANCE ORGANIZATIONS (HMOS)

Group Health Association of America
1129 Twentieth Street, NW
Suite 600
Washington, DC 20036
202-778-3200

Health Resources and Services Administration Bureau of Health
   Maintenance Organizations and Resources
Office of Health Facilities
5600 Fishers Lane
Rockville, MD 20857
800-492-0359 (English and Spanish, within Maryland)
800-638-0742 (English and Spanish, outside Maryland)

HOME HEALTH CARE

American Federation of Home Health Agencies
1320 Fenwick Lane
Suite 100
Silver Springs, MD 20910

National League for Nursing
8600 Rockville Pike
Bethesda, MD 20894
800-638-8480

Visiting Nurses' Association of America
3801 E. Florida Avenue
Suite 806
Denver, CO 80210
800-426-2547
(referrals to over five hundred local VNAs)

HOSPICE

Hospice Education Institute (national referral and information
   service)
5 Essex Square
P.O. Box 713
Essex, CT 06426
Hospice Link: 800-331-1620

National Hospice Organization
Suite 901
1901 N. Moore Street
Arlington, VA 22209
703-243-5900
800-658-8898 (Helpline)

HOSPITAL

American Hospital Association
840 N. Lakeshore Drive
Chicago, IL 60611

American Nurses' Association
600 Maryland Avenue, SW
Suite 100
Washington, DC 20024

Living Wills

Choice in Dying (formerly Society for the Right to Die and
    Concern for Dying)
250 W. Fifty-seventh Street
New York, NY 10107
212-246-6973

Dying With Dignity
175 St. Clair Avenue W.
Toronto, Ontario
Canada M4V 1P7

Physicians

American College of Physicians
Independence Mall West
Sixth Street at Race
Philadelphia, PA 19104
800-523-1546

American College of Surgeons
55 E. Erie Street
Chicago, IL 60611
312-664-4050

American Medical Association
535 N. Dearborn
Chicago, IL 60610
312-464-5000

National Second Surgical Opinion Program
200 Independence Avenue, SW
Washington, DC 20201
800-492-6603 (within Maryland)
800-638-6833

Society of Critical Care Medicine
8101 E. Kaiser Boulevard
Anaheim, CA 92808
714-282-6000

Suicide

American Association of Suicidology
2459 S. Ash
Denver, CO 80222
303-692-0985

Survivors of Suicide
Suicide Prevention Center Inc.
P.O. Box 1393
Dayton, Ohio 45401-1393
513-223-9096
Hotline: 513-223-4777

Invaluable information, referrals, and many other services can be obtained by calling local and state offices of the following agencies and organizations: Department of Health, Department of Human Services, Department of Insurance, Meals on Wheels, Medicaid, Medicare, Office on Aging, and the senior resource center in your community.